Influencing Early Childhood Education

Influencing Early Childhood Education

Key figures, philosophies and ideas

Linda Pound

 Open University Press

KH

Open University Press
McGraw-Hill Education
McGraw-Hill House
Shoppenhangers Road
Maidenhead
Berkshire
England
SL6 2QL

email: enquiries@openup.co.uk
world wide web: www.openup.co.uk

and Two Penn Plaza, New York, NY 10121-2289, USA

First published 2011

A catalogue record of this book is available from the British Library

ISBN13: 978 0 335 24156 9 (pb)   978 0 335 24155 2 (hb)
ISBN10: 0 335 24156 5 (pb)   0 335 24155 7 (hb)
eISBN13: 978 0 335 24157 6

Library of Congress Cataloging-in-Publication Data
CIP data has been applied for

Fictitous names of companies, products, people, characters and/or data that may be used herein (in case studies or in examples) are not intended to represent any real individual, company, product or event.

Typeset by Aptara Inc., India
Printed in the UK by Bell & Bain Ltd, Glasgow

Mixed Sources
Product group from well-managed forests and other controlled sources
www.fsc.org Cert no. TT-COC-002769
© 1996 Forest Stewardship Council
FSC

The **McGraw·Hill** Companies

6/8/12

Contents

Introduction

A culture should know where its beliefs originate.

(Kramer [1961] 1995: x)

The development of theories and practices related to the rearing of young children is a fascinating subject. Around the world societies and cultures have chosen to bring up their young in ways which correspond to what they believe about the nature of young children and the nature of the society in which they wish to live. This has led to wide diversity.

While the history and philosophy of early childhood care and education used to be considered a vital element of the training of teachers and other practitioners in Britain, it fell out of favour in the latter part of the twentieth century and came to be regarded as an unnecessary frill. More recently, practitioners and trainers alike have, however, come to recognise the importance of understanding something of the legacy of giant thinkers like Piaget and pioneer practitioners such as the McMillan sisters. An understanding of theory can:

- help practitioners to shed light on what they do and help them to understand why they do what they do;
- promote reflective practice which supports constant improvement;
- enable practitioners to evaluate new theories or innovative practices, weighing up their effectiveness and relevance.

This book seeks to explore some of the theories of such thinkers. It will:

- plot the development of relevant theories from the nineteenth century;
- discuss the ways in which particular theories influence practice;
- identify the links between theories; and
- consider both the limitations of theories and their impact on practice and on future theories.

Theory or philosophy?

It is interesting to speculate on whether what lies behind these ideas and practices is a theory or a philosophy. The word theory stems from Greek and is linked to ideas of viewing or looking at. In everyday conversation we often say to one another things like 'I've an idea – I don't know whether it will work. It's only a theory'. Alternatively we label opinions as theories – 'my theory about why so and so does that is . . .'. In both cases we are acknowledging that theories are not infallible but are ideas being shaped. In normal conversation, we accept that theories are not facts but explanations of things that we have noticed or observed. This view of theories being based on observation, what we see or observe, also covers theories which go beyond the trivial. Susan Isaacs' theories and writings (see Chapter 6) offered an explanation of the learning she observed in children at Malting House School.

Philosophy, on the other hand, stems from Greek words whose meaning implies a love of knowledge. But this is by no means the whole story. Theory may be thought of as a set of beliefs – or perhaps a philosophy which guides action. In the case of Steiner Waldorf education (see Chapter 4) or Montessori education (see Chapter 5), the philosophy is based on a set of theories which guide practice. Some beliefs are not recognised as theories but they still guide our actions. Our theories or views of how children learn or what they should learn are often informed and shaped by culture. It is likely that what guided practitioners in foundational (Miller and Pound 2011) or traditional contexts was a philosophy – a set of values about the nature of children, their learning and the contexts in which they learn most effectively. There was no theoretical or empirical data which guided their views other than the evidence of their own eyes (Board of Education 1933). The pioneers of early education developed practice which was based on firmly held philosophies and personal theories.

Within what have been called the traditions of early childhood education (Blackstone 1971; Clift et al. 1980; Tizard 1974), risk has often been regarded as an important element of early childhood education. Woodwork benches and real tools were standard equipment for nursery schools and classes well into the 1980s and 1990s – and still are in some areas. In Steiner Waldorf practice for example, from a very early age – perhaps 2 – children are given opportunities to use knives (Heckmann 2008). This practice is mirrored in forest schools. Rogoff (1990) provocatively uses a picture of a child of less than one year of age wielding a machete in order to cut fruit – an image which frequently evokes cries of horror from audiences of English practitioners. Risk-taking is an area about which contemporary thinkers from many different disciplines have expressed concern. While on the one hand tighter and tighter constraints are imposed to prevent harm to children, others express deep concern about the absence of opportunities for young children to learn to manage risk by exploring risky situations safely (see for example Furedi 2001; Lindon 1999; Tovey 2007). A failure to learn to manage risk safely results in a loss of independence and autonomy (see for example Walsh 2004).

Personal or informal theories

Whether we recognise it or not we all hold personal theories. Keenan and Evans (2009) write about formal and informal theories. They suggest that formal theories have sets of linked laws or hypotheses, can be expressed in a variety of ways including mathematically and are logical in their structure. Informal or implicit theories, on the other hand, 'may be little more than organized sets of intuitions or expectations about our world' (Keenan 2002: 18). They go on to claim that although developmental psychology has no formal theories, its informal theories 'are somewhat more developed than the intuitive expectations about human behaviour that we all hold' (Keenan 2002: 27).

These views raise some interesting questions. The first relates to the nature of human development, an area in which all who work with young children must have some interest. Throughout this book, reference will be made to many different theories of development and no further exploration is needed at this point. The second question is about the nature of intuition. Claxton (2000: 50) suggests that intuition gives practitioners the ability to:

- function fluently and flexibly in complex domains;
- extract intricate patterns of information;
- make subtle and accurate judgements;
- detect and extract the significance of small, incidental details of a situation that others may overlook;
- take time to mull over problems in order to arrive at more insightful or creative solutions;
- and to apply this perceptive, ruminative, inquisitive attitude to one's own perceptions and reactions.

It is the ability and willingness to reflect (or ruminate), that helps to prevent our implicit, informal theories about children and learning from becoming prejudice or dogma. Gardner (2006) asserts that no one in any field of employment can claim to be a professional unless they are prepared to become a reflective practitioner. He goes further in suggesting that anyone who fails to do so should be counselled out of their chosen profession. Nowhere can this reflective approach be more necessary than in the field of early childhood – where practitioners are working with young children who are in many ways amongst the most vulnerable members of any society and are therefore determining the shape of society.

The third question is about the extent to which theories of child development should or do inform practice. Writing about the primary curriculum around the time of the introduction of OFSTED, Alexander et al. (1992: 18) reminded teachers that 'teaching is not applied child development. It is a weakness of the child-centred tradition that it has sometimes tended to treat it as such and, consequently, to neglect the study of classroom practice'. In the years since Alexander et al. wrote their report, the term child-centred has largely been replaced by the idea of learner-centredness. This is perhaps in part a response to what was seen as a derogatory overtone in the use of the term child-centred, perhaps most closely associated with Piaget. However it is undoubtedly also a reflection of the impact of the work of Urie Bronfenbrenner (see Chapter 12) who developed an ecological systems theory (1979). Within that theory children are seen as being central to a series of systems, beginning with the close family (microsystem) and moving out to what Bronfenbrenner terms the macrosystem, which includes the attitudes and ideologies of the culture within which the child is growing up (Pound 2009).

Pedagogy

This in turn raises the issue of pedagogy. For many writers (see for example Siraj-Blatchford et al. 2002; Collins et al. 2001) pedagogy relates mainly to teaching or:

- the instructional techniques and strategies which enable learning to take place;
- the interactive process between teacher and learner;
- the actions of the family and community.

(based on Siraj-Blatchford et al. 2002: 10).

Other writers cite the long-established tradition of pedagogy in Europe, seeing it as a more holistic and theoretical pursuit, involving social responsibility for the well-being and development of children. In this tradition, the pedagogue regards care and education as being of equal concern – with changing nappies seen as part of the process of promoting development, and mealtimes as part of the teaching process (Petrie et al. 2009). Whichever view you take, throughout this book the terms pedagogy, teacher or teaching imply an integral relationship between care and education.

The development of theories

At the heart of this book is a desire to explain (and therefore better understand) the way in which theories about how children develop and learn have evolved. The process by which theories become accepted, or not, is sometimes difficult to understand. The work of Bronfenbrenner, for example, helped to change views of learning from being largely child-centred to placing the child as learner at the heart of community and culture. Outside academic circles Bronfenbrenner is largely unknown. However, on his death he was described as the person 'whose theories profoundly altered the understandings of what children need to develop into successful adults' (Pound 2009: 11, citing the *LA Times* obituary for Bronfenbrenner).

Often the impact of a theory depends a great deal on external influences. In Bronfenbrenner's case he, an American, began writing at the time of concern about the rise of Soviet influence and anxiety about the state of education in the United

States. His view that children and their development need to be seen as the focus of a society struck a chord. It is speculated that it was social conditions that initially led to the popularity of John Bowlby's ideas (Riley 1983). As men returned from the war, nurseries were closed and women were once again expected to become home-based in order to ensure employment for men. Bowlby's ideas of maternal attachment (explored more fully in Chapter 9) complemented the social imperative and thus gained favour. The McMillan sisters famously began developing provision for young children in response to the widespread poverty and accompanying misery at the turn of the nineteenth to twentieth century which they claimed society regarded 'without perturbation' (Nutbrown et al. 2008: 45, citing McMillan 1927). It was only when the impact of poverty prevented sufficient soldiers being recruited for the Boer War that politicians and other policy-makers began to see the need to take action.

Theories develop in relation to current constructions of childhood. James et al. (1998) hypothesise two distinct clusters of views of childhood – the presociological and the sociological. The first category includes:

- *the evil child*, who requires strict discipline and punishment, may also be the subject of institutionalised violence as adults strive to restrain childish impulse. This view may be recognised in the doctrine of original sin, but is still current in, for example, the media treatment of the two boys convicted of murdering Jamie Bulger, and in the popularity of boot camps.
- *the naturally developing child* is linked to the theories of Piaget which have been described as containing 'the secrets of human learning and knowledge hidden behind the cute and seemingly illogical notions of children' (Pound 2005: 38, citing Papert).
- *the unconscious child,* derived from Freudian theories but ironically while opening up 'adult self-exploration . . . (it) has done little to broaden our understanding of children' (James et al. 1998: 20).

These views are not discrete and may be mingled with 'sociological' views of children (James et al. 1998) where understanding has grown of:

- the socially constructed nature of childhood;
- the view of childhood from children's own perspectives;
- the politicisation of childhood.

Many of these aspects will be returned to later in this book (see Part 5).

The structure of the book

This book is designed to be easily dipped into but it also sets out to provide a bigger picture of the ways in which thinking about early childhood has been shaped by new theories and by social and cultural events. It is divided into six parts. Each part has an introductory section, followed by a series of chapters relating to individual theorists or groups of related theories. Part 1 focuses on nineteenth-century developments in thinking about and provision for early childhood. Part 2 details the many progressive and pioneering ideas (including those of Steiner and Montessori – still household names today) which arose in the first half of the twentieth century. Part 3 highlights psychoanalytical theories, beginning with Freud and including contemporary ideas about the emotional aspects of development. Part 4 considers the competing roles of behaviourism and constructivism in shaping practitioners' views of children's learning. In Part 5, the many theoretical challenges which emerged, mainly over the second half of the twentieth century, will be considered. These include postmodern analyses, the de-schooling movement and discussion of the deconstruction of developmental theories. Part 6 differs from the other five in that it focuses not on theories relating to the care and education of young children but on the nature of evidence.

Each part will include some key dates to give a context to the theories and to provide a sense of chronology. Each chapter and the introductions to sections will offer ideas for further reading and some reflective questions. Broadly in each set of questions, the first two are aimed at readers new to this area of study while the second two aim to deal with more complex issues.

Conclusion

This introductory chapter attempts to highlight the complex nature of the theories and philosophies which have shaped early childhood care and education. In the chapters that follow many of the themes that have emerged in this introduction will be returned to. The ideas may sometimes be confusing but there is often a mismatch between:

- what we say and do;
- what we understand from what others say and do;
- the informal or implicit views in our heads and the explicit formal theories which are shared with others.

In a book on a topic such as this, it would be impossible to ignore the fundamental importance of our beliefs about the relative role of nature and nurture, genetics and experience on learning and development. These areas will arise over and over again. Finally it is important to remember the different stakeholders or audiences for which theorists and thinkers are writing or outlining their ideas. Owen (see Chapter 1) was primarily a philanthropic employer – he was foregrounding the lives of his employees. The McMillan sisters (see Chapter 3) were political animals, members of the Fabian Society, anxious to improve the lot of the poor but with a wider vision, going beyond those with whom they were working. So as you read consider not only the theories and philosophies themselves but who they were aimed at.

Reflective questions

1. What might your personal theory about children and learning include? Take some time to reflect on this.
2. Where did your ideas come from? It may have been a carer or teacher that had a particular influence on your thinking. Perhaps it was some insights gained as a child or as an adult about when learning seemed effective.
3. What views of children and childhood seem most prominent at the moment in media and policy documents?
4. What are the differences between teaching and pedagogy in your view?

Further reading

Holland, P. (2004) *Picturing Childhood: the myth of the child in popular imagery.* New York: Tauris and Co. Ltd.

Keenan, T. and Evans, S. (2009) (2nd edn) *An Introduction to Child Development.* London: Sage.

Part 1
Thinking about early childhood in the nineteenth century

In many ways it would have been appropriate for this book to begin much earlier in thinking about the ways in which societies have thought about young children and their learning. Ancient Greek and Chinese philosophers have undoubtedly influenced ideas about education and learning today (Pound 2008). Indeed it is claimed that their ideas have shaped the whole pattern of eastern and western thinking (Nisbett 2003). However, it is Comenius, born in 1592, who is described as 'the father of modern education' (Nutbrown et al. 2008). He was amongst the first to develop picture books for children, publishing an illustrated text book in 1658. More importantly he recognised the holistic nature of children's development and the important role of sensory experience in promoting learning. It was he who encouraged adults to 'teach gently', ensuring pleasure for both child and adult (Nutbrown et al. 2008: 24).

But James et al. (1998: 14) have asserted that the work of Rousseau in the seventeenth century might be the most relevant starting point since it is his work that highlights the need for society to take responsibility for children. If, as Rousseau believed:

> childhood innocence is to be nurtured at all costs, then we must attain publicly recognizable standards in the treatment of children; all adults must assume responsibility for children ... Children can no longer be routinely mistreated, but neither can they be left to their own devices. ... *Our contemporary concern for children's education begins therefore, with Rousseau and with a childhood that is recognizable through encouragement, assistance, support and facilitation.* [Author's italics.]

Eighteenth-century influences on nineteenth-century theories

Two philosophers, both born in Switzerland in the eighteenth century, have had an immense influence on the way in which theories and philosophies of early childhood have developed in western Europe in particular.

Jean-Jacques Rousseau

Jean-Jacques Rousseau was born in 1712 in Geneva. He died 66 years later but the influence of his writing was to impact on thinking about childhood for much longer. One of his contemporaries, Madame de Stael, suggested that he 'had succeeded in restoring happiness to childhood' (Jimack 1974: xxv). Other more critical contemporaries blamed the publication of Rousseau's renowned book *Emile* for the 'provoking, obstinate, insolent, impudent, arrogant' children of Paris (Jimack [1762] 1974: xxv). These are not the only anomalies in Rousseau's story. As indicated in the introduction to this book, it was Rousseau's ideas about liberty (James et al. 1998) that led to views of children as innocents. He regarded children as part of nature, corrupted only by human society and he made other people believe that children were worthy of attention.

Despite these worthy views and the recognition which Rousseau received for his ideas, their impact on his own life appears minimal. His best known book *Emile* was written after his own failed attempts to tutor two young boys. Later he writes of the importance of kindness but it is said that, as a result of his writings, many parents bathed their children in cold water and dressed them flimsily, in order to rear them, 'à la Jean-Jacques', more closely attuned to nature. He himself had five children all of whom were to be placed in an orphanage soon after birth, apparently against the wishes of their mother, and unsurprisingly, an action he is said to have later regretted (Jimack [1762] 1974).

Rousseau's work is often contrasted with that of John Locke. It has been suggested that Locke's writing influenced that of Rousseau (Slentz and Krogh 2001). One suspects that if true, this can only have been in a negative way, since their views appear diametrically opposed. For Rousseau, nature was what drove development while for Locke all learning was driven by experience. It may be easier to think of eighteenth-century thinking on this subject, as Ezell (1983) does, as a kaleidoscope with many brightly coloured elements – the pattern being imposed externally through reflection rather than regarding the parts themselves as having an order. Perhaps the truth is that we are all influenced, positively or negatively, by the theories that have preceded us.

Nonetheless Slentz and Krogh's (2001: 40) simple characterisation of these widely differing and complex views may give pause for thought:

> A teacher who prefers materials designed for teaching correct answers or procedures is one who believes that the environment has a strong influence and that children's learning progress is, in large part, the result of the ways in which the teacher prepares and manipulates the environment. This teacher has been influenced by Locke, whether aware of it or not. On the other hand, a teacher who prefers open-ended activities and materials as well as an unstructured day and believes that children grow best if allowed to play and learn freely, largely through their own direction, whether aware of it or not has been influenced by the thoughts of Rousseau.

Johann Pestalozzi

Johann Pestalozzi was born in Zurich in 1746. He, like Rousseau, believed that education should be in tune with nature. So much did he admire Rousseau that he named his only son, Jean-Jacques, after Rousseau. Like Rousseau, Pestalozzi is regarded as making a major contribution to modern approaches to the education of young children. His work has been described as 'the starting point for modern educational theory and practice' (Green and Collie 1916: 1). Unlike Rousseau whose work was essentially theoretical, Pestalozzi made several attempts to link theory and practice. Some were successful – his school at Yverdun in Switzerland for example attracted many notables including Friedrich Froebel and Robert Owen. Pestalozzi [nd] suggests that adults should focus on:

> not a perfection in the accomplishments of the school, but fitness for life; not the acquirement of habits of blind obedience and of prescribed diligence, but a preparation for interdependent action.

Sadly, despite the fact that Pestalozzi has been described as being more practical than Rousseau (Slentz and Krogh 2001), all his schemes eventually ended in failure. This may have been because although he promoted the importance of a practical education, Pestalozzi was not himself a very practical man (Pound 2005). He was however committed to providing a similar education for rich and poor. This aim of providing for the needy has been reflected in the use of his name in the establishment of Pestalozzi Children's Villages around the world, caring for orphans, refugees and war victims.

Nineteenth-century contexts

In the chapters that make up Part 1 of this book, the focus will be on two key figures in this period, Robert Owen and Friedrich Froebel. Both were strongly influenced by the work of Pestalozzi, and indirectly by that of Rousseau. Before considering the work of these two men it may be useful to think about the broader context within which their work was developing. The strongest influence, as we shall see – certainly for Robert Owen – was that of the Industrial Revolution, accompanied as it was by 'deprivation, squalor, hardship and suffering' (van der Eyken 1967: 59).

European models

It was a country pastor in Germany working in a rural community who is credited with inspiring the first nursery provision. Johann Oberlin, visited by Robert Owen, has been called the 'founder of the nursery school movement', setting up as he did provision for children of mothers working in the fields, in 1779. The village in which he worked was in Alsace, then part of Germany. He developed teaching methods which included educational visits, the use of story and a focus on play. In Paris, the first crèche was set up in 1844 for working mothers by Firmin Marbeau and by 1869 there were 68 crèches throughout Paris. Similarly, *jardins des enfants* were established in Belgium. Compulsory education was introduced in Britain in 1870. In a political 'fudge' provision for children under 5 years of age was left ambiguous, a decision which was to have long term effects – as will be seen in Part 2. By 1908, half of all Belgian children aged between 2 and 5, and a quarter of those in France were already attending nurseries. Britain was decrying the state of health of the poor working classes and simultaneously embracing policy on the care and education of the young which was to leave most of them in inappropriate and poor quality conditions.

The broader context

The nineteenth century was a remarkable period of change and development. In addition to the impact of the Industrial Revolution there was dynamic thinking at work. Charles Darwin and his most famous work, *On the Origin of Species,* although not published until 1859, impacted on thinking. Amongst these ideas was a view of human development as a biological process – the privilege of nature over nurture. Darwin was interested in eugenics, a theory put forward by his cousin Francis Galton. He was also fascinated by the development of his own children. This is reflected in the publication, shortly before his death, of observations that he had collected of the development of one of his sons. Changing views of the role of women in life outside the home are also evidenced by the work of Florence Nightingale and Mary Seacole. Mary's work is less well known than that of Florence Nightingale but her active presence in battle hospitals of the Crimean War, demonstrates changing attitudes.

Reflective questions

1. Consider Slentz and Krogh's comparison of Locke and Rousseau. Where do you think your informal theories and practice fit within those ideas?
2. What evidence do you see in today's provision for young children of a desire to be in touch with nature?
3. Which in your view has had more influence, the ideas of Rousseau or the practical implementation of those ideas by Pestalozzi?
4. To what extent do you think that rich and poor children in the eighteenth and nineteenth centuries would have benefitted from being educated together?

Key dates

1592–1670	**John Comenius**
1632–1704	**John Locke**
1658	Publication of Comenius's illustrated text for children
1712–1778	**Jean-Jacques Rousseau**
1740–1826	**Johann Oberlin, founder of the first nursery school**
1746–1827	**Johann Pestalozzi**
1762	Publication of Rousseau's book *Emile*
1771–1858	**Robert Owen**

1779	First nursery school established in Germany by Oberlin
1782–1852	**Friedrich Froebel**
1792–1866	**Samuel Wilderspin**
1798–1875	**Firmin Marbeau, founder of day care movement in France**
1805	Pestalozzi opens school at Yverdun
1805–1881	**Mary Seacole**
1808	Froebel works with Pestalozzi at Yverdun
1809–1882	**Charles Darwin**
1816	Owen establishes New Lanark infant school
	Froebel establishes Universal German Educational Institute in Griesheim
1818	Owen visits Yverdun
	James Buchanan, teacher at New Lanark, opens the first English infant school
1820	Samuel Wilderspin opens infant school at Spitalfields, as master
1820–1910	**Florence Nightingale**
1837	Froebel's Play and Activity Institute opened at Bad Blankenburg
1840	Froebel renames Play and Activity Institute at Bad Blankenburg *Kindergarten*
1844	First crèche established in Paris by Marbeau
1854	Froebelian training begins in England
1859	Publication of Darwin's *On the Origin of Species*
1860	Florence Nightingale establishes the Nightingale Training School for nurses at St Thomas's Hospital in London
1877	Darwin publishes observations of his son Doddy's childhood

Further reading

Blackstone, T. (1971) *A Fair Start: the provision of pre-school education.* London: Allen Lane/LSE. (See Chapter 2.)

1 Robert Owen 1771–1858

Robert Owen was a businessman and philanthropist. He has been described by one of his biographers as 'one of the most important and controversial figures of his generation' (Donnachie 2000: ix). In an era when employers widely believed that profit could not be made unless workers were paid the bare minimum, Owen paid high wages to those working in the mill at New Lanark. Moreover he provided homes for them, made provision for the education for children and adults alike and perhaps most radically and philanthropically of all refused to employ children under the age of 10. At that time mill-owners regularly employed boys under the age of 6 for a pittance, but Owen was prepared to step outside the contemporary convention. At New Lanark:

> Instead of children being admitted at nine years of age to work in cotton mills twelve and a half hours a day, with only an hour and a half for meals and recreation, no child should be admitted to work in any manufactory before ten years of age and not for more than six hours per day until he is twelve years old.
>
> (van der Eyken 1967: 62, citing Owen)

It was this bold and essentially moral move (together with a range of similar actions described by one biographer as 'mad') which were to lead to reforms in child labour, to the spread of socialist ideals and to the development of trade unions.

Owen's theories

The school that Owen built in New Lanark opened in 1816, one year after the mill itself had been set up. It says much about his educational ideas that he called it, not a school, but the Institution for the Formation of Character. At the opening of the institution he declared that it had been set up to support working parents, which has today earned it the title of the first UK workplace nursery. However, Robert Owen also wanted to prevent children 'from acquiring any bad habits' and to help them 'learn the best' (van der Eyken 1967: 63).

His book *The New Moral World* was published in 1836, twenty years after New Lanark had opened. In it Owen highlights some important aspects of his philosophy of education. He firmly asserts that learning begins at birth and continues until death, and that qualities of character depend on external factors. In this, Whitbread (1972) suggests, he was influenced by the work of John Locke. Owen, like Locke, favours the view that it is nurture which is of the greatest importance in development. He writes:

> the constitution of every infant, except in the case of organic disease, is capable of being formed or nurtured, either into a very inferior or a very superior being, according to the qualities of the external circumstances allowed to influence that constitution from birth.
>
> (Whitbread 1972: 9, citing Owen 1836)

However, he also sympathised with the views of Pestalozzi in his belief in the importance of nature. In any case it is clear that Owen's educational philosophy differed greatly from many of his contemporaries:

> He was not concerned with breaking wills and creating individuals satisfied with their station. Nor was he concerned with saving souls, or even teaching the principles of Christianity. He wished with the aid of informal teaching and physical activity to create an individual who would be a useful citizen later.
>
> (Blackstone 1971: 17)

Radical as his approach may have appeared in the UK, Owen was aware of alternative approaches. He was aware, for example, of the work of Oberlin, the founder of the nursery school movement in Germany. He visited a number of experimental schools across Europe and was sufficiently impressed with Pestalozzi's views on education, to send some of his sons to a school run by a follower of Pestalozzi (Donnachie 2000). The philosophy of their school at Hofwyl in Switzerland had two elements which particularly appealed to Owen. One was that children were taught practical life skills which would enable them to earn a living. The other was that it aimed for greater social cohesion, bringing rich and poor together – a rare concept at that time.

His personal philosophy is further reflected in his establishment of a 'community of equality'. In 1825, he bought an American village and renamed it New Harmony. He set up a constitution which focused on equality of both rights and duties; freedom of speech and cooperation; sincerity, kindness, courage and order; as well as the importance of health and knowledge. Perhaps of particular interest to twenty-first-century readers is his objective on 'the practice of economy, or of producing and using the best of everything in the most beneficial manner' (Donnachie 2000: 237).

Linking theory and practice

Robert Owen had, by the age of 7, been a pupil-teacher and by the age of 9 had left school. However, he believed firmly in the power of education and set up what was for the time radical provision for young children. Some interesting features of the provision he set up included:

- *a focus on geography.* This perhaps reflects his socialism, with a recognition that different societies might do things differently. Wall maps were a feature of the environment.
- *a focus on morality.* Although an emphasis on morality was not unusual in Victorian England, Owen's view was unusual in that it included concern for equality – an aspect in which he was certainly ahead of his time. Donnachie suggests that even the geography taught had 'a strong moral undertone' (2000: 169) with an emphasis on respecting others.
- *excitement and conversation.* Whitbread (1972) describes the school as being filled with images and natural objects designed to promote children's curiosity and interest, creating 'an animated conversation between the children and their instructors'. Owen himself wrote in 1858 of:

> instruction by the inspection of realities and their qualities, and these explained by familiar conversations between the teachers and the taught, and the latter always allowed to ask their own questions for explanation or additional information.
>
> (Blackstone 1971: 18, citing Owen)

- *outdoor provision and physical activity.* There were:

> no regular indoor hours for school, but the teachers to discover when the minds of the taught or their own minds, commenced to be fatigued by the indoor lesson, and then to change it for out-of-door physical exercise in good weather; or in bad weather for physical exercise undercover, or exercises on music.
>
> (Blackstone 1971: 18, citing Owen)

- *music and dance.* Descriptions of singing, dancing and marching to fifes in the open air give an image of vibrant and lively provision. It has been suggested however that Owen believed that 'by promoting cheerfulness and content-ment' (Donnachie 2000: 170), he could keep children from bad habits.
- *an absence of books.* This perhaps the most remarkable aspect of Owen's curricu-lum. He himself wrote that 'the children were not to be annoyed with books' but there was to be an emphasis on first-hand, sensory experiences of 'the uses and nature and qualities of the common things around them' (Blackstone 1971: 17, citing Owen 1858).
- *a focus on well-being.* Blackstone (1971: 17) suggests that Owen 'anticipated modern psychological theory'. He wrote of a need to create 'real affection, and full confidence between the teachers and the taught' (Blackstone 1971: 17, citing Owen 1858). He instructed the teachers employed at New Lanark, James Buchanan and Molly Young, that:

> they were on no account ever to beat any one of the young children, or to threaten them in any manner or word or action, or to use abusive terms;

but were always to speak to them with a pleasant countenance, and in a
kind manner and tone of voice. That they should tell the infants and children (for they had all from one to six years under their charge) that they
must on all occasions do all they could to make their playfellows happy.

(Whitbread 1972: 10, citing Morton)

A critique of Owen's theories

The effects of the Industrial Revolution and of the land clearances in Scotland (from
which many of Owen's workers were refugees) were brutal. Owen created what must
have seemed at the time almost Utopian conditions. He offered work on what has been
termed the 'economics of high wages' (van der Eyken 1967). This meant that, despite his
contemporaries' disbelief, he turned concern for the welfare of his workers, rather than
the brutalising impact of 'sweated labour', to profit. It might be possible to criticise
Owen for his motives – did he act altruistically or was he just interested in profit?
However he seems to have acted with genuine philanthropic intent. He believed in
equality, he believed in social cohesion and he believed that kindness would be repaid
with kindness, sincerity with sincerity.

Alongside his concern for the plight of the poor and his belief in equality, there is
a whiff of paternalism. In saving the poor from 'vicious habits' or from 'things that are
vile and degrading' (Donnachie 2000: 170, citing Griscom) there is an assumption that
somehow the poor need more than improved conditions and an escape from poverty
to improve their lot. Writing at a time in the 1960s when there was a very low level of
provision for under-5s in Britain, van der Eyken (1967: 59) identifies this as an issue,
writing:

> it is perhaps unfortunate that the idea of nursery education has become so
> inevitably associated in the public mind with rescue work, and overlaid with
> emphasis on remedial treatment, for it has made harder the task of convincing
> society as a whole that the early years of any child are too important to be left
> unattended.

Owen has also been criticised for admitting children to the New Lanark school
from as young as 1 year of age. Like Locke, he believed that character is formed early
and that an early start in good social and moral habits would be nothing but a benefit
for young children. Again one must ask whether his undoubted altruism might have
been tinged with a desire to get the mothers of young children back to work?

The legacy of Owen's theories and practice

There can be no doubt of the impact of Owen's social experiment on social consciousness in relation to child labour and working conditions more generally. It is also

undoubtedly the case that Owen's work sparked an interest in what were then called infant schools (catering for children up to the age of about 6). Many visitors, including members of parliament, were attracted to New Lanark. By 1824, three infant schools had been established in London. A few of these schools, such as one set up in Bristol, favoured the approach put forward by Owen. In Glasgow, close to New Lanark, David Stow founded two infant schools (in 1826 and 1828). Although he favoured class instruction, he placed an emphasis on understanding and outdoors used physical play equipment and wooden building blocks. Whitbread (1972: 12) suggests that Stow preceded Froebel in favouring free play 'and understood Owen's aims better than the various English exponents of infant teaching'.

Best known amongst the English exponents is Samuel Wilderspin. James Buchanan, teacher at New Lanark, had opened the first English infant school in 1818. Wilderspin opened the second in 1820 but subsequently went on to establish about 150 infant schools in the next ten years across the country (Whitbread 1972). He and Owen were bitter rivals. Where Owen's ideas were based on strong philosophical and ideological principles, Wilderspin saw no link between education and social reform and is described as having no 'unifying pedagogical theory' (Whitbread 1972: 13). This is perhaps reflected in Whitbread's (1972) description of Wilderspin's provision.

She describes the tiered, galleried seating which he provided, perhaps familiar today from the stories which later emanated from twentieth-century reformers, such as the McMillans. This inevitably meant that the focus was on rote learning, a far cry from the excited and animated conversations described at New Lanark. He, in contrast to Owen, emphasised the methods employed in elementary schools. However he did suggest in his manual, published in 1823 and entitled *On the Importance of Educating the Infant Children of the Poor*, that children should spend half of their time in school outdoors – playing with swings, ropes and wooden blocks in playgrounds containing trees and flower beds.

Owen's legacy is the introduction of a developmental approach to the care and education of young children – an approach which took account of the 'imperatives' of early childhood (DES 1990). His conflict with Wilderspin marks the beginning of a conflict which continues to be waged today. Teachers, knowing that children would be leaving school at the age of 8 or 9, may have felt compelled to begin instruction early. Poor parents, in an age without social benefits of any kind, needed to work. Industrialisation had taken many people away from their communities and brought them to cities where they were often without the support of family. Schools – whether providing appropriate or inappropriate education – offered a form of day care which was desperately needed. Establishment figures who had been instrumental in setting up infant schools believed that they would act as a preparation for elementary school and for the world of work. This preparation was very different from that offered by Owen, who saw the best preparation as being the formation of a spirit of cooperation, equality and respect. However, sadly, 'Robert Owen was a lonely voice in an England convulsed with a search for power and quick wealth' (van der Eyken 1967: 63).

It was, as is so often the case, government intervention which was to delay the development of effective care and education for young children in the UK. It had become traditional, in the absence of other provision, that children under 5 could attend elementary school. At the beginning of the twentieth century, reformers began to voice concerns about the quality of provision for these children. In 1905, legislation enabled local authorities to refuse admission to them, but failed to require that nursery provision be offered. Van der Eyken (1967) offers statistics which highlight the impact of this decision. In 1900, 43 per cent of under-5s were attending school. By 1926, only 13 per cent were. While it could be seen that removing children from an inappropriate setting might be a good thing, the social reality was that 30 per cent of young children were all too often condemned to inadequate care and education.

Reflective questions

1. What do you think children learn from singing and dancing?
2. Identify some of the benefits to children and families and to the employer of an early admission to nursery (or infant) school.
3. The work of Robert Owen is known and admired in contemporary China. Why do you think this might be?
4. What reasons can you suggest for the widespread interest in Wilderspin's ideas as opposed to those of Owen?

Further reading

Donnachie, I. (2000) *Robert Owen: Owen of New Lanark and New Harmony.* E. Lothian: Tuckwell Press.

2 Friedrich Froebel 1782–1852

Owen and Froebel represent two strands of the movement to provide care and education for young children – a working-class and a middle class strand (Blackstone 1971). Owen is widely regarded as being representative of the philanthropists who responded to working-class need while Froebel may be seen as a key member of the group addressing middle-class need. Blackstone (1971) suggests that working-class needs were identified primarily as protection for young children both from exploitation and the impact of poverty. Middle-class needs, on the other hand, were focused on the benefits of provision outside the home. For middle-class families (Blackstone 1971: 14):

> a new educational theory came into being, which pointed to problems which had previously received little consideration. How might the young child's social and educational development be enhanced? The early Froebelian kindergarten indicated the possibilities of extra-familial communal activity, of guided and organized play as aids to the development of the young child. This appealed to a small section of the liberal-minded bourgeoisie, and a sprinkling of intellectuals as the deficiencies of life in the nursery became plain to them.
> *[Author's note: 'nursery' here refers to part of the home where children and their nanny resided.]*

Friedrich Froebel is widely credited with developing the term *kindergarten*. In fact he had earlier dabbled in the education of older children, and it was not until around 1840, that the first kindergarten officially came into being. He was the youngest of a large family and his mother died when he was just 9 months old. Throughout his life he had a deep interest in plants and nature becoming, when he left school, an apprentice forester. He worked with Pestalozzi and this experience was undoubtedly to underpin the value he later placed on outdoor provision. His experience of working with older children convinced him of the importance of early education (Whitbread 1972).

Froebel's theories

Froebel's book first published in 1826, *The Education of Man*, set out much of his philosophy. Froebel's writing, even in German, is 'open to misinterpretation' (Whitbread

1972: 32), since both the style and ideas are complicated. Froebel shared many of the ideals of Rousseau and Pestalozzi with a focus on the 'unfolding' of the child. The use of the metaphor of the *kindergarten* with its dual meaning of 'children's garden' or 'garden of children' highlights his view of children and childhood. Nicol (2007: 5) adds that in German 'garten' also carries the sense of transformation or metamorphosis. She suggests that Froebel intended its use to inspire the notion of 'a paradise garden'.

His notion of the child as an integral part of nature who should be left to blossom is clearly closely linked to this romantic view. Likening children to small flowers, Froebel emphasised his belief in nature, rather than nurture, as the basis of human development, writing:

> We grant space and time to young plants and animals because we know that, in accordance with the laws that live in them, they will develop properly and grow well; young animals and plants are given rest, and arbitrary interference with their growth is avoided, because it is known that the opposite practice would disturb their pure unfolding and sound development; but the young human being is looked upon as a piece of wax, a lump of clay which man can mold into what he pleases.
>
> (Froebel [1826] 2009: 8)

Millar (1968: 13–14) cites the value given by both Plato and Aristotle to play but acknowledges something of Froebel's role – a role that his translator Hailmann (Froebel [1826] 2009) suggests led to a true understanding of the value of play:

> Following the great educational reformers, from Comenius in the seventeenth, to Rousseau, Pestalozzi and Fröbel in the eighteenth and early nineteenth centuries, teachers increasingly accepted the idea that education should take account of the child's natural interests and stage of development. This culminated in Fröbel's stress on the importance of play in learning. An unhappy childhood lead him to take an interest in young children and his admiration for . . . romanticist philosophy . . . made the idea of freedom and self-expression almost an article of faith with him.

Also linked to play was the notion that learning essentially comes about by doing. Building on Pestalozzi's philosophy, Froebel placed an emphasis on the role of language as a way of understanding concepts. Furthermore he believed that language should be linked to actual sensory experiences (Whitbread 1972) and not reduced to mere verbalisation.

Play was also given spiritual importance since he believed that 'spontaneous play derived from a mystic notion of play as "the highest level of child development"' (Whitbread 1972: 32). He identified three forms or strands in play – forms of life which represent experience; forms of beauty by which we discover pattern; and forms of knowledge which help to make the abstract tangible (based on Read 1992: 5).

In fact, spirituality lay at the heart of play and of Froebelian philosophy. He wrote that:

> The purpose of education is to encourage and guide man as a conscious, thinking and perceiving being in such a way that he becomes a pure and perfect representation of that divine inner law through his own personal choice; education must show him the ways and meanings of attaining that goal.
>
> (Froebel [1826] 2009: 2)

Linking theory and practice

The complexity and inaccessibility of much of Froebel's theories are not reflected in his efforts to translate theory into practice. Millar (1968: 14) writes that:

> His sympathy with children, and his practical experience as a teacher, enabled him to realize that the kind of play children enjoy, and the toys they find most attractive could be used to gain their attention, and to develop their capacities and knowledge. His ideas were of great practical value.

Not only has Froebel been described as the first to have a philosophy of education (Aspin 1983), he was perhaps the first person to develop a comprehensive theory linked to practical activities and experiences (Pound 2005). Like Owen's provision, Froebel made use of singing and dancing. He published many songs, including a book of one hundred songs for playing with a ball (www.heidecksburg.de). The most famous are his mother-songs, designed to develop a child's physical and sensory awareness in fingerplay and physical action. Bruce (in press) writes that rhymes like 'Pat a cake' (which Froebel wrote) were 'aimed at the emerging symbolic life of the child' and that he valued the mothers' role in bringing up their children.

Froebel is perhaps most renowned for his focus on outdoor provision and has been described as giving it 'the same status as learning indoors' (Bruce 2011). Read (2009, cited by Bruce in press) describes Froebel's first kindergarten at Bad Blankenburg as providing a garden plot for each child as well as a community garden. Although in sympathy with Pestolozzi's emphasis on outdoor education, Froebel believed that he had placed insufficient emphasis on physical development and this influenced both his approach to the garden but also to the Gifts and Occupations.

For Froebel, Gifts and Occupations formed the link between work and play (Hailmann [1887] 2009). Occupations were a series of craft activities such as paper folding, sewing on punched cards and weaving, all designed to support the development of fine motor skills. Exercises based on the way in which Froebel had observed children drawing and using soft clay, wet sand and pieces of wood were devised. In his early writing Froebel emphasised play with large sets of around five hundred wooden blocks. He writes of them in *The Education of Man* (Froebel [1826] 2009: 283):

> The material for building in the beginning should consist of a number of wooden blocks whose base is always one inch square and whose length varies from one to twelve inches. If, then, we take twelve pieces of each length, two sets – e.g., the pieces one and eleven, the pieces two and ten inches long,

etc. – will always make up a layer an inch thick and covering one foot of square surface; so that all the pieces, together with a few larger pieces, occupy a space of somewhat more than half a cubic foot. It is best to keep these in a box that has exactly these dimensions; such a box may be used in many ways in instruction, as will appear in the progress of a child's development.

Over time, his emphasis became increasingly on what he termed the Gifts. Gift 1 was a box of six small woollen spheres. Gift 2 was a wooden cube, cylinder and sphere, while Gift 3 was a two-inch wooden cube divided into eight one-inch cubes. Gifts 4 to 6 were three eight-inch wooden cubes, each differently divided into cubes, half cubes, cuboids, and triangular prisms. The Gifts were:

> presented in a highly structured way. Children had to take the Gift carefully from the box and 'every block within the Gift had to be used and any new construction made by transforming the existing one, rather than knocking it down and starting again' (Read 1992: 5). A special table was provided, marked in one-inch squares to encourage careful and symmetrical working. When they had finished, children had to replace the blocks in the box.
>
> (based on Pound 2005: 15)

A critique of Froebel's work

Froebel was interested in development as he observed children at play. However 'there was little systematic knowledge of child development in Fröbel's time, and his conception of play as the "unfolding of the germinal leaves of childhood" does not explain anything' (Millar 1968: 14). This did not prevent Froebel from seeing the value of play. His interpretation of play as the work of God has led to some criticisms – but it must be remembered that he was writing from a nineteenth-century European perspective.

Blackstone's (1971) assertion that Froebel's practice addresses middle-class needs highlights a complex argument about the policy, theory and practice surrounding early childhood education. Van der Eyken (1967), as highlighted in Chapter 1, has suggested that provision designed to meet the needs of poor working-class children prevented early childhood care and education being seen as anything other than a remedial service. Blackstone (1971) on the other hand suggests that the education offered by Froebel created demand from middle-class parents for nursery schools which cultivated not merely family life, but 'the forming of national life and even of all humanity' (Singer 1992: 52). This argument remains familiar in the twenty-first century as evaluations of Sure Start demonstrate (NESS 2005).

There is also a question as to whether Froebel's work did actually only focus on middle-class need. Weston (1998: 15) writes that many of the children registered at Bad Blankenberg 'had first to be washed in the fountain in the market place before starting school'. But other writers (see for example Singer 1992; Whitbread 1972) question whether, in England, plans to broaden provision for poor families actually came to fruition. Some queried whether Froebel's approach was appropriate for all children – believing it would prove too expensive for working-class children (Black-stone 1971). Woodham-Smith (1952: 5) highlights once again the dilemma raised in Owen's time but still familiar today:

> One party said 'take time by the forelock, teach infants their prescribed tasks before they are legally required to repeat them; by mere reiteration the tasks will become familiar.' The other party said 'develop the infant's powers; teach him to attend, to construct; and "change" the standards.'

Despite his emphasis on free play, the instructions for the use of the Gifts and Occupations appear to twenty-first century eyes very rigid and formal. Bruce (2011) suggests that this is in part to do with misinterpretation. She writes 'People yearn for tangible ways forward and simple ways of working with children. But teaching is a subtle and often intangible process and set of skills'. The history of Froebelian education (Brehony 2000) demonstrates the tendency for practice to become ossified when insufficient attention is paid to underpinning philosophies. This was addressed around the turn of the nineteenth and twentieth centuries when a group of so-called 'revisionists' worked to take Froebel's work back to first principles. This gap between theory and practice is mirrored in Wilderspin's infant schools (see Chapter 1) – where Owen's philosophy was not reflected in Wilderspin's work.

Froebel's own childhood is widely described as unhappy. The death of his mother and the apparent subsequent neglect by his father inevitably coloured his view of moth-erhood and family life. Bruce (in press) reminds us of the legacy of Froebel's work in encouraging women to work with young children and will be considered in the next section of this chapter. Blackstone (1971: 19) suggests that much of the provision aimed at working-class families in the early part of the nineteenth century, which was often in overcrowded and 'appalling conditions' was run by men. However, some writers have claimed that this shift in practice was to lead to a situation where only women worked with young children in what Whitbread (1972) describes as 'entrenched' practice.

The legacy of Froebel's work

Froebel is internationally recognised and the word *kindergarten* is internationally un-derstood. However, many of the things for which Froebel may be criticised are also part of his legacy. While Bruce (in press) suggests that efforts to offer free places for working-class children in Froebelian nurseries marked 'the beginning of the Nursery School Movement', there is some doubt about the extent to which this actually hap-pened in Britain (see previous section of this chapter). Nonetheless, as with the philoso-phies of Owen and Pestalozzi, the aim of greater equality may be applauded. Two other aspects of Froebel's legacy – child development and the role of women – were by the end of the twentieth century to have been the subject of much critical thinking.

Child development

Although knowledge of child development was embryonic at that time, Froebel's fascination with child development was part of a wider interest in how children

develop. A century before Darwin published his documentation of his son's development, Pestalozzi had written *A Father's Diary* containing observations of his three year
old son (Bartholomew and Bruce 1993). Froebel was by no means alone in his interest
but was perhaps pioneering in developing his understanding by attempting to link it
to practice. His work was said by a contemporary (Singer 1992: 50; citing van Calcar
1879) to have created 'the basis of human development':

> It is the mother's wisdom that can take humanity further than all the wisdom
> of men put together. But she has to know what she can do, and do what
> she knows. A new science has been discovered for her, designed by Froebel –
> the science of mothers which can and must become the science of women
> generally.

The role of women

This also highlights the criticism of placing too heavy an emphasis on the role of
women in educating young children. This should be seen as part of a wider movement.
In this period, Florence Nightingale was, for example, opening up career opportunities
and training for nurses (Bostridge 2008, cited by Bruce 2011). Froebelian training for
women teachers began in Britain in 1854, and Nightingale began training nurses in
1860. Bruce (2011) highlights the importance of Froebel's efforts to bring women into
the profession since there were very few career paths open to women. Work in a kindergarten bridged the divide between home and work, since it mirrored the role of mothers
in caring for young children. Froebelian training was offered in many parts of England
in the second half of the nineteenth century (Whitbread 1972). In addition to the
many teacher training courses, the Norland Institute was opened in 1892, still today
acclaimed as offering training for elite nannies to elite families.

Research

The Froebel Institute in London (now part of Roehampton University) has played an
important role in furthering Froebel's legacy. The work of Chris Athey, then a lecturer at
the Froebel Institute, in developing schema theory arose in part out of funding from the
Council of Management of the Froebel Educational Institute. The research itself took
place from 1972 to 1977. It aimed to build on the findings of a project (1971–2), also
based on Froebelian principles, which claimed success in children's individual progress
but was unable to find more general principles about children's learning. Athey (1990:
218) writes that this project 'revealed a need for detailed research into the more minute
units of psychological growth'.

The second project was set up, the full details of which are outlined in Athey's
(1990) book *Extending Thought in Young Children*. An experimental group of children
was observed daily in an effort to identify developments in thinking; developments
in symbolic representation (including physical representations) and consider curricular implications. The teacher working with the experimental group was Tina Bruce –
offering a curriculum in the spirit of Froebelian practice but with an updated content involving 'participation in cooking, movement, dance and music, constructing,

creativity and play, in an atmosphere of community with purpose, with a garden' (Bruce in press). The project continues to have an enormous impact on practice – both in this country and internationally as schemas are seen to have relevance in young children's learning (Bruce 2005; Meade and Cubey 2008).

In addition to all the work that has emerged in relation to the role of schema in young children's thinking and development the study has had a great impact on thinking about the importance of partnership between home and family (Whalley 2001). In fact the work of early excellence centres which acted as trailblazers in progress towards integrated provision was built on the work of Pen Green. Pen Green has employed both Tina Bruce and Chris Athey as pedagogues supporting the development of staff at the centre.

The second seminal research project to develop from Froebelian practice was the Blockplay Project. This has been well-documented by Pat Gura (1992). The development of wooden blocks is widely attributed to Froebel, although as was seen in Chapter 1, Wilderspin and others were using them before Froebel's kindergartens were set up in the British Isles. In *The Education of Man* Froebel writes:

> Building, aggregation, is first with the child, as it is first in the development of mankind, and its crystallization. The importance of the vertical, the horizontal, and the rectangular is the first experience which the child gathers from building; then follow equilibrium and symmetry. Thus the child ascends from the construction of the simplest wall with or without cement to the more complex and even to the invention of every architectural structure lying within the possibilities of the given material.
>
> (Froebel [1826] 2009: 281)

Reflective questions

1. In what aspects of your practice can you see evidence of Froebel's legacy?
2. What do you believe that children learn from the use of blocks and from outdoor play?
3. In what ways do you think Froebel's theories influenced thinking about child development?
4. Do you think that Froebel's insistence on women as the teachers of young children has or has not been helpful in promoting equality between the sexes?

Further reading

Bruce, T. (2011) Froebel today. In L. Miller and L. Pound (eds) *Theories and Approaches to Learning in the Early Years*. London: Sage.

Part 2
Progressive ideas of the twentieth century

Part 2 takes up the story of the development of educational theories and philosophies at the beginning of the twentieth century. This was a time when middle-class kindergartens were apparently thriving nationally and internationally – although the numbers actually attending are unclear. Provision for working-class children remained mired in dreadful conditions, with widespread – but often patronising – concerns. It is into this scenario that a range of progressive and innovative approaches begin to emerge. In the chapters that follow the work of some of the influential pioneers of early childhood education of the twentieth century will be explored.

The period up to the Second World War was marked by a range of radical and progressive approaches to education for children of all ages. Some of the innovations in the early years were, as Owen's ideas had been, a response to socio-economic deprivation but many represented an effort to improve the quality or effectiveness of education. More than a century later this still finds echoes in public concerns. Physical conditions may have improved but a clear sense of direction too often remains elusive. Although not specifically written about the education of young children but about education in general, Claxton (2008: vi–vii) states that:

> The purpose of education is to prepare young people for the future. Schools should be helping young people to develop the capacities they will need to thrive ... but they are not getting it. ... This is shocking and it is dangerous. Education has lost the plot, and it urgently needs to recover its core purpose.

Provision for under-5s

Compulsory education was introduced in 1870 for all children over the age of 5. Under-5s were not included – partly because members of the ruling classes feared that the widespread introduction of what were then called infant schools 'would lead to the insubordination of the working classes' (Blackstone 1971: 23) and partly because there was a widespread belief that children under the age of 5 should, or perhaps would, be at home with their mothers. Blackstone (1971: 23) outlines the contradictory positions (perhaps not very different from those of today) held at the time:

The attitudes of the Victorian middle class were neither uniform nor consistent. They varied from the belief that all children, rich and poor, should attend educational institutions outside their home at an early age, to the assertion that the home was the only place suitable for young children. Between these two poles lay a number of intermediate attitudes including one that recommended that educational provision should be made for the children of *working* mothers, or the children of the destitute.

The fact that compulsory education was to begin at the age of 5 in contrast to the start of education in so many other countries is said to have been selected so that children could begin work at the age of 10 (Blackstone 1971, citing Stretzer). Others claimed that 'an early start would prevent the exploitation of young children in the home and remove them from the unhealthy physical conditions of the slum house and the dangers of the street' (Blackstone 1971: 23). The decision to allow children to enter school before the age of 5 and its impact has been referred to in Part 1. No notion of developmental appropriateness was employed in making this decision – an omission which was compounded by the introduction of the principle of payment by results in 1862. In order to achieve the desired standard by the age of 7, instruction began at an increasingly early age 'on the principle that constant repetition produces results' (Blackstone 1971: 23). Despite the many advances that have been made in understanding about children and learning, these ideas with all of their inconsistencies still abound.

Kindergartens run by Froebelian trained teachers flourished throughout the second half of the nineteenth century amongst middle-class families. Parents who could pay the hefty fees were encouraged to think of the benefits for their children of being in touch with nature, and suggesting that the kindergarten provided a bridge between home and school. In the 1870s two free kindergartens for the working classes were established in Manchester. Although free, and despite claims that Froebelian principles of play and rest were employed, up to 500 children were accommodated in settings. As Blackstone (1971: 27) comments rather drily 'it appears that standards were sacrificed in favour of numbers'. Froebelian in name but not in character.

The first free kindergarten in Woolwich in London was established thirty years later, in 1900, by Adelaide Wragge. She was the principal of the Blackheath Kindergarten Training College and was apparently jolted into action by:

> visitors from America (who) were shocked to find no Kindergartens in England, but only large classes of poor little automatons sitting erect with 'hands behind' or worse still 'hands on heads,' and moving only to the word of command.
>
> (Murray and Brown Smith nd)

Wragge's free kindergarten was not actually called a kindergarten but a mission because it was linked to the work of Adelaide's brother who was a minister. It was also not actually free because parents were expected to contribute one penny per week. Wragge (cited by Murray and Brown Smith nd) herself wrote that:

The neighbourhood was suitable for the experiment; little children, needing just the kind of training we proposed to give them, abounded everywhere.... The Woolwich children were typical slum babies, varying in ages from three to six years; very poor, very dirty, totally untrained in good habits. At first we only admitted a few, and when these began to improve, gradually increased the numbers to thirty-five. They needed great patience and care, but they responded wonderfully to the love given them, and before long they were real Kindergarten children, full of vigour, merriment and self-activity.

These and many other similar acts of philanthropy, undoubtedly of varying quality, give an indication of the concern in some quarters about the health and well-being of the nation's children. Recruitment for the Boer War highlighted the scandalous ill-health of the population and 'pioneers had been campaigning for systematized preventive medicine, such as school medical inspections for some years' (Blackstone 1971: 27). Even when Margaret McMillan successfully campaigned for the introduction of school health checks, which were finally established in 1907, children under 5 were excluded. It was this omission which encouraged her to set up the first nursery school.

In addition to concerns about young children's health, there were similar misgivings about the educational approaches employed. In an article entitled *The Need for Nurseries,* an inspector highlighted the physically uncomfortable, developmentally inappropriate and educationally ineffective conditions in which very young children were being kept. She writes:

The discipline expected is military rather than maternal, and can only be maintained at the expense of much healthy, valuable and as far as the children are concerned necessary freedom.

(Blackstone 1971: 29, citing Bathurst 1905)

In the same year (1905), *The Report on Children Under Five Years of Age in Public Elementary Schools*, was published. The authors' summary recommended:

It will be seen that there is complete unanimity that the children between the ages of three and five get practically no intellectual advantage from school instruction. The inspectors agree that the mechanical teaching in many infant schools seems to dull rather than awaken the little power of imagination and independent observation which these children possess.

'No formal instruction' is the burden of all the recommendations 'but more play, more sleep, more free conversation, story telling and observation'. The aim ... is too often to produce children who have mastered the mechanical difficulties of Standard 1 work. It should be to produce children well developed physically, full of interest and alertness mentally and ready to grapple with difficulties intelligently.

> It would seem that a new form of school is necessary for poor children. The better parents should be discouraged from sending children before five, while the poorer who must do so, should send them to nursery schools rather than schools of instruction.
>
> (Board of Education document cited by Blackstone 1971: 29)

John Dewey (1859–1952) – bridging cultures and philosophies

The work of the American philosopher, psychologist and teacher, John Dewey, may serve to bridge the early pioneers such as Owen and Froebel with the work of what Selleck (1972) has called the 'progressives'. Certainly he spans the two centuries chronologically and in terms of philosophy he also offers some interesting links. His theories, like those of Owen, emerged at the time of the Industrial Revolution – the impact of which was felt later in America than in Europe. In addition, like Margaret MacMillan, Susan Isaacs, Rudolf Steiner and Maria Montessori, he is regarded as a progressive. Ideas of democracy and citizenship which permeated English practice in the period between the two world wars were central to and inspired by Dewey's thinking and writing. Moreover, because he lived so long he was still writing at the time when Piaget's constructivist theory began to have an impact on educational practice.

Apple and Teitelbaum (2001) suggest that Dewey's greatest contribution was his prolific writing. A pragmatist and a philosopher, he believed it to be his duty to offer social criticism. He believed that democracy was not primarily about government but about citizens actively and equitably engaging in all aspects of society including culture and economics. He regarded change as the natural order of things and saw schooling as the key to social progress. In 1896 he established what he termed a laboratory school, an elementary school where he put his ideas into practice.

He believed that schooling should be seen not as a preparation for life, but as part of life itself. He was critical of many child-centred approaches which he saw as giving the teacher a 'negligible role'. While old approaches cast the role of the teacher as a dictator, what he saw as necessary was the teacher as 'the intellectual leader of a social group' (Dewey 1910). He wrote that:

> the most effective curriculum . . . would attend seriously to the present interests of children, not as a motivational strategy but as a way to teach the essential relationship between human knowledge and social experience.
>
> (Apple and Teitelbaum 2001: 180)

Like Froebel, he believed that children learn by doing. It was this together with his focus on children's interests which led to him being widely identified with what is termed a project approach. He recognised the importance of social contact which he saw as stimulating curiosity and rejected the idea of children as merely individuals. For Dewey, schools shape society and must help children to live in a society. Somewhat ironically since he rejected the ideas of socialism, reportedly calling Marxism 'unscientific utopianism' (Apple and Teitelbaum 2001: 181), Dewey's ideas have been highly influential in China.

Admired by progressive thinkers in the field of early childhood education, Dewey's most significant contribution may have been the development of the notion of reflective professional practice (Pound 2005). This particular legacy is one which bridges the nineteenth and twenty-first century. Howard Gardner (2006) in a book entitled *Five Minds for the Future*, for example, highlights the importance of reflective practice for *all* professionals. Dewey identified distinct stages in the process of critical reflection:

- being perplexed
- finding a tentative explanation or interpretation
- a more careful observation
- an elaboration, or firmer explanation
- testing the hypothesis.

(based on Pollard 2002: 4–5)

Despite influencing so many thinkers, Dewey is not without his critics. Some critics suggest that such a project approach can lead to trivialisation of curriculum content. This would of course be avoided in practice by engaging fully in the reflective practice that Dewey recommended. A more fundamental criticism has been developed by Egan (2002). He argues that Dewey's ideas came from Herbert Spencer (1820–1903) whose work Egan suggests is flawed in a number of ways – beyond the scope of this account. Primarily though, Egan challenges the notion that any educational approach can be based on ideas about how children learn – since, in his view, our knowledge will never be sufficient. What is actually needed to improve education he suggests is that practitioners 'make (children's) minds most abundant by acquiring the fullest array of the cultural tools that can, through learning, be made into cognitive tools' (Egan 2002: 184).

New approaches to education

The publication of two books influenced the development of progressive education in Britain. One was *What is and What Might Be* ([1911] 2008) by Edmond Holmes and the other was *The Play Way* (1917) by Caldwell Cook. The first is believed to have marked the beginning of progressive education in Britain. Holmes was a school inspector until the publication of this book but claimed that he was unable to achieve the necessary change from within the system (Selleck 1972). The book offered a model of an education in which children could feel joyful and free – rather than being hedged around by the 'blind, passive, literal, unintelligent obedience ... on which the whole system of Western education has been reared' (Selleck 1972: 23, citing Holmes). Caldwell Cook's book set out to spread play-based approaches throughout all schools, including secondary – which he declared was 'the one thing upon which my heart is fixed ... to make this dream come true in our England' (Caldwell Cook 1917: 2). His aim in this was to establish an approach to education which emphasised learning, focusing on joy, activity, interest and democracy (Pound 2008).

From a wealth of figures who contributed to the development of progressive ideals in this country, two others should not be omitted. One is Homer Lane (1875–1925) who was described by contemporaries as 'determined to excel, ebullient, unpredictable and restless' (Pound 2008: 61). This colourful figure was brought from the United States by the Earl of Sandwich to establish what was termed the Little Commonwealth – a co-educational learning community for difficult children. In America he had successfully worked with young delinquent boys. The Little Commonwealth was based on the assumption that giving children a combination of freedom and trust could lead to an ordered community. He is said to have achieved remarkable results – albeit for a short period of time.

Summerhill, A. S. Neill's school, was established in 1921 and is still running today – though not without controversy. Neill (1883–1973) was a mainstream teacher but unhappy with what he was able to provide, he became influenced by Homer Lane. The central philosophy of the school was that children's happiness was the most important element in learning and that it arose from a sense of freedom. Both Homer Lane and A. S. Neill held Freudian views (see Part 3) – and these often conflicted with mainstream views urging repression of sexual drives and strict Victorian values. Like other progressives Neill believed in democratic education – a view which is still central to the school's philosophy.

Forest schools

Forest schools are widely believed to have been developed in the 1950s in Scandinavia (Pound 2005) – and the ideas imported to Britain in the 1990s. However there are many earlier precedents. Froebel's initial training was as a forester. In 1916, Ernest Westlake, a progressive thinker devised the Order of Woodcraft Chivalry. Children from 4 to 8 years of age were included, known in the movement as 'elves'. The order was based on ideals of 'religion, ritual, tradition, discipline and mystical expression, all coming together in a radical movement opposed to the given social structures' (van der Eyken and Turner 1975: 134). Westlake believed that:

> the child who has been rooted and grounded in Woodcraft will be able to use the higher crafts without injury, and books without pedantry. In this way traditional learning and social culture will have full opportunity to complete the wisdom and refinement necessary to his highest functioning.
>
> (van der Eyken and Turner 1969: 134, citing Westlake)

From this beginning, following his father's accidental death, Aubrey Westlake with three others established the first forest school in the New Forest. It ran from 1929 to 1938 and inspired the development of many other progressive schools such as Bedales and Dartington – both still running today. The life, though basic in many ways, was also idyllic in that children lived much in the open air. If they did not want to attend lessons they could help with farming tasks.

Ideas about intelligence and the education of children with cognitive impairment

Throughout the nineteenth century interest in mental disability grew. Jean Marc Gaspard Itard, who was born in 1775, is perhaps best known for his work with Victor of Aveyron – a child of about 12 years of age who had been left in the wild since early childhood. (Victor's story subsequently was made into a film by Truffaut entitled *The Wild Child*.) The boy was taken to the National Institute for the Deaf in Paris, where contemporary scientific interests focused on the differences between animals and humans. Itard believed the major differences to be around empathy and language. When study of the boy failed to produce the results scientists were seeking, Itard took him in and although he was able to produce some changes in his behaviour there was not sufficient development to fit the child for an independent life.

Early in his career Edouard Seguin worked with Itard at the National Institute for the Deaf. Seguin's focus was less on deafness and more on cognitive impairment. He set up the first private school for children with mental disabilities in 1840. In 1846 he wrote what is thought to be the first systematic textbook on the subject. In 1848, he moved to the United States of America where his work continued, working to improve conditions for disabled people. In 1866 he published a book entitled *Idiocy: and its treatment by the physiological*. This outlined what was termed Seguin's Physiologial School, in which he demonstrated a belief in the importance of self-regulation and independence. Both Margaret McMillan and Maria Montessori were influenced by the work of Edouard Seguin.

A third Frenchman Alfred Binet (born Binetti in Nice, now part of France but then part of the Kingdom of Sardinia) contributed a great deal to the development of thinking about intelligence. Late in his career, working with his student Theodore Simon, he was charged by the French government with developing tests which would allow those considered unfit for mainstream education to be identified and given special education. In 1905 the first Binet-Simon intelligence test was published and this, in many revised forms, has provided the basis of intelligence testing to this day. Piaget worked with Binet. (The influence of ideas about intelligence will be explored further in Part 6.)

Reflective questions

1. Consider the views expressed about early education at the beginning of the twentieth century. To what extent are these views still current?
2. The 1905 report argued that children should be 'well developed physically, full of interest and alertness mentally and ready to grapple with difficulties intelligently'. To what extent do you think these are still appropriate priorities? How well do early childhood practitioners to day address these aims?
3. Why is reflective practice important?
4. What do you think the purpose of education is? To what extent do you agree with Claxton that education has 'lost the plot'?

Key dates

1850–1936	**Edmond Holmes**
1859–1952	**John Dewey**
1860–1931	**Margaret McMillan**
1861–1925	**Rudolf Steiner**
1870–1952	**Maria Montessori**
1875–1925	**Homer Lane**
1883–1973	**Alexander Sutherland Neill**
1885–1939	**H. Caldwell Cook**
1885–1948	**Susan Isaacs**

Further reading

Selleck, R. (1972) *English Primary Education and the Progressives 1914–1939*. London: Routledge and Kegan Paul.

Van der Eyken, W. and Turner, B. (1975) *Adventures in Education*. Harmondsworth: Penguin Press Ltd.

3   Margaret McMillan 1860–1931

Rachel and Margaret McMillan, sisters, spent most of their working lives together. Despite working so closely, it is Margaret who is most widely known since Rachel suffered ill-health for many years. Although they were born in New York, their mother returned with them to their native Scotland after the death of her husband and youngest daughter. Both the father and daughter had died of scarlet fever which Margaret had also contracted but which she survived. The disease however caused her to be deaf for nine years from the age of 5. Margaret McMillan later wrote that their mother became shadow-like after these sad events and appeared to be ashamed of being a widow (Pound 2005).

The two sisters had deeply held Christian and socialist views. Their political interests led them to see the impact of both rural and industrial poverty at first-hand. They were astute in realising that 'social welfare required political action' (Whitbread 1972: 61). They saw for themselves the devastating amounts of disease and deformity prevalent in poor families which could have been prevented in early childhood if their parents had had more money and knowledge (Blackstone 1971). In Bradford, Margaret was able to persuade fellow school board members to appoint a medical officer in 1894. In 1897 she gave Bradford another first – the first school bath in the country, which she believed 'would reveal curved spines, crooked legs and other defects of malnutrition and inadequate physical care, as well as eliminate vermin' (Blackstone 1971: 35). These advances were to lead to (as noted above in the introduction to Part 2) the achievement of a statutory medical service for children of school age (1907) and school meal provision (1906).

The sisters' combination of astuteness and determination enabled them to persuade a reluctant London County Council and a philanthropic American industrialist to join with them in establishing the first school clinic in 1908. However, they quickly realised that although they could provide some remedies for endemic poor health, their work was not preventing disease. Their curative approach included vast numbers of tonsillectomies and a remedial gym which was seen to improve children's health and strength. But, in 1911, they set up a night camp in a churchyard in Deptford which they believed would help to minimise the spread of tuberculosis. More than 50 children slept in open air shelters for nine months of the year. Van der Eyken (1967: 67) gives a vivid picture of the early days of the initial camp:

a nearby garden . . . (was) converted into a camp for the children, to give them an opportunity to escape from the claustrophobic, unventilated and polluted atmospheres of their homes. What the sisters wanted to provide was fresh air, light and space. They put up canvas awnings over fixed gas pipes and turned an outside drain into a shower bath. More canvas was turned into camp beds, and in this improvised camp seventeen girls spent a whole year sleeping in the open without a single one of them catching pneumonia.

It is in this context that the educational work of Margaret McMillan should be seen. Between 1913 and 1914 an open air nursery was also established in Deptford where their work was to flourish. The school still exists today, the Rachel McMillan Nursery School. The classes are still called shelters and there is still one of the original baths.

McMillan's theories

Rachel McMillan regarded much of their early work as little more than remedial. For her, much more radical solutions were needed. Margaret McMillan wrote, following Rachel's death:

> The injury done to the child of poor streets and slums is not to be remedied by any form of literary . . . education. New environment, and a new study of organic subjects involving the speech centres, the middle brain and the respiratory and circulatory systems – these must come first. These won, it is possible to build a new structure, to aim at a wider education, to attempt the unfolding of a new personality.
>
> (McMillan 1927: 128)

Margaret shared this interest in the brain. Like Montessori, she was interested in the work of Edouard Seguin. Working in Paris and subsequently America, Seguin was interested in what were then called 'defectives' – children with mental disabilities. For Margaret the relevance of Seguin's work was that she believed that the 'poor streets and slums' of which Rachel had spoken were the starting point for many 'subnormal traits' (McMillan [1904] 1923). She wrote of the impact of:

> nasal complaints that prevented children from learning to speak properly, early deformity at two or three 'through having been obliged to sit with their legs tucked under a table'. . . and fingers almost atrophied because they never had an opportunity to use them.
>
> (Whitbread 1972: 61, citing McMillan 1923: 34)

Despite their shared concern for the needs of the poor, the McMillans did not see nursery education in itself as a remedial venture. They refuted the idea put forward in the report of a consultative committee in 1908 that nursery schools were not necessary for richer families. 'The open-air Nursery School is here for rich and poor' they insisted, continuing 'it is ... the thing, lacking which, our whole educational system was like a house built on the sand' (Curtis 1963: 335, citing McMillan 1930).

Whitbread (1972) describes McMillan's educational theories as eclectic. She describes the Rachel McMillan Nursery School as being in the Owenite tradition. She, like Owen, thought it important to educate the whole child and to fit children for their future life. She believed, like him, in a developmental approach – fitting the pedagogy to the child's needs. Although essentially practical, her writings often reflect her deep spirituality which Owen, while holding strong moral and social values, did not share. She is widely reported as having suggested that 'we must try to educate every child as if he were our own and just as we would educate our own' (see for example Whitbread 1972: 63). In this too, there is a link with Owen, since he sent some of his own children to a school on which he modelled New Lanark. Certainly her socialist, or even Marxist (Whitbread 1972) views were strongly linked to those of Owen.

On reaching London in the final years of the nineteenth century, Margaret joined the Froebel Society, and by 1902 she had become a member of its council. She undoubtedly shared with Froebel the sense of importance of being in touch with nature and its spiritual qualities. Whitbread (1972) claims that McMillan 'derived many of her educational ideas from Pestalozzi and Froebel'. She was also influenced by the theories of other progressives, including Dewey (Blackstone 1971). Despite sharing an interest in Seguin's work and despite facing many of the same issues, she disagreed with aspects of Montessori's philosophy.

However with another of the European progressives, Rudolf Steiner, McMillan felt she had much more in common. In 1904, McMillan published a book entitled *Education Through the Imagination* ([1904] 1923). This showed the influence of William Morris and John Ruskin – both of whom were very involved in the Arts and Crafts Movement. The influence of the Arts and Crafts Movement lasted from around 1880 until 1910. The Society of Arts and Crafts which was set up in 1897 was committed to the use of natural materials, reliance on traditional craftsmanship rather than machines and to economic reform. It is easy to see why the McMillan sisters, constantly campaigning as they were against the impact on children of the Industrial Revolution were drawn to this. Steiner was invited to give lectures in England. On his arrival he was given a copy of *Education through the Imagination*. Steiner describes his pleasure at what McMillan had written:

> she is led to say that the wonderful power of Imagination is not to be found only in the minds of scientists and artists, but that it is also the driving force in all that we do in our daily life.... The brain of every grown man and every child is in its way a world in which a degree of creative force is revealed. As soon as a man expands beyond mere routine the imaginative creative power which carries him as a thinking being through life, enters into him. In the child whose activity is not yet hampered by routine, imagination reveals itself as the real driving power of the soul and this it is that the trainer and educator should make use of.
>
> (Steiner [1904] 1923: 142)

The philosophy developed by the McMillans had at its heart:

- the fairness and social justice demanded by their socialist views;
- the sense of hope and the drive to make things better, motivated by their faith; and
- the sense of beauty drawn from their views of the importance of nature and simplicity based on the diverse views of Ruskin and Morris on the one hand and Froebel on the other.

Since they observed children closely, their philosophy also included an under-standing of the need for children to be children – given 'time and space' (words fundamental to their philosophy) to run and jump, play and imagine. The unwritten motto of Steiner Waldorf education is 'here we have time ...' (Nicol 2007: 74). Guy Claxton (1997) highlights the importance of enabling learners to take their time. This runs contrary to OFSTED advice that so often praises 'pace' and yet we know that adults regularly fail to allow children time to gather their thoughts in speech (DCSF 2008).

Linking theory and practice

For the McMillans the principle objective of nursery schools was to promote children's physical, emotional and intellectual well-being. 'Time and space' described vital aspects of the provision which emerged from the experience and thinking of them both. In her book *The Nursery School* (McMillan 1919) Margaret describes the space needed by young children. The classrooms, or shelters, were light and airy with windows that folded right back in order to maximise the sense of contact with the outdoors. She wrote that:

> from the age of one to seven, space, that is ample space, is almost as much wanted as food and air. To move, to run, to find things out by new movement, to feel one's life in every limb, that is the life of early childhood. And yet one sees already dim houses, behind whose windows and doors thirty or forty little ones are penned in 'Day Nurseries'. Bare sites and open spaces are what we need today.
>
> (Curtis 1963: 333–4, citing McMillan 1930)

A sense of having time, she insisted, could be provided through free activity. In an address to the Nursery Schools Association of Great Britain and Northern Ireland, given at the time she was elected its first president in 1923, she argued, somewhat controversially for a longer nursery school day with extended hours. She stated that:

> Underlying all mental and bodily development lies the need for free activity. Without it neither healthy growth of body and spirit, nor training in self-control is possible. . . . Free activity involves the provision of spontaneous and purposeful activity in spacious open-air conditions . . . as well as an atmosphere of love, joy and freedom. . . . The daily routine must provide for the right

alternation of rest and activity through the day.... It is undesirable to accept the hours of the ordinary school day as the limit for nursery school.

(Pound 2005: 25, citing McMillan [1904] 1923)

Fresh air is at the heart of McMillan's approach. She described the garden as 'the essential matter', continuing:

> ...not the lesson, or the pictures or the talk. The lessons and talk are about things seen and done in the garden, just as the best of all the paintings in the picture galleries are shadows of originals now available to children of the open air ... (which) should make them ready for the later work of 'lessons' by letting them learn in a natural way from the first.
>
> (McMillan 1930: 2).

The fresh air and exercise which the outdoor provided was part of an overall belief in the need for education to take part in a nurturing atmosphere. 'Nurture included nourishing food, therapeutic physical activity including music and movement, fresh air and sunshine' (Blackstone 1971: 39). However, physical nurture was only a starting point – the starved intellect and emotions had also to be nurtured. Food and rich experiences (including music, stories, play and free movement) were regarded as being of equal importance.

A critique of McMillan's theories

The McMillan sisters have been criticised for favouring large institutions. It was their belief that if provision was not too expensive, more would be provided. Efficiencies could more easily be achieved if children were placed in large groups. At one stage, the school in Deptford catered for 500 children – not all of nursery age. Today, most people would regard that as inappropriate provision for such young children. However, children were not organised into classes but in small groups of 6 under-5s or 12 over-5s. Each group was assigned a helper, who assisted the trained teacher in her work. By this time, training establishments were widespread – indeed Margaret McMillan established one adjacent to the school. These establishments had already become the realm of women – the view that the field of early childhood was women's work having become in Whitbread's word 'entrenched' (1972). (See also Chapter 2.)

In a similar vein, Margaret was criticised for the long hours that children attended the nursery school – from 8.00 am to 5.30 pm each weekday. As indicated earlier in this chapter, she countered this criticism by asserting that normal school hours were not long enough to do all that needed to be done with very young children. Blackstone (1971: 38) suggests that McMillan regarded these long hours as necessary 'to make listless and undernourished children strong and healthy'. McMillan (1919) described the nursery school as a 'healing agency', arguing that unless firm foundations including health and well-being were established, money spent on education at any age would be wasted.

The saddest critique is that, despite the many successes of Margaret and Rachel, they failed to achieve their utopian view of what could be achieved through high quality nursery education. The Education Act of 1918 contained a clause that allowed children who were attending nursery schools to delay attendance at elementary school until the age of 6. By 1928 only one in a thousand children was in nursery school. Van der Eyken (1967) draws out the similarities with the Plowden Report (CACE 1967) which suggested raising the age of entry to primary school. The McMillan dream had been that nursery schools for all would:

> make a new Junior School possible because it will send out children who are equipped for a much easier and more rapid advance than is the average child of today. . . . The modern world of interest and movement and wonder will be ajar for him already.
>
> In short, if it is a real place of nurture, and not merely a place where babies are 'minded' till they are five, it will affect our whole educational system very powerfully and very rapidly. The Bastilles will fall at last – by the touch of a little hand.
>
> (van der Eyken 1967, citing McMillan 1927)

The legacy of McMillan's theories

This failure to achieve their major dream should not be allowed to blind modern readers to their very real achievements. Margaret was a powerful and persuasive speaker. She gained the support of many rich, influential and famous people. She and Rachel together made a difference to many young lives. They worked with and for parents and community. They succeeded in changing attitudes to health provision for children, including the introduction of school meals. They brought to the attention of policy-makers and government, who might otherwise not have noticed, the plight of young children.

Although they did not create the major social reform that Dewey, for example, sought they continue to influence practice even today. The focus on the importance of the nursery garden (Bilton 2010; Tovey 2007; White 2008) and the development of forest schools (Blackwell and Pound 2011; Knight 2009) owe much to their pioneering ideas. During the first half of the twentieth century their views shaped the way in which nurseries were set up. Chelsea Open Air Nursery was set up in 1929 for children whose lives were regarded as too advantaged and sheltered. Whitbread (1972: 72) suggests that 'it took months to train children who had had nannies to be independent in dressing, washing, and use of the lavatory'. The children were said to be nicknamed 'Kensington Cripples' (Whitbread 1972) or 'the cripples of Chelsea' (Pound 1986). Ideas such as this marked a shift away from the clear class lines along which nursery education had evolved.

Reflective questions

1. Do you think the McMillan sisters had different objectives in promoting outdoor play from those of Owen or Froebel? What were their main aims?
2. In what ways did the McMillan sisters believe that a focus on health would improve children's learning?
3. In what ways does imagination support learning?
4. What, in your view, is the importance of space and time in young children's learning?

Further reading

Lowndes, G. (1960) *Margaret McMillan: the children's champion.* London: Museum Press Ltd.

4   Rudolf Steiner 1861–1925

Rudolf Steiner was born in a part of Austria (which is now Croatia). He was a philosopher described by Taplin (2011) as

> an artist, with a scientist's interest in the natural and the man-made world, and a person with an inner life so rich and deep that he initiated and inspired innovative work in areas ranging from education, through medicine, social development and agriculture to theatre and design.

He established anthroposophy in 1912, sometimes described as 'a science of the spirit', the human struggle for inner freedom, or the study of humanity. The World Anthroposophical Society, set up in 1923, is based in Switzerland and has 70 branches world-wide. The organisation's website (www.anthroposophy.org) states that its aim is to create an 'association of people who would foster the life of the soul, both in the individual and in human society, on the basis of a true knowledge of the spiritual world'.

Emil Molt, director of the Waldorf Astoria cigarette factory, was so impressed with Steiner's thinking that in 1917, he asked for his help in setting up a school which would cater both for middle-class families and for the children of the factory workforce. The school was established in 1919. Now, almost 100 years later Steiner-Waldorf schools are to be found in 60 countries around the world. Overall there are around 900 schools catering for children up to the age of 18 or 19, and 1,800 kindergartens. In order to be known as a Steiner-Waldorf school, the school must 'support all pupils to develop their potential for clear thinking, sensitive feeling and motivated doing' (Taplin 2011), and teach in line with the Steiner Waldorf curriculum.

Steiner's interest in education began early. At the age of 14 he gained employment as a tutor. In 1864, at the age of 23 he was employed by a family with several sons. In *The Education of the Child* (1996, first published in 1907), Steiner describes his part in the successful education of one of the boys who had hydrocephalus. When Steiner became his tutor, the 10-year-old boy's academic skills were minimal but within two years he was able to enter secondary school with his peers, passing an examination for the Gymnasium (similar to a grammar school). The boy subsequently became a doctor – although he went on to die in the First World War. Steiner describes the way in which he observed the boy, seeking to tune into his needs – and this experience awakened his interest in education.

Steiner's theories

Steiner's educational theories sprang not initially from concern for the plight of the poor, nor with concern for children disadvantaged by their own social and economic advantage but with a single child whose education and approach to learning presented a challenge. His aim was to create an education system for children of all ages which rested on a series of what he regarded as developmental stages – each lasting approximately seven years. For the first seven years of life, he believed it to be important for children to develop strength of will. Seven to 14-year-olds were to be developing sensitivity of feeling while the next seven years are described as the time when humans may attain clarity of thought. It is seen as the job of educationalists to work with these stages as they emerge or unfold, making provision for the changing needs of the child.

In a document entitled *Guide to the Early Years Foundation Stage in Steiner Waldorf Early Childhood Settings* (Steiner Waldorf Education 2009: 5), the authors offer the following explanation of the theories underpinning Steiner Waldorf education:

> The Steiner Waldorf early childhood approach takes as given the interdependence of physical, emotional, social, spiritual and cognitive development. It takes account of the whole child, including his/her soul qualities, and believes that children's learning flourishes in a calm, peaceful, predictable, familiar and unhurried environment that recognises the child's sensory sensitivities. Young children need to experience the relevance of their world before they separate themselves from it and begin to analyse it in a detached way.

A third and equally recent view of Steiner's theory or approach is described by Trevor Mepham who is currently the principal of the Steiner Academy that has been set up in Hereford. In the introduction to *Meeting the Child* (Drummond and Jenkinson 2009: 7) he writes:

> Perhaps it is not too far-fetched to describe the human condition in the following terms: as we live, we eat; we partake of the world and all that is in it – whether by looking, by breathing, by meeting, playing or working. As we encounter the world and all that life has to offer we are nourished. Immersed as we are in this process of engagement and nourishment, the steps that follow are transformation, assimilation and expression. The task of 'eating' the world leads from universality to individualization, the shaping of the human being; nowhere is it more tender or potent than in early childhood.

Linking theory and practice

Based on deeply held principles, Steiner Waldorf early childhood settings endeavour to offer:

> an education that supports the young child to understand and love him or herself, other people and the earth. The intention is not to preserve children in an idyllic version of the past, but to prepare them for the future by building secure foundations.
>
> (Taplin 2011)

Firm principles on which this aim rests are described by Nicol (2007) as the 3Rs of Steiner Waldorf early education; namely rhythm, repetition and reverence. Taplin (in press) identifies the following principles:

- imitation and example
- imagination
- purposeful activity and free movement
- rhythm and repetition and
- child observation.

Imitation and imagination

These principles translate into practice through an emphasis on play and imitation up to the age of 7. Play is self-initiated and adults do not engage directly in it. Their role however is to make appropriate provision and to provide an anchor, acting as a model which children may imitate. Heckmann (2008: 20–1) suggests that:

> Small children refer to the center all the time, and the adult is their center or gravity. If the adult leaves the room, the children stop what they are doing and follow.... I always advise adults to do visible work in close proximity to the child, for example cooking, cleaning, and hanging up the laundry, things that are necessary for the well-being of the family and need to be done. Children often enjoy participating in these tasks in their own way and at their own pace.... These tasks have a completely different effect on the child's play and ability to relate than so-called activities.... The more children trust their center, the more courage they have to go out into the periphery. If children know their mother will stay there ironing they are not afraid to make an excursion into the next room.... When you maintain a peaceful state of mind in yourself, it creates security within them.

Play incorporates imitation and imagination but is also fed by practical experiences such as gardening and cooking. Formal schooling does not begin until the age of 7, but informal learning in a calm and purposeful atmosphere is highly valued. Stories are told rather than read and music is regarded as an important element of provision – with a focus on vocal sound and the use of a lyre or small glockenspiel. Electronic devices are not used and all play materials are made from natural materials – wood, wool and so on. What is termed 'warm technology' or hand-manipulated tools, such as drills and whisks are encouraged (Steiner Waldorf Education 2009: 28). Much of the activity (as well as the resources and environment) is reminiscent of the work of The Arts and Crafts Movement, which was discussed in Chapter 3. This should not be surprising since although in another country Steiner was developing his curriculum around the same time as Margaret McMillan.

Imitation is regarded as developing in three stages during the first six or seven years of life (Nicol 2007). It involves the development of the child's will which Nicol (2007: 9) describes as follows:

> Will activity is very individual, and we can observe this in the different ways children imitate. For example, everyone has the same thing in front of them, but their reactions are quite different. Some children immediately start to imitate, or to play nearby the adult, taking in the atmosphere of the working activity, while other children don't get the impulse at all. Within imitation there is freedom.

The first stage or phase of imitation is described as occurring up to the age of 2 and a half years of age. Steiner practice suggests that playthings should include 'natural organic forms such as wooden logs, shells conkers etc' in order to 'stimulate the child's formative and imaginative forces' (Nicol 2007: 14). The second stage runs from 3 to 5 years of age when imagination and memory develop. Experience is reflected or imitated in play – as natural objects become play props, such as wheels, food or animals. From 5 to 7 years of age, what Steiner practitioners term 'the will forces' lead the child to self-initiated activity; play becomes planned. Nicol (2007) suggests that the space and time that McMillan highlighted as vital are necessary to children of this age in order to allow them to observe and reflect the world, rehearsing (or representing) what they have experienced over and over again in their efforts to make sense of it.

The environment

The environment is regarded as part of the curriculum. Drummond et al. (1989: 59) have described a typical setting:

> The teacher attempts to engage the child's whole being in what they do, in as an artistic way as possible, by providing a warm and joyful environment in which the child can feel nurtured and at ease, happy to explore and play, be busy and be still.... The room is painted and in a warm colour, has few hard rectangular corners, and is often furnished with soft muslins to mark off a different area, or draped over a window to give a softer light. The quality of sound is that of human voices rather than mechanical toys. The materials in the room are natural and are at children's level, and stored in aesthetic containers such as simple baskets or wooden boxes which may themselves be incorporated into the play.

Repetition and rhythm

Rhythms are identified not only in physical action but in the passing of time, within a single action like preparing a meal or hand-washing; within the day; the cycle of the year both in terms of festivals and in relation to the natural order to seasons and growth. All of these are regarded as of vital importance since health, well-being, and 'the feeling of coherence . . . is strengthened through rhythm and order (which) bears fruit in adulthood in increased resources of resistance and resilience' (Patzlaff and Sassmannshausen 2007: 32).

Reverence for the child

The reverence to which Nicol refers is for each other, for the environment, for food and for each child as an individual. Practitioners use three questions as what Nicol (2007: 43) describes as 'meditative study' to enable them to focus on each child:

- Where has this child come from?
- Where is he or she going?
- What can I do to support this?

Observation is an important part of the work of the adult. Steiner (1920, cited in Steiner Waldorf Education 2009: 35) exhorted practitioners to realise

> what I accomplish with this child, I accomplish for the grown up in his twenties. What matters is not so much a knowledge of abstract educational principles or pedagogical rules. . . . What does matter is that a deep sense of responsibility develops in our hearts and minds and affects our world view and the way we stand in life.

Steiner Waldorf Education (2009) refers to observation as 'picture building'. Observation is to be of the whole child and should rely on insight and the development of an intuitive understanding of the child. It should attempt to interpret what is seen, thereby increasing understanding of the unfolding person. Perhaps more difficult for the non-Steiner trained practitioner to understand is the emphasis on 'inner work' – a process of holding the child in a meditative fashion in his or her thoughts.

A critique of Steiner's theories

The response of many English early childhood practitioners when they hear that print is not introduced to children in Steiner schools until the age of 6 or 7 is often incredulity. In a country that has favoured an early start to the more formal aspects of schooling this feels impossibly late. While in many other European countries an introduction to literacy has generally come later, many people in this country have maintained the view that in order to get ahead children have to begin earlier. In the history of early education in England, the roots of this belief are evident – payments by result, an early entry into the labour market and so on. However, this view has been widely maintained in the face of evidence to the contrary.

Research in New Zealand by Suggate (2009a) for example shows no significant differences in reading ability by the age of 11, between children taught to read at 5 and those at 7 years of age. He suggests (Suggate 2009b) that the most important factors in later reading ability are play, language and interaction with adults and that taking time away from these things in the early years may disadvantage children in the longer term (see also Paley 2004). This is reflected in, for example, standards of achievement in Finland where although formal schooling does not begin until the age of 7, children there consistently outstrip children who have made an earlier start.

Criticism is often made of Steiner Waldorf Education for its absence of modern technology. The argument is often that since we are educating children for the twenty-first century, it is necessary to employ the tools of the twenty-first century. However Alexander (2010) in his review of the primary curriculum has criticised the government initiated review of the primary curriculum (Rose 2009). He suggests that there is a danger that computers and other information technologies become 'a tool without apparent substance or challenge other than the technical'. He is not alone in urging caution. The extent to which technology is tied into commercialism is worrying – but when used by young children, particularly worrying because they are likely to be more susceptible to its influence. Secondly, long hours spent in front of a screen do not help to 'build intelligent muscles' (Healy 1999). It is not only Steiner Waldorf Education which has identified the importance of physical activity for young children – it is not experience of a virtual world which is needed, but real and sensory experience. Speech therapists also suggest that the use of television and video with very young children should be limited (Chonchaiya and Pruksananonda 2008). In addition, neuroscientist Professor Susan Greenfield has warned of the dangers of ICT:

> The mid-21st century mind might almost be infantilised, characterised by short attention span, sensationalism, inability to empathise and a shaky sense of identity.... If the young brain is exposed from the outset to a world of fast action and reaction, of instant new screen images flashing up with the press of a key, such rapid interchange might accustom the brain to operate over such timescales.... Real conversation in real time may eventually give way to these sanitised and easier screen dialogues.... It is hard to see how living this way on a daily basis will not result in brains, or rather minds, different from other generations.
>
> (Greenfield's evidence to the Cambridge Primary Review team, Alexander 2010: 270)

The legacy of Steiner's theories

Perhaps the greatest legacy of Steiner's theories is the fact that they have endured. Changes in policy and pedagogy have come and gone but Steiner principles and practice have been consistently adhered to, not just in this country but throughout the world. Although often regarded as rather marginal or unconventional, the philosophy is widely respected. An interim study for the Alexander report (Conroy et al. 2008) highlighted the importance of what are still seen as alternative approaches. (This report also commented favourably on the contribution to leadership which Steiner philosophy and practice can make.) This respect is also reflected in Mary Jane Drummond's (1999: 58) writing:

> I am not a Steiner educator, nor ever will be. I have no intention of settling and putting down roots within the Steiner community of discourse.... My intention here is to take stock of what I have learned ... from my friends and colleagues in the Steiner movement, and to outline the ways in which my notebooks full of observations have shaped my present understanding. I do so in the hope that other educators, in any of the great variety of settings where children live and learn, may here find some support for their continuing advocacy of children's play.

When Margaret McMillan and Rudolf Steiner were alive they admired one another's work (Steiner [1904] 1923). They shared a view on the importance of play, of observing and tuning into the 'child-mind', delaying a beginning to formal education and so on. Over the years those who followed and built on McMillan's ideas in the mainstream faced new challenges. Policy and curricular changes have forced developments which often made good sense but over time may be seen to have eroded the simple truth that children's needs must be judged from what they do rather than from a set of predetermined objectives. Steiner practice and philosophy has remained the same, against the onslaught of OFSTED inspections and requirements to adhere to EYFS curriculum demands.

Steiner philosophy has kept alive the belief that children do not have to begin to read at 5, do not have to use a computer before they can walk. It has challenged the over-protection of children by enabling 2-year-olds to cut with real knives and 6-year-olds to whittle with sharp implements. Perhaps above all they have kept the faith in and with children. Drummond (1999: 57) writes that:

> It seems to me that Steiner educators express in every line and every utterance their fundamental trust, in both children and adults. They trust in the pedagogical value of what children spontaneously do in their play, in a harmonious and supporting environment; ... and they trust as completely in the value of their own, adults activities – their story telling, their sewing, their music-making, their calm, sensitive watchfulness, their joyful loving presences – as they consciously shape the environment in which the children learn by living.

Mepham (Drummond and Jenkinson 2009: 7) takes up this theme. He writes of the belief that Steiner practitioners have in children, belief:

deriving from love and commitment, rather than simply accepting proposi-tions that might be either robust or dubious ... however we help, guide, live and work with young children. It is a huge and worthy belief to hold and to nurture.

He concludes by welcoming 'the continued probing and exploration of Steiner's ideas on education – both the theory and the practice'.

Reflective questions

1. What differences do you think there might be between the observa-tions you make of children and the kinds of 'picture-building' in which Steiner practitioners engage?
2. What might you do to your learning environment to make it calmer?
3. What activities do you offer children that enable them to meet and manage risk? What do they learn from these opportunities? How could they be extended?
4. Review some of the ideas about literacy learning. What can you learn from these ideas?

Further reading

Nicol, J. (2007) *Bringing the Steiner Waldorf Approach to Your Early Years Practice.* London: David Fulton.

Taplin, J. (2011) Steiner Waldorf Early Childhood Education – offering a curriculum for the twenty-first century. In L. Miller and L. Pound (eds) *Theories and Approaches to Learning in the Early Years.* London: Sage.

5   Maria Montessori 1870–1952

Maria Montessori was a remarkable woman. In 1896, she became the first woman in Italy to receive a degree in medicine. Her subsequent hospital work led to her interest in children with intellectual impairment. This in turn led her to study the work of Edouard Seguin. By the age of 30, Maria Montessori had already been teaching medicine and education, been given an award for her outstanding work in hospitals and led a school of 'mentally deficient' children in Rome. After visiting elementary schools she decided that their methods of teaching were inferior to those she used, and that she herself achieved better results with what were regarded as much less able children. Applying these methods to 'normal' children would, she believed, set their personalities free (Montessori 1919).

Her first mainstream school the Casa dei Bambini (Children's House) for 3 to 6-year-olds, opened in Rome in 1907. Bradley et al. (2011) suggest that her aim of keeping the children of working mothers off the streets and reducing vandalism is parallelled by the cooperation between Rudolf Steiner and the Waldorf Factory owners. A second Casa dei Bambini was opened in Milan in the following year, 1908. The first in the United States of America opened in 1911 and interest was already developing in England. In 1916, the London Borough of Acton decided that all its provision for young children should be based on Montessori principles and practice. This influence on mainstream provision was to continue for many years, right up to the Second World War – with Montessori advising the London County Council on its provision in nursery and infant schools (Curtis 1963).

Montessori's theories

Montessori was amongst the first early childhood theorists to claim a scientific basis for her theories. She identified sensitive periods, suggesting a small window of opportunity when particular things could be learned most effectively (see also Part 6 of this book). These particular things for which critical periods existed, she suggested, were co-ordination of senses, language, awareness of order and small detail, refinement of the senses and socialisation (Bradley et al. 2011). She believed strongly in freedom of choice and independence for children. That freedom stemmed from the adults' willingness to observe and plan from their observations. Failure to do this limited children's freedom (MacNaughton 2003).

Her view of freedom has much in common with Steiner's theory. For her it must be limited only by respect for others and for the environment. This she believed would support the development of self-discipline which in turn would lead to self-motivation, and bring about enhanced concentration and perseverance.

Just as Steiner identified specific stages of development, Montessori suggested that there were four main developmental stages. The first lasts from conception to the age of 6. The second, from 6 to 12 years of age is regarded as a period when the child is hungry to find things out. From 12 to 18 is thought of as a creative period while the stage from 18 to 24 was identified as a period of 'calm expansion' (Bradley et al. 2011). The first stage, up to the age of 6 which is the focus of this book is characterised as being focused around an absorbent mind, sensory experience and self-creation 'when the child begins to develop their own view of the world within their culture' (Bradley et al. 2011).

Montessori's careful observation of children led her to believe that young children had a number of characteristics which should be nurtured in order to support their development and independence. She believed that they:

- were capable of extended periods of concentration;
- enjoyed repetition;
- 'revelled in freedom of movement';
- preferred work to play;
- were self-motivated and self-disciplined;
- enjoyed silence and harmony; and
- were capable of learning to read and write.

(based on Isaacs 2007: 6)

Linking theory and practice

These perceived characteristics hold a number of implications for practice. The notion that children can concentrate for long periods of time is linked to practice by ensuring that children have extended periods of time in which to concentrate. Sessions are not, for example, broken by snack times and story times since these are seen as an unwarranted intrusion into the child's 'work curve'. Montessori (1948: 95–6) suggests that:

> children need a cycle of work for which they have been mentally prepared; such intelligent work with interest is not fatiguing and they should not be arbitrarily cut off from it by a call to play. Interest is not immediately born, and if when it has been created, the work is withdrawn, it is like depriving a whetted appetite of the food that will satisfy it.

The environment, indoors and out, is carefully arranged so that children can choose from an appropriate range of structured learning materials. Order and an absence of clutter are thought to minimise distractions. Children select structured apparatus from a range provided and are given the opportunity to repeat the same experience time after time. Montessori observed that children used a particular activity or exercise, then repeating it several times, rather than moving to a new one. It was work for its own sake, not for reward. The curriculum focuses on:

- daily living;
- sensory education;
- language development;
- mathematics; and
- an exploration of the world which is designed to integrate 'mathematical, linguistic, sensory and daily living activities' (Pound 2005: 31).

Daily living is reflected in a range of activities such as cooking, gardening, dressing and cleaning. Sensory experience is seen as important and a wide range of structured materials are used to heighten olfactory, oral, visual and kinaesthetic awareness and discrimination (for examples see www.absorbentminds.co.uk). Language development is focused on all four aspects – talking, listening, reading and writing. A widely recognised feature of Montessori practice is the use of sandpaper letters – reflecting the focus on sensory and phonic learning.

A critique of Montessori's theories

Montessorian approaches are sometimes criticised for being overly prescriptive and rigid. This means that practice, rather than being dynamic and open to change can become ossified, or over-rigid. This is understandable when it is remembered that Montessori was catering for a group of children whose slum conditions often made their lives chaotic and disordered. What is interesting about this however is that while Montessori education is very much a product of the working-class movement for early childhood education, in the latter part of the twentieth century and on into the twenty-first century it has become very much a middle-class movement. Princess Diana, for example, chose a Montessori pre-school for her son William.

Montessori's views about work and play perhaps also have their roots in similar concerns about the challenging home lives of the children with whom she was working. She believed that the children with whom she worked needed to learn about meaningful tasks and ought not to be distracted by fanciful ideas. However, for many early childhood practitioners, Montessori's apparent rejection of play and imagination poses difficulties. Modern analyses (see for example Montessori St Nicholas 2008) suggest that the apparent conflict of ideas arises from historical interpretations and that today 'freedom of choice, the exercise of will and deep engagement, which leads to concentration' (Montessori St Nicholas 2008: 21) are seen as common to both work and play.

A third area of criticism concerns the focus on phonics. Montessori's contemporary, Susan Isaacs, was highly critical of both Montessori's views on play and imagination (Smith 1985) and on phonics. Isaacs suggested that:

> it is the paucity of other games in the Montessori schools which makes the children take to this new occupation. In the Froebel kindergartens, with their incomparably greater variety of occupations to exercise the child's powers of intuition and imagination, his interest and independence, as a general rule, scarcely any instances of liking for reading and writing exercise are to be observed.
>
> (Smith 1985: 255, citing Isaacs)

This is an interesting area since as Bradley et al. (in press) point out an early introduction to phonics and print is entirely in line with many policies, including the Early Years Foundation Stage in England (QCA 2007). However, as Steiner Waldorf theory and practice highlight, this is not without controversy. It might also be relevant to consider that Italian, the language in which Montessori developed her ideas, is entirely phonetic while written English is not at all regular.

The legacy of Montessori's theories

Montessori education, like Steiner Waldorf education, has stood the test of time. Conroy et al. (2008) praise Montessori education as they do Steiner Waldorf education for the alternative and principled approach which both bring to mainstream thinking. Like Steiner Waldorf it remains very popular. However, unlike Steiner Waldorf which continues to cater for children up to the age of 19, it remains much less active in the later years of schooling – although there are examples both in the United States and in this country. Unlike Steiner Waldorf education its approaches are clear and direct for practitioners to follow. The equipment that Montessori devised is widely used in other forms of pre-school provision. The resources are generally made of wood and are aesthetically pleasing as well as offering a range of sensory experience. As indicated in the next chapter Susan Isaacs initially used Montessori materials.

The effectiveness of Montessori teaching methods has most recently been demonstrated by the results of a study published in the US journal, *Science* (Lillard and Else-Quest 2006). Along with Steiner Waldorf education it was also highlighted by Conroy et al. (2008) as offering particular benefits from which mainstream practitioners might learn. In a study which looked at children at 5 and at 12, Lillard and Else-Quest (2006) conclude that when compared with a control group from the mainstream Montessori education gives children:

- an advantage in reading and in mathematics;
- improved behavioural and academic skills; and
- an enhanced sense of justice and fairness.

The authors conclude that 'when strictly implemented, Montessori education fosters social and academic skills that are equal or superior to those fostered by a pool of other types of schools' (Lillard and Else-Quest 2006: 1894). In addition, many parents report that it gives children the ability to behave quietly and purposefully as they go about their self-chosen activities.

Reflective questions

1. What aspects of Montessori's approach do you think makes children successful in learning mathematics?
2. What are the drawbacks in trying to use an approach to education devised for children with learning difficulties in mainstream groups?
3. Do you think an approach to reading that is based entirely on phonics can work with children learning to read English?
4. What are the overlapping characteristics of work and play?

Further reading

Bradley, M., Isaacs, B., Livingston, L., Nasser, D., True, A-M. and Dillane, M. (2011) Maria Montessori in the United Kingdom. In L. Miller and L. Pound (eds) *Theories and Approaches to Learning in the Early Years*. London: Sage.

Isaacs, B. (2007) *Bringing the Montessori Approach to Your Early Years Practice*. London: David Fulton.

6   Susan Isaacs 1885–1948

Susan Isaacs may be thought to hold a pivotal role amongst the twentieth-century progressives. She was critical of her contemporaries such as, as we have seen above, aspects of the work of Montessori. A psychologist by training, she favoured psychoanalytic theory working closely with Anna Freud and Melanie Klein (an aspect of her work which will be explored further in Part 3). Unsurprisingly in the light of this interest, Isaacs was also critical of the work of Piaget, who largely ignored the role of emotions and feelings in learning. Isaacs visited Piaget's research centre in Geneva and Piaget visited the Malting House School in 1927. In 1929, although Isaacs had left the Malting House in 1927, Piaget was amongst several distinguished educators and thinkers of the day who attempted to rescue the school from insolvency (van der Eyken and Turner 1969).

In 1933, Susan Isaacs became the first head of the Department of Child Development – now London's Institute of Education. Thus, numbered amongst the progressives she, like Montessori, was developing a science of pedagogy. Although she resisted any involvement in research projects (van der Eyken and Turner 1969) the detailed and extensive observations collected during her time at the Malting House underpinned her subsequent theories and writings. Isaacs wrote extensively for parents. From 1929 to 1936 she wrote a column addressing parents' anxieties and queries in *Nursery World*, under the pen-name of Ursula Wise.

Isaacs' theories

Isaacs' theories followed Froebel's belief that children learn by doing and that play is of great importance. She was also influenced by John Dewey, sharing his views about the importance of social interaction and of following each child's interests. This is reflected in this extract from *The Nursery Years*, published in 1929:

> Not all (the child's) play, however, is directed to exploring the physical world or practising new skills. Much of it is social in direction, and belongs to the world of phantasy. He plays at being father and mother, the new baby sister, the policeman, the soldier; at going for a journey, at going to bed and getting up,

and all the things which he sees grown-ups doing. Here also his play makes it easier for him to fit himself into his social world. When he becomes the father and the mother, he wins an imaginative insight into their attitude to him, and some little understanding of their sayings and doings; and momentarily feels their powers and great gifts (as they seem to him) as his own. All the things he may not do and cannot be in real life, he is able to do and be in this play world.

(Isaacs 1929: 10–11)

These words also reflect the strong impact of psychoanalytic theory (see Part 3 of this book) on her educational and developmental theories. In 1933 she, jointly with Cyril Burt, gave evidence to the government's *Report on Infant and Nursery Schools* (Board of Education 1933) in which her focus on the importance of the emotional aspects of children's development is highlighted. The following quote is taken from the report but the chapter which included these words was written by Susan Isaacs and Cyril Burt:

Quiet, positive encouragement, showing the child what to do and how to do it, is far more important than scolding or punishment, or emphasis on what he should not do. Successes should be emphasised; failures should be minimised; and above all any feeling of shame or hostility should be avoided.

(Board of Education 1933, cited by Smith 1985: 58)

Isaacs' cooperation with Burt throws up a perhaps unexpected aspect of her theory. Despite placing a strong emphasis on challenging environments and interactions (which might suggest a nurture stance in the nature/ nurture debate), she believed with Burt that intelligence was a fixed element within each child.

Linking theory and practice

The Malting House School was small, generally catering for around ten children (most of whom were boys) who were generally aged from 3 to 7. It had two main aims:

- to stimulate the active enquiry of the children themselves rather than to teach them ...
- to bring within their immediate experience every range of fact to which their interests reach out.

(Tovey 2007: 46, citing Isaacs 1930: 17)

When first setting up the Malting House School, Isaacs had described it as a Montessori school and purchased substantial amounts of Montessorian structured apparatus (Smith 1985). These remained as part of the school's indoor provision but the real focus of Isaacs' practice was the garden. Her psychoanalytic training led her to place an emphasis on freedom, arguing for the role of play as having 'the greatest value for the child when it is really free and his own' (Isaacs 1929: 133). Her contemporary Lawrence (cited by Smith 1985: 73) describes the happiness of the children reflected in 'shrieks and gurgles and jumpings for joy'. A journalist who had been invited to see a film of the work of the Malting House declared that there 'children's dreams come true' adding 'after having seen this film, I came away wishing with all my heart that my own dull schooldays had been as theirs were, and that education could be made such an adventure for every child' (text from the *Spectator*, cited by van der Eyken and Turner 1969: 56–7).

The garden can only be described as extraordinary. It had a range of stimulating, features (some familiar – others less so) which included:

> grass, fruit trees, a climbing frame, slides, movable ladders, trees for climbing, flower and vegetable gardens with individual plots for each child and a range of animals, including chickens, guinea pigs, as well as snakes and salamanders.
>
> (Tovey 2007: 47)

Tovey (2007) includes a number of examples from contemporary writers and subsequent historians of the activities in which children were engaged outdoors. She writes of children climbing on the summer house roof – but only one at a time. Children were allowed to build fires – but were only allowed one box of matches and were not allowed to build their fires near the wooden summer house. Descriptions (included in Tovey 2007 and in van der Eyken and Turner 1969) paint a picture of children mending, exploring, climbing, making and in short *doing* all manner of things which might be considered as dangerous. Isaacs believed that freedom created a sense of responsibility and enabled children to learn to be safe. She wrote:

> The children climbed trees and ladders, used tools and handled fire and matches far more freely than is commonly allowed, and with complete immunity – partly no doubt, because of our careful supervisions but largely also because their skill and poise become so good under these conditions.
>
> (Isaacs 1930: 25)

Isaacs' theories led her to create an environment in the Malting House School in which the emphasis was on:

- curiosity and finding out
- talk to promote thinking, and
- paying attention to children's emotional needs.

Her practice addressed all three of these aspects of provision and despite only being at the Malting House for three or four years, Isaacs' practice was to have immense influence.

A critique of Isaacs' theories and practice

In this part of the book the focus is very much on child-centred provision but the twentieth century characterised by some as 'the century of the child' (Smith 1985: 59) was not without its detractors. Many contemporary writers were critical of Isaacs' theories and the way in which they were translated into practice. Smith (1985: 59) suggests that concerns about free methods which 'especially in untrained hands, can look sometimes more like chaos than school' may have come from many quarters:

> working-class parents may realistically emphasize vocational training, not self-expression and harmonious development for their children, while middle-class parents, anxious for their children to rise, may push for examination-governed methods and curricula, so as to improve the chances of university acceptance. Freer methods may seem like a luxury or at least a waste of valuable time to people with these practical or personal concerns.
>
> (Smith 1985: 59–60)

Smith also highlights the view, familiar from arguments about the appropriateness of statutory schooling, that working-class children ought not to be taught to think as this might make them dangerous (1985). Further criticisms relate to the romantic nature of Isaacs' theories:

> Education philosophy had become dangerously romantic since the (1914–18) war, the more dangerously so because it was encouraged by, for instance, the American school of Dewey to clothe its romance in the trappings of science and to dignify it by the title of psychology.... Believing thus in free development it believed also that the individual's capacity for development was predetermined at birth and that its limits could be measured in advance. The individual's 'intelligence quotient' could be ascertained at an early age ... and it was unalterable.... Those who cannot believe in the daylight fact of original sin fall easy victims to the calvinistic nightmare of predestination.
>
> (Smith 1985: 60, citing Percy 1958)

Current reviews of Isaacs' work are often surprised by her belief in the notion of fixed intelligence, referred to in Percy's words. Smith (1985) underlines the contradiction to be found in Isaacs' work – being at once a hereditarian, seeing intelligence as fixed; and an environmentalist, bringing out children's potential. Isaacs was also aware of contradictions, discussing with psychoanalyst Klein the difficulties she faced in managing children's freedoms. Graham (2009) gives examples of individual children's unhappiness and Isaacs' own conflict in supporting such children from the choices of other children – which were making them unhappy. These difficulties were resolved as she explored the concept of autonomy – but not without a great deal of heart-searching as she struggled to put into practice deeply held beliefs.

Isaacs' views of intelligence need to be seen in the light of current thinking at that time. Cyril Burt, with whom she worked, was in the mid-twentieth century well-respected for his work on intelligence but was later discredited for having apparently falsified his findings of the inherited (or otherwise) nature of intelligence.

Finally Isaacs' work may be criticised for the fact that her theories rested on work with a small number of children, all of whom were highly advantaged in coming from rich and academic families. The children were mostly boys and considered to be of high intelligence; many demonstrated difficult or challenging behaviour (van der Eyken and Turner 1969).

The legacy of Isaacs' theories

Despite these criticisms it is difficult not to see Issacs as having left a strong legacy for early childhood education. Drummond (2010: 2; citing Isaacs 1932: 113) sees her as of great importance in the development of early childhood education:

> Susan Isaacs changed our way of seeing children, rather than our ways of providing for them. She was passionately interested in children and their learning. She emphasised . . . that they too are passionately interested in the whole world and everything and everyone in it. . . . Let us give Susan Isaacs the last word . . . 'the thirst of understanding springs from the child's deepest emotional needs . . . [it is] a veritable passion'.

Isaacs' ideas have influenced generations of practitioners and parents. This is in part through her books and articles which remain highly readable. It is also because of her work in the Department of Child Development, which was apparently set up in order to harness Isaacs' talents (Graham 2009). Now called the Institute of Education at London University, this institution continues to have a great impact on theory and practice – not only nationally but internationally. The EPPE study (Sylva et al. 2004) for example – a longitudinal study of children's experience of early childhood care and education and its impact – was undertaken there.

Let's not forget the impact on outdoor provision which Isaacs' work has had. Her vision of children's ability to manage risk and create challenges for themselves has much to teach today's risk averse society. Walsh (2004: 108) reminds us that:

> what children can do at any given historical and cultural moment depends a great deal on cultural constraints – what is accessible and not accessible, valued and not valued, and so on. The norms themselves become constraints that both enhance and restrict as society sets strong expectations about what children can and cannot, and should and should not do. Missing is the sense of the possible.

Isaacs saw what was possible because she observed children carefully but also because she believed in their abilities.

Reflective questions

1. What aspects of Susan Isaacs' garden could you incorporate into your outdoor space?
2. What do you think are the benefits of the imaginative play that Isaacs encouraged?
3. Do you agree with Isaacs' view that a child's need to understand the world is 'a veritable passion'.
4. Do you agree that freedom creates a sense of responsibility which in turn enables children to learn to be safe?

Further reading

Graham, P. (2009) *Susan Isaacs: a life freeing the minds of children.* London: Karnac Books Ltd.
Smith, L. (1985) *To Understand and to Help: the life and work of Susan Isaacs (1885–1948).* London: Associated University Presses.

Part 3
Psychodynamic theories and their impact

The chapters that follow in this section of the book, Part 3, will focus on the psycho-analytical work of Freud; on those such as Anna Freud, Klein and Winnicott whose work focused most specifically on young children, and on the development of thinking about attachment. Finally a chapter will focus on recent developments in bringing together emotional and cognitive development.

This will by no means cover the whole field, which would require many volumes of its own. It will inevitably give insufficient emphasis to key figures in the movement such as Carl Jung [1875–1961] and Erich Fromm [1900–1980] both of whom have made important contributions to thinking about and understanding the development of personality and the role of emotions and feelings. Throughout the chapters that follow in Part 3, it is however likely that these names will feature. Jung was closely associated with Freud but the two were irreconcilably divided as it became clear that Jung's work was focusing more and more on religion and the supernatural, while Jung believed that Freud overstated the sexual influences on human development. It should be remembered (Manning-Morton 2011) that for Freud and his followers 'sexual influences' included other sources of bodily pleasure. Jung developed the idea of extroversion and introversion – terms widely used today in everyday conversation. Fromm disagreed with Freud's view that humans are at the mercy of their unconscious drives.

The beginnings of psychology

The roots of psychology, as we know it today, lie in physiology and in philosophy (sometimes described as mental philosophy). In America, William James (1842–1910) published a book entitled *Principles of Psychology* (1890) which focused on topics such as emotion and habit. In Europe, Hermann von Helmholtz (1821–1894) was perhaps the first experimental physiologist to venture into fields which we now identify as psychology but it is Wilhelm Wundt (1832–1920) who is known as the 'father of experimental psychology'. Wundt worked initially on apperception – that is, studying the point at which things we have not consciously perceived come into our consciousness, and in 1874, published a book entitled *Principles of Physiological Psychology*. Meanwhile in France Jean Martin Charcot, a neurologist, was influencing many people who were to remain as renowned figures in psychology well into the twenty-first century. Amongst his students was Itard whose work with Binet was discussed in Part 2 of this book, and Freud who was initially drawn to Charcot's work on hypnotism.

In Britain, there was less overt focus on this new science of psychology. The work of philosophers like John Locke (see Part 1) and John Stuart Mills remained favoured explanations of the workings of the mind. However, the first academic psychology journal *Mind* was published in Britain, beginning in 1876. Francis Galton, Charles Darwin's cousin (discussed in Part 1 and Part 6), collected large amounts of physiological data as part of his interest in eugenics. This enabled him to contribute scientific expertise about statistics to the field of psychology.

The beginnings of psychodynamic theories

The term *psychodynamic theories* covers a very wide range of ideas. The term *psycho-analytical theories* is closely associated with the work of Sigmund Freud, (which will be explored in Chapter 7). The twentieth century marked the emergence of psycho-dynamic theories. It is widely thought that the publication of Darwin's ideas about evolution (see Part 1) freed thinkers and theorists to think of humans as another type of animal and therefore open to scientific investigation. Such an approach would be unthinkable if humans were primarily regarded as being made in the image of God.

Essentially, psychodynamic theories seek to explain the forces and dynamics that shape human behaviour and are generally thought to be more influential in therapy than in developmental theory. Psychodynamic theories are considered by some to have had a narrow impact on theories and practices of early childhood care and education. Yet as Manning-Morton (2011) reminds us, these theories have highlighted the causal link between childhood experiences and adult life. The sense of self, the ability to form intimate relationships and what is now widely termed 'emotional intelligence' all are shaped by early childhood experiences and it is for this reason that early childhood practitioners are drawn to explanations of human development which highlight the social and the emotional.

Psychodynamic theories as a whole have brought into everyday usage a range of ideas and concepts which are familiar to the man or woman in the street. The uncon-scious, defence mechanisms, projection and attachment are terms with which most people are comfortable. Most early childhood practitioners happily discuss transitional objects, or the use of play as a means of dealing with feelings. These are all ideas which have emanated from Freud and his followers. Not all of those who followed Freud stuck by his ideas, but his were the giant's shoulders on which they stood.

Reflective questions

1. Do you think that the man and woman on the street are aware of psychodynamic theories? In what ways is this reflected in their use of language?

2. How many ways can you identify as indicating that psychoanalytical theory has an influence on early childhood practice?
3. What relationship can you see between physiology, philosophy and psychology?
4. Do you agree that sources of bodily pleasure are the motivation for young children's actions?

Key dates

1821–1894	**Hermann von Helmholtz**
1832–1920	**Wilhelm Wundt**
1842–1910	**William James**
1856–1939	**Sigmund Freud**
1875–1961	**Carl Jung**
1895–1982	**Anna Freud**
1900–1980	**Erich Fromm**
1902–1990	**Erik Erikson**

Further reading

Manning-Morton, J. (2011) Psychoanalytic ideas and early years practice. In L. Miller and L. Pound (eds) *Theories and Approaches to Learning in the Early Years*. London: Sage.

7 Sigmund Freud (1856–1939) and the development of psychoanalytical theories

Sigmund Freud was born in Moravia, then part of Austria, but now part of the Czech Republic. He studied medicine at the University of Vienna and in 1885 went to Paris. There he was introduced to the work of Charcot which strongly influenced his future career. Although rejecting Charcot's ideas about the application of hypnosis he became interested in his theories about free association and hysteria – also a focus of Charcot's work. He developed and practised his theory of psychoanalysis in Vienna, writing a number of books on the subject. Because they were a Jewish family, Freud's daughter Anna was imprisoned by the Gestapo and his sisters died in concentration camps. However, Freud was allowed to leave with his wife and children in 1938 – when he came to England. Freud died shortly after, in 1939.

Freud's theories

Freud proposed five stages of development, all of which, he suggested, revolve around erogenous zones:

- the oral stage, where pleasure is centred around the mouth – biting, chewing, sucking;
- the anal stage, where the focus is on faeces;
- the phallic stage, said to emerge around the ages of 3 to 6, in which pleasure is derived from the genitals. This is the source of the Oedipus complex, a period or state during which there is sexual attraction to the parent of the opposite sex;
- the latency stage, pre-puberty where the focus is on social and cognitive drives;
- the genital stage, which emerges in puberty and in which the focus of interest is peers rather than family members.

At the core of Freud's theories is the belief that personality emerges from the conflict between things we want – our unconscious drives – and what reality makes possible. He saw personality as having three parts:

- the id, sometimes referred to as the pleasure principle. Freud saw the id as dominating babies' behaviour, needing desires to be met immediately.

- the ego which is formed as the baby comes to realise that needs cannot or will not always be met. The ego helps us to address our needs but in socially acceptable ways. It mediates between the demands of the id and those of the superego.
- the superego emerges as we learn to take account of the values and expectations of parents and society.

Consciousness was also seen as having three parts:

- the conscious or things to which we are paying attention;
- the preconscious – things which we are not currently paying attention but to which we can choose to pay attention; and
- the subconscious – the things in our mind which influence our behaviour but of which we are generally unaware.

Psychoanalytic theory suggests that the conflicts inherent in the struggle between id, ego and superego at different stages of development are the cause of anxiety. In order to minimise that anxiety, he hypothesised that we develop a range of coping strategies or *defence mechanisms*. These include:

- *repression* – the mind may push uncomfortable memories or experiences into the unconscious;
- *denial* – behaving as though whatever is causing the anxiety never happened or does not exist;
- *projection* – placing blame somewhere else;
- *regression* – finding security in a less mature stage of development;
- *rationalisation* – finding spurious reasons for uncomfortable things that have happened;
- *compensation* – overshadowing what one feels to be a negative by excelling at something else;
- *sublimation* – turning unacceptable desires into something acceptable.

(Talay-Ongan 1998)

Linking theory and practice

The work of Freud himself was therapeutic, often stereotyped as catering for rich, hysterical women. True or not, the focus of his work was not the application of his theories to other fields or disciplines. Whether or not we agree with his analysis, it is clear that an understanding of the defence mechanisms outlined above can be of great value in work with young children. This understanding should encompass insights into our own behaviour as well as that of colleagues, parents and children (Manning-Morton 2011).

Table 7.1 Defence mechanisms in practice

Defence mechanisms	Examples in adults	Examples in children
Repression	As adults many victims of child sexual abuse may claim to have forgotten the incidents.	Victims of child abuse may 'forget' traumatic incidents.
Denial	Parents of children with disabilities may deny that there is anything wrong with their children.	Children may deny, for example, wetting the bed – not lying but having come to believe that they did not.
Projection	If late for work, adults may claim that the traffic was bad – even though they left later than usual – blaming traffic rather than their own tardiness.	A child who has, for example, struck another may claim that he or she was hit – not the other way round.
Regression	Adults regress – often in arguments, for example, reverting to abusive or aggressive verbalisations instead of rational, adult discussion.	This is commonly seen after the birth of a new baby in the family or when any particularly challenging event – such as moving house has taken place. It may take the form of bed-wetting or wanting a baby bottle of milk at bedtime. Many children also regress by using baby-talk.
Rationalisation	An adult who fails to get a particular job may come to believe that he or she didn't want it anyway!	'A child not invited to a birthday party states . . . that she hates her and wouldn't have gone anyway.'
Compensation	When adults feel that they are not good at something such as writing they may seek to compensate by either setting themselves increasingly difficult writing challenges, or by seeking to become excellent at something else.	'A child with reading difficulties may excel in dance.'
Sublimation	Taking the proverbial cold shower when sexual desires cannot be met is a form of sublimation.	When we encourage children to punch a cushion or hammer when they're angry we're suggesting a form of sublimation.

Source: based on Talay-Ongan 1998: 10.

Although David et al. (2003) have suggested that psychoanalytical theory has had little impact on early practice, Manning-Morton (2011) disputes this. Because so much of Freud's thinking has permeated popular thinking it is perhaps difficult to identify. In addition, many of the aspects of practice and provision which have been shaped by psychoanalytic or psychodynamic theory have been developed by Freud's followers. Many of these will be examined in the chapters that follow.

A critique of Freud's work

While Freud is widely regarded as a giant or a titan (Bruner 1986) amongst thinkers, on whose shoulders rest the work of vast numbers of subsequent theorists, he has large numbers of critics. There was widespread public outrage at the work of Freud in the 1920s which was described as a 'public danger' (Graham 2009, citing Lawrence 1923). James Joyce, like Lawrence, was also scathing about psychoanalytical ideas. He is said to have written about Freud and Jung as 'the Viennese Tweedledee and the Swiss Tweedledum' (Graham 2009).

Despite the fact that much of Freud's work was with women, his theories are widely criticised particularly by feminist theorists, as being too heavily focused on male perceptions and ideas. This can be clearly seen in the fact that he labelled the third stage of development as 'phallic', and wrote about the Oedipus complex. Boys competed with their fathers for their mothers' affection while women could only engage in penis-envy!

Many of Freud's techniques and interpretations have been discredited – too lengthy (and therefore expensive), too subjective, and too unscientific. Free association and dream analysis were important elements of his approach. A number of writers have underlined the fact that Freud's views cannot be scientifically tested or validated (see for example Keenan and Evans 2009). In addition, just as Piaget's theories of staged development (see Part 4) have been criticised, so have those of Freud. Freud himself voiced some misgivings about any notion that development could easily be mapped. He wrote:

> So long as we trace the development from its final outcome backwards, the chain of events appears continuous, and we feel we have gained an insight which is completely satisfactory or even exhaustive. But if we proceed in the reverse way, if we start from the premises inferred from the analysis and try to follow these up to the final results, then we no longer get the impression of an inevitable sequence of events which could not have otherwise been determined.
>
> (Freud 1955: 167)

The use of terminology in psychodynamic theory is often criticised. The work of Freud and many of the early psychoanalytic theorists was written in German and works in translation are probably less accessible than when read in the language in which they were written. However the work is difficult to read and this has inevitably led to misunderstanding, ambiguity and misinterpretation.

The legacy of Freud's work

It would be difficult to overestimate the impact of Freud's work on twenty-first century thinking. It has inspired other theories both in the field of psychodynamics and in the field of developmental psychology. It has given a platform for new thinking. Even when not thoroughly understood, the notion of defence mechanisms for example can help us to better understand human motivation. It can help us to empathise when others behave unexpectedly or inappropriately and perhaps most importantly of all it can help us to understand our own actions better. Such understanding can also play a role in developing the reflective practice explored by, for example, Dewey, Steiner and many other theorists yet to be examined in this book.

The work of Freud highlighted the importance of early experiences and the way in which they impact on the child's future life. It showed human development to be 'shaped by the dynamics of the conflict between the individual's biological drives and society's restrictions on the expression of these drives' (Keenan and Evans 2009: 25). It changed the popular view of children and their emotions (Goleman 1996).

Albeit indirectly, Freud's interest in stages of development contributed to the widespread interest in developmental psychology. It is clear that Freud's influence went way beyond psychoanalytical theory. Gardner (1993) documents the meeting between American philosopher and psychologist William James and Freud in 1909. Although Freud's visit to America coincided with the rise of behaviourism there, James is reported to have said to Freud 'the future of psychology belongs to your work'. The declining impact of behaviourism and the growing interest in emotional or affective aspects of learning since that time make it difficult to ignore James's assertion.

Reflective questions

1. What evidence of their developing conscience have you observed in the children you work with?
2. To what extent are you aware of repression, denial, projection, or sublimation in the children and adults you work with? How aware of your own defence mechanisms are you?
3. What strategies can help you to deal with defence mechanisms in yourself and others?
4. Do you agree with William James that the future of psychology will focus on the unconscious aspects of thinking?

Further reading

Bateman, A. and Holmes, J. (1995) *An Introduction to Psychoanalysis: Contemporary Theory and Practice*. London: Routledge.

8 Psychodynamics and young children

In this chapter the focus will be on some psychodynamic theorists, the impact of whose work has been particularly strongly felt in the field of early childhood care and education. The London (later to be termed British) Psycho-Analytic Society was set up in 1913. Despite the criticisms (outlined above):

> psychoanalysis became widely accepted, even beyond medical circles, especially after the First World War, until it became an important influence on intellectual circles and, to some extent, in the popular press.
>
> (Smith 1985: 191)

Melanie Klein (1882–1960), like Freud and his family, was Jewish. She became a psychoanalyst in Vienna where she was born but left for Berlin in 1919. She began psychoanalysing children but found life difficult in what was then a very male-dominated area of work. Moreover, unlike Freud himself and many of his followers, Klein had at that time no medical or academic qualifications. In 1926, invited by the founder of the London Psycho-Analytic Society, she came to England where she met Susan Isaacs with whom she was to collaborate over many years. Their collaborative work involved a study of the impact of evacuation during the Second World War on young children.

Susan Isaacs (1885–1948), (described in Chapter 6 of this book), is probably best known for her work in the Malting House School and at the Department of Child Development. However her first employment had been as a lecturer in psychology at a teacher training college. In 1921 Isaacs was in therapy, published a book entitled *Introduction to Psychology* and became the assistant editor of the *British Journal of Psychology* (Smith 1985). In the following year she became a member of The British Psycho-Analytical Society and began taking patients for therapy. During her time at the Malting House School she began to explore the emotional development of children. Klein's arrival in London introduced Isaacs to analysis techniques with young children. So impressed with this was she that Isaacs re-entered therapy, this time with a Kleinian therapist.

Anna Freud (1895–1982), Sigmund Freud's youngest daughter, is perhaps most well known in the field of early childhood care and education for her work on the importance of observation. Anna came to London in 1938, but her disagreements with Melanie Klein were well established before that. Once in London, she and Melanie

Klein disagreed so significantly that the British Psychoanalytical Society broke into three camps (in which it remains) the Kleinian; Anna Freudian and independent.

Donald Winnicott (1896–1971) worked closely with Klein on object relations theory (see below). Despite this, when Klein and Anna Freud caused a split within the British Psychoanalytical Society, Winnicott became an independent member. A paediatrician by training, he remains a highly respected psychoanalyst particularly revered for his insights into work with children.

Erik Erikson (1902–1994) was a student of Anna Freud. He was the first of the psychoanalysts to leave Vienna when life became difficult for Jewish families and his working life was mainly in the United States of America where his work is particularly influential. He put forward a theory, psychosocial theory (details below), in which human development is characterised as being shaped by social and cultural forces.

Psychodynamic theories focusing on young children

A number of important theories and applications arose from these theorists. In this section some of the theories are outlined.

Object relations theory

The idea of projection (discussed in Chapter 7) is perhaps most commonly associated with Melanie Klein. Manning-Morton (2011) points out that Klein's object relations theory suggests that 'the internal world of the infant is populated by the self, its objects and the relations between them' (objects in this context refer to the mother or main carer). The theory is described as follows by Manning-Morton (2011, citing Bateman and Holmes 1995):

> Klein believed that very young babies do not have a concept of a whole object but only images in their minds of part objects. She developed the idea of splitting to explain how an infant will defend themselves against the anxiety that arises from internal feelings of disintegration by dividing objects into good and bad part objects. When good experiences are projected the carer is idealised but experiences and feelings that feel bad such as frustration in feeding or anger at the objects absence, are also split off and projected into the carer, who is then felt to be threatening. In object-relations theory, ego development occurs through a process of (mental) separation, in which children differentiate themselves from their carer and individuation in which they start to establish their own personality traits.

Winnicott built on Klein's theory emphasising that 'the determining influence on a child's personality is their *actual* experiences of feeding and holding' (Manning-Morton 2011). He summed up his feelings on the relationship between mother and baby with the words 'there is no such thing as a baby, only a mother and a baby' (Winnicott 1960: 39). For Winnicott, holding is a particularly important part of his theory – the adult holds the child, emotionally and physically, providing secure dependency until the child is able to move towards independence.

Containment and attunement

From the difficult concept of object relation theory come three important and relatively familiar ideas – containment, attunement and attachment. The latter will be examined more fully in the next chapter. Containment is the process by which an adult picks up on children's distress and, as Manning-Morton (2011) describes it, keeps the baby 'in mind', 'holding' him or her emotionally. Positive interactions help the child to manage anxiety. Affect attunement is similar to containment. Siegel (1999) suggests that when the carer is able to respond to the baby's communications, the baby feels understood and is able to connect with the mind of the carer. It is this process which supports emotional well-being, psychological resilience and thought (Manning-Morton in press).

Gerhardt (2004: 124) writes about the impact of a mother's depression on her baby – a situation where the mother's own needs prevent her from containing or attuning to those of the child. She writes:

> One study ... found that the normal state of play between a mother and baby is to fluctuate between positive and neutral interactions – about equally divided. But depressed mothers are very different. They offer very few positive interactions. About 40% of the time they are unresponsive and disengaged, whilst much of the rest of the time they are angry, intrusive and rough with their babies. When the mother is being overtly or covertly angry, these babies look away a lot. They can't actually leave the room, of course, but perhaps they would like to. For a baby, the most painful experience of all seems to be not being able to get mother's attention. Babies make the most protest when their mother's attention is switched off as if this is even more unbearable than maltreatment. But either way, babies of depressed mothers experience more negative than positive feelings.

Gerhardt (2004) goes on to point out that Melanie Klein (1988) believed that babies harbour overwhelming feelings of envy and greed – a theoretical stance that Winnicott was unable to share. Gerhardt queries this assumption and suggests that Klein herself suffered a negative relationship with her mother. Gerhardt (2004: 124) concludes that 'it is probably more accurate to think of the hostility and envy of the depressed mother towards her baby than vice versa'. It is interesting to speculate on the psychology of Klein, as Gerhardt does, apparently taking the blame for her own mother's shortcomings.

Winnicott's writing (1967) highlights the importance of the interface between mothers and their babies. He focuses particularly, like Gerhardt, on depressed mothers. Depression, he suggests, prevents the baby from seeing anything other than the mother's face and mood. The baby's creative capacity begins to atrophy, and in some way or other they look around for other ways of getting something of themselves back from the environment ... [resulting in the breakdown] of that which might have been the beginning of a significant exchange with the world.

(Winnicott 1967: 7)

Wright (2001), one of Winnicott's followers, picks up on Winnicott's concerns and highlights the importance of facial expression in communicating with babies. Unlike other aspects of a baby's experience expression can only be perceived visually not through tactile handling. This relies on pattern recognition and an ability to identify small changes in and between faces – a competence which twenty-first century neuroscientific investigation shows to be the case (Slater and Quinn 2001).

As the baby becomes a toddler his or her sense of self as an individual begins to emerge. The psychoanalyst Lacan refers to this as 'the mirror stage' (Manning-Morton 2011) and it is a stage that is reflected in developmental theories. In a well-known experiment Lewis and Brooks (1978, cited by Talay-Ongan 1998), demonstrated that by the age of 21 months it was clear that toddlers could recognise the image in a mirror as themselves. By around the same age they can identify and name themselves in a photograph. They also express emotions such as pride or embarrassment, indicating some level of self-awareness.

Psychosocial theory

Erikson differed from Freud in proposing a life-long theory of development. For him development rested on interactions between:

- the somatic system (concerned with physical and biological processes);
- the ego system (concerned with thinking and reasoning processes); and
- the societal system (concerned with the ways in which individuals become part of their society or culture).

Erikson's theory put forward eight stages of psychosocial development. The stages rested on a series of conflicts (or crises) which were believed to lead to the dynamic forces which produce change and development. For example, if adolescents fail to discover their true selves or identities they will continue to experience confusion. Similarly in old age, those who have not previously resolved earlier stages are likely to have a negative (or despairing) view of their lives. The stages are described as follows:

- basic trust v. mistrust (from birth to 1 year of age)
- autonomy v. shame and doubt (1 to 3 years)
- initiative v. guilt (3 to 6 years)
- industry v. inferiority (6 to 11 years)
- identity v. identity diffusion (adolescence)
- intimacy v. isolation (young adulthood)
- generativity v. stagnation (middle adulthood)
- ego integrity v. despair (old age).

Linking theory and practice

The theories of Sigmund Freud were probably not intended to influence directly practice with young children. However they did influence many psychoanalysts and pscychotherapists who in turn applied their theories to work with children.

Transitional objects

Transitional objects are arguably the most well-known of the applications of psychoanalytic theories. Early years practitioners are familiar with the concept of encouraging young children to use objects which symbolise security, such as a security blanket or a familiar toy. These transitional objects (Winnicott 1957) represent the beginning of feeling separate rather than merged with their mother. In using this object as symbolising mother or home, Winnicott (1971) believed that the child developed the ability to play – which he believed was essential to later abilities to discovering ourselves and our potential. He described transitional objects as 'the first thing in the world that belongs to the infant, and yet is not part of the infant' (1971: 167) and thus 'the beginning of the infant's creation of the world' (1971: 169).

Child therapy

Both Melanie Klein and Anna Freud made a major contribution to the development of child therapy. For Klein, while children's language competence constrained the use of the free association routinely used in adult therapy, she believed their play was a window to the unconscious mind of young children. She theorised that using play in this way enabled her to work with strong feelings such as rage and fear of abandonment. For her, 'the whole gamut of feelings must be expressed, in play or in words, and then interpreted by the analyst' (Smith 1985: 194).

Winnicott, in 1962 already a renowned paediatrician, described his introduction to Klein's theories and the impact of play therapy on his work with children:

> [I was] astounded by the insight which psycho-analysis gave me into the lives of children ... it made sense and joined up my case history detail with psycho-analytical theory ... specific play with the toys was a projection from the child's psychic reality which is localized by the child, localized inside the self and the body [and which] provides glimpses into the child's inner world.
>
> (Winnicott 1965: 173, cited by Smith 1985: 196)

Anna Freud is perhaps seen as the foremost figure in child therapy. Bromfield (2003: 1–2) declares that 'if Sigmund Freud was the father of psychoanalysis, then Anna Freud was child therapy's foremost mother.' She disagreed with Klein about the use of play in place of free association. She believed that the defences employed by the child's unconscious (see Chapter 7) enabled them to deal with difficult experiences and that change could only come about as the child became able to explore them consciously.

Anna Freud was responsible for establishing Child Guidance clinics in England (Wardle 1991). Her work on children's emotions and feelings took into account their health and ability, as well as their family context.

The role of adults

The major source of disagreement between Melanie Klein and Anna Freud was their differing views about the superego (Smith 1985). Freud believed that the superego developed later while Klein believed that the superego developed early and that the very young child internalized 'external adult forces', perceiving them as harsh:

> even the most gentle forms of education and the kindest adult cannot keep the child from its attacks; indeed, being kind and gentle may make dealing with frustrations actually more difficult for him, since such (kind) adults clearly deserve his aggressive behavior so little. Then massive repression occurs, and complexes arise.
>
> (Smith 1985: 194)

It is here that the disagreement grew. Klein strongly attacked Anna Freud's view of the role of the therapist – suggesting that she sought to deflect conflict in order to safeguard the child's relationship with the parent or even to attach the child to herself. Although Kleinian views were more popular in Britain and Susan Isaacs was regarded as Kleinian in outlook, in her practice and in her writing:

> she carefully distinguishes between the different roles played by a child's analyst and his or her teacher. With regard to the analyst, her description is entirely Kleinian. But the role played by the teacher, the mild-but-firm authority, who controls the child's most aggressive behaviour since it is still too libidinized for him or her to handle, is very close to the 'educative' role that the analyst plays, for Anna Freud.
>
> (Smith 1985: 197)

Isaacs applied her belief in psychoanalytic theories for the popular press. Under the pen name of Ursula Wise, Isaacs provided accessible advice for parents in dealing with behaviour problems, nightmares and so on. Her down to earth common sense approach when for example giving advice to parents bears all the hallmarks of her psychoanalytical training but is easy to understand. In a section on obedience for example (Isaacs 1929: 101–2) she writes:

> obedience is not an end in itself. It is a means of education, not a final purpose ... Many people's difficulties come from not being clear.... If we are muddled in our own minds as to why we want obedience, and when and how we want it, we are very likely to ask for it when it isn't really valuable ... when we say the child 'should obey', we clearly can't mean that he should never do anything without being told, never have any way of his own. Nor that we

want him to be docile to our mere whim and fancy. That would be sacrificing the whole of his future to our present convenience, and what a useless sort of person it would make him.

The impact of psychosocial theory

Erikson's theory has been arguably more influential in care and education contexts than other psychodynamic theories, whose influence has been almost exclusively therapeutic (Keenan and Evans 2009). Robert Havinghurst has put forward a *developmental tasks theory* which builds on Erikson's work and makes it more accessible and practical (Keenan and Evans 2009). He suggests that there are three types of task:

- those arising from physical maturation such as walking and talking;
- those arising from personal views and experiences;
- those arising from the demands and culture and society.

He highlights six age periods and identifies corresponding developmental tasks. Unfortunately his analysis, undertaken in the 1950s, is from the perspective of a white middle-class American. The strength however is in highlighting the conflicts which Erikson presented along with examples which could help parents to understand and support children in dealing with particular issues at particular stages.

A critique of psychodynamic theories and theorists focusing on young children

The breakdown of relations in the British Psycho-Analytic Association has had long-term and far-reaching consequences. It reflects the strength of feeling which underpins deeply held views and philosophies. Like Freud's work, the work of the theorists working with young children may often be seen to be mired in language which is inaccessible.

Some criticisms are of a personal nature. Klein is widely condemned for her practice of psycho-analysing her own children – something which would today be seen as wholly inappropriate. Winnicott, was described by Adam Phillips as 'exemplary as a psychoanalyst' (2007: 17), but Singer (1992: 99) sheds an interesting and surprising light on his thinking. She writes that:

> Winnicott argued that society had to choose to help the relatively healthy children from 'normal' families. The illegitimate and homeless children were supposedly too badly disturbed to be helped. 'Deprived children', according to Winnicott, were a threat to society and cost more than they could return. They supposedly lacked any form of self-control and were totally uninhibited. For that reason, he said they would be better off in large institutions, without individual attention and under a dictatorial regime.

The legacy of psychodynamic theories focusing on young children

Psychodynamic theorists have left many practical legacies – play therapy, child guidance, the use of transitional objects and the importance of play as a vehicle for exploring feelings. This goes beyond the specifics of play therapy and is widely seen as part of day-to-day practice – a hospital corner in a setting where a child has had a serious illness; or opportunities to care for dolls in a group where a number of baby siblings have recently been born. It may also be argued that Isaacs' belief in the importance of the garden was part of her focus on the emotional well-being of children.

Both Anna Freud and Susan Isaacs were trained teachers in addition to being psychoanalysts (Graham 2009). Both used observational techniques which are part of the legacy of psychoanalysis – carefully observing children in order to better understand them. Manning-Morton (in press) describes in detail the technique used by analysts at the Tavistock clinic. The child is observed at home for an hour at a time over an extended period. No notes are taken at the time but written up later and discussed in a group – a practice which Manning-Morton commends to early childhood practitioners. Winnicott valued observation too greatly. Casement (1992) suggests that Winnicott saw his observations as key to understanding and thus supporting children.

Developmental psychoanalysis

Mayes et al. (2007) have drawn attention to the unexpected parallels in the work of Anna Freud and Arnold Gesell. Both were making a distinct contribution to the study of child development – Anna Freud through her work on child observation and Gesell through his studies of the benchmarks of normal development (Mayes et al. 2007: 2). Although it seems that the two never actually met, it led to a collaboration between the two study centres that they established. Their collaboration in turn led to a programme which brings together 'psychoanalysts and developmental cognitive and neuroscientists' in order 'to address ... basic mind-brain, body-and-mind issues with shared perspectives' (Mayes et al. 2007: 3). Mayes and his colleagues have named this shared field as developmental psychoanalysis. They suggest that psychoanalysis has long been concerned with:

> how young children learn the language of the social world with its intertwined biological, genetic, and experiential roots and how infants translate thousands of intimate moments with their parents into a genuine, intuitive, emotional connection to other persons. Basic developmental neuroscience and psychology has also of late turned to these basic questions of affiliation: of how it is that as humans our most basic concerns are about finding, establishing, preserving, and mourning our relationships. These are key areas to understanding our capacities for resilience across life or our vulnerabilities to life's hardships.

Reflective questions

1. How can you ensure that children's transitional objects are accessible but protected?
2. In what ways do you regard play as therapy in your practice?
3. To what extent do you agree that human development is a lifelong process? Do you agree with Erikson's description of stages? Do they still work for people in the twenty-first century?
4. Why do the psychoanalytic theories outlined here place such a strong emphasis on observation?

Further reading

Phillips, A. (2007) *Winnicott.* London: Penguin Books.

9 John Bowlby (1907–1990) and attachment theories

Bowlby's first degree from Cambridge was in psychology and he subsequently qualified as a medical doctor. Later studying at the Tavistock Clinic, he became a psychoanalyst. His own mother appears to have been a remote figure and he was brought up, along with his five siblings, by a nanny. At the age of 7 he was sent to boarding school and it is claimed (Schwartz 1999) that he later said that he wouldn't impose such a fate on a dog. However with a characteristic emphasis on the importance of age he sent his own son to boarding school at the only slightly older age of 8!

Bowlby's emphasis on maternal deprivation came to light at the end of the Second World War when he was commissioned by the World Health Organisation (WHO) (Bowlby 1951) to examine the impact on children of being orphaned or homeless. His work focused on the importance of nurture since he believed, along with other psychoanalysts, on the strong role of early care in shaping children's future. He was also interested in developmental aspects of children's growth – seeing, for example, the age of 3 as a stage when children could tolerate separation from their mothers or main carers. His interest in the role of nature is underlined by the posthumous publication of his biography of Charles Darwin (Bowlby 1992).

Bowlby's theories

Bowlby studied the bonding, or as he termed it *attachment relationship*, which occurred between caregivers and babies. Attachment theories seek to explain bonding and its impact on subsequent mental health. They look to it as the means by which attachment is developed and maintained. His theories were drawn from psychoanalytic theory, as well as from developmental psychology. Bowlby also drew on ethological theory, based on Darwin's work on evolution (Keenan and Evans 2009). Keenan and Evans (2009: 32) describe this link with evolution and with animal behaviour by stating that 'Bowlby argued that infants have a built-in signalling system to which mothers are geared to respond, a system which is designed to promote nurturance and protective behaviours by the parent'.

Talay-Ongan (1998: 83) describes attachment as follows:

Attachment is a mental representation of how the world and the interpersonal relations in it are viewed by the growing child, and it spans a lifetime. We carry it with us, unless a wilful attempt is made (self-discovery, counselling or psychotherapy) to change our belief, understanding and representation of the cognitive notion. Attachment research is a cornerstone of developmental psychology.

Bowlby identified three stages in attachment. His student Mary Ainsworth added a fourth. These are outlined in Table 9.1 opposite overleaf. Bowlby (1973) also identified what he termed an *internal working model* which is a mental model or representation of experiences with their main attachment figure (Keenan and Evans 2009). He suggested that this model changes over time as experiences change and that it influences relationships for the rest of the child's life. In Chapter 5, Montessori's belief in critical periods was raised. Certainly Bowlby believed that attachment could best be achieved in the early years. This view is echoed by Siegel (1999) who suggests that neuroscience indicates relatively few critical periods since the brain is plastic – able to change and modify. However, Siegel states that although not entirely irreparable, the damage which stems from failure to form a close attachment very early in life is difficult to repair at a later stge.

Pugh (2002) echoes this view. She suggests that Bowlby's theories have been mis-interpreted as 'requiring mothers to stay at home full-time to care for their pre-school children' (Pugh 2002: 112). Pugh explores his work on attachment in order to find ways to examine its role in supporting resilience. She writes that:

> Children who are unable to form secure and dependable attachments to their parents – who find their parents cold or hostile or lacking in empathy, or to-tally unpredictable in how they respond to them, perhaps due to depression or abuse of drugs or alcohol – will find it more difficult to form trusting rela-tionships with their peers or with their future partners or, in time, with their own children.
>
> (Pugh 2002: 112)

Bowlby built on and challenged Freudian theory. This development is described by Bretherton and Waters (1985), who suggest that his analysis of the role of the mother may owe more to Vygotsky than to Freud. Bowlby describes the mother as acting as the young child's ego and superego:

> She orients him in space and time, provides his environment, permits the sat-isfaction of some impulses, restricts others. She is his ego and his super-ego. Gradually he learns these arts himself, and as he does, the skilled parent trans-fers the roles to him. This is a slow, subtle and continuous process, beginning when he first learns to walk and feed himself, and not ending completely until maturity is reached. . . . Ego and super-ego development are thus inextricably bound up with the child's primary human relationships.
>
> (Bowlby 1951: 53)

Bowlby described a series of stages of attachment – work which was refined and developed when Ainsworth, an American, came to work in London as a researcher

Table 9.1 Phases of attachment

	Age indicated	Bowlby 1969 (cited by Talay-Ongan 1998)	Ainsworth's amendments (Ainsworth et al. 1978 and Keenan and Evans 2009)
Non-focused orienting and signalling	newborn	Through innate mechanisms, the newborn is building expectancies, schemas, and the ability to discriminate mother and father from others by crying, eye contact, clinging, cuddling and responding to parents' efforts to soothe. However, these early *proximity-seeking* behaviours are simply emitted, rather than being directed to a particular person.	Ainsworth describes this as the *preattachment* phase and suggests that it is present during the first two months of life.
Focus on one or more figure(s)	2/3 months – 7 months	From 3 months, the baby starts to smile indiscriminately to her caregivers, although no-one in particular has yet become the safe base, nor is *separation anxiety* and fear of strangers evidenced at separation from the parents.	Ainsworth describes this as *attachment-in-the-making*. She describes it as running from 2 to 7 months – a period in which babies show a preference for the attachment figure and differentiate between familiar and unfamiliar figures.
Secure base behaviour	6/7 months – 2 years	By 6 months of age the now sitting baby is able to signal the caregiver, as well as proceeding to approach her in *proximity-seeking* behaviours. A caregiver has been chosen (usually the mother) as the safe	*Clear-cut attachment* begins at 7 months. Babies show clear preferences for attachment figures and may be upset when they leave.

(continued)

Table 9.1 Phases of attachment (*continued*)

Age indicated	Bowlby 1969 (cited by Talay-Ongan 1998)	Ainsworth's amendments (Ainsworth et al. 1978 and Keenan and Evans 2009)
	base/most important person, although the infant may exhibit attachment behaviours with a number of caregivers, such as the father, older siblings, grandparents or babysitters. By 10 months, social referencing has begun to occur: she checks the facial expression of the parent before venturing on a novel experience. Fear of strangers and separation anxiety are present.	
2 years +		Ainsworth et al. identify a fourth phase beginning at 2 years of age, namely *goal-corrected partnership*. At this stage the child becomes more aware of the attachment figure's part in the process, and better able to communicate their thoughts, thus playing a more active role in maintaining the relationship.

Source: based on Talay-Ongan 1998: 81 and Keenan and Evans 2009: 251, citing Ainsworth et al. 1978.

with him. Ainsworth developed an experimental approach which she termed *strange situation* (Ainsworth et al. 1978). From this she devised a theory intended to in some way measure children's attachment. Table 9.2 explains the phases and accompanying stages proposed by Bolwby and Ainsworth.

The *strange situation* experiment involves a series of short events described by Bretherton and Waters (1985) as a half-hour drama. The sequence of events is as follows:

1. Mother and baby enter an empty room
2. Mother sits while baby plays
3. A stranger enters and talks to mother
4. Mother leaves
5. Stranger comforts baby if upset
6. Mother returns for three minutes (comforting baby if necessary)
7. Stranger leaves
8. Mother leaves room leaving baby alone
9. Stranger returns and comforts baby if necessary
10. Mother returns, greets and comforts baby.

(based on Talay-Ongan 1998)

Depending on the babies' reactions, they are categorised as shown in Table 9.2. (The right hand column identifies the source of some criticisms of this work.)

Table 9.2 Categories of attachment

Type		Description	% incidence (in middle- (class American children)
A	Avoidant attachment	Reactions to stranger and mother are similar. Mother's physical comfort is not rejected nor is it sought.	20%
B	Secure attachment	Babies may cry while mother is absent clearly preferring her to the stranger. On her return they actively seek contact and crying lessens straight away.	65%
C	Anxious/ resistant attachment	Before mother leaves babies seek contact but on her return they may appear angry. They remain difficult to comfort.	10–12%
D	Disorganised/disoriented attachment (identified by Main et al. 1985)	Babies in this category are said to reflect the greatest insecurity. They may look away when held, and cry unpredictably.	−5%

Source: based on Talay-Ongan 1998: 82

Linking theory and practice

The applications of attachment theory are numerous.

Hospitalisation of children

James Robertson and his wife Joyce had worked with Anna Freud during the Second World War. Working at the Tavistock Clinic, they became concerned about young children in hospital. A survey in 1949 indicated that most hospitals only had visiting in children's wards on one afternoon a week. The thinking at that time, strange as this may seem in the twenty-first century, was that increased visiting merely distressed children unnecessarily. The Robertsons set about filming children away from their main carer in hospital or in foster care. The footage (described in detail on their website www.robertsonsfilms.info/) was extremely influential. Hospital regulations about visiting children in hospital were radically changed. Parents were enabled to stay with young sick children. James Robertson was described by Bowlby:

> as a remarkable person who achieved great things. His sensitive observations and brilliant observations made history, and the courage with which he disseminated – often in the face of ignorant and prejudiced criticism – what were then very unpopular findings, was legendary. He will always be remembered as the man who revolutionised children's hospitals, though he accomplished much else besides. I am personally deeply grateful for all that he did.
>
> (Bowlby nd)

Key person approach

The key person approach, now a requirement of the EYFS (QCA 2007) is underpinned by attachment theory (see for example Elfer et al. 2003). The theory has informed practice and there is a recognition that children need to develop sustained relationships with the adults who care for them. But this does not mean that the policy is without difficulties. Manning-Morton and Thorp (2003) highlight the difficulties. They suggest that often practitioners

- can find the relationship emotionally draining and may therefore actively avoid contact with the child by keeping too busy to interact effectively;
- may believe that if they form too strong a bond with the child it will damage the child's relationship with his or her parents (a view refuted by Bowlby, 1969);
- may have emotional difficulties of their own which make it difficult for them to interact with some children.

Manning-Morton and Thorp (2003: 33) go on to suggest that practitioners need to have:

- a high level of self-acceptance;
- an ability to understand how, as adults, we may see ourselves in particular children and them in us;
- an ability to separate out traits and feelings that belong to the adult and not the child.

In a later publication Manning-Morton (2011) writes that 'we have psychoanalytic theory to thank not only for the concept of the key person approach but also for a way of understanding the barriers that inhibit its full and positive implementation'. This in turn means that supervision procedures need to be in place in order to support the well-being of the adults taking on these emotionally draining roles.

Strange situation experiments

Strange situation experiments have been used to identify parenting approaches which successfully support the growth of attachment. These include:

- affectionate physical and verbal interactions with the baby;
- rapid response to distress with appropriate strategies;
- mother's responsiveness to the baby's utterances;
- frequency and stimulating nature of play with baby.

(Bretherton and Waters 1985)

These characteristics in turn are said to induce in children:

- higher self-esteem and popularity with others;
- coping skills and resilience;
- skills for dealing with mistakes or failure;
- learning dispositions (e.g. persistence, curiosity, enthusiasm);
- a sense of agency;
- an absence of behaviour difficulties (e.g. aggression or anxiety).

Mary Main was one of Ainsworth's researchers. She identified the *disorganised/disoriented* stage of attachment and explored the correlation or relationship between the way in which a child was classified in the *strange situation* and the account that a parent gave of his or her own childhood.

Pugh (2002) comments on the application of these insights from research. In providing early childhood care and education, society has the opportunity to develop characteristics in children and families which will support emotional well-being. The longitudinal study of HighScope (see Part 6) which motivated the development of Sure Start in England underlines the role that support for parenting and high quality early education together can play in improving children's life chances.

A critique of attachment theories

Bowlbyism, as it is sometimes termed, was heavily criticised by those interested in feminism and women's rights (see for example Scarr and Dunn 1987). In 1983 for example Denise Riley published a book entitled *War in the Nursery* in which she charts the rise of Bowlbyism, linking it to the economic pressures of the post-war period. She highlights the government's desire to 'discourage mothers of children under two from going out to work' (Ringen 1997: 72, citing a 1945 Ministry of Health circular). At that time this was seen as being about creating employment opportunities for men. Over time, this became linked to Bowlby's theories with a widespread view that young children ought to be at home with their mothers.

The criticisms outlined by Riley and many other like-minded people was that attachment was being used as an excuse to provide employment for men at the expense of women – who throughout the war had been expected to do their duty and work outside the home. The fact that between 1940 and 1943 the numbers of nurseries rose from 14 to 1,345 and that by 1965 the numbers had fallen again by two thirds underlines that view. Similar conclusions may be drawn from the fact that 62,000 nursery places were available in 1944 while in 1988 less than half that number were available (Ringen 1997). To this calculation might be added the fact that while most places in 1943 would have been full day places, by 1988 most places would be part-time only.

The impact of this policy was widely felt. During the 1980s, the policy arising from Bowlbyism was challenged. Scarr and Dunn (1987) write scathingly about Bowlby's theories – arguing that his use of ethological theories was inappropriate since babies are not animals and do not have the same instincts. Psychiatrist Michael Rutter, declared that Bowlby's theory of 'maternal deprivation' was 'scientifically untenable' (Singer 1992: 102) and argued that there was no evidence that day care had bad effects. He suggested that:

> [It] is clear that early claims that proper mothering was only possible if the mother did not go out to work and that the use of day nurseries ... has a particularly serious and permanent deleterious effect on mental health were not only premature but wrong.
>
> (Rutter 1972: 3)

Bruno Bettelheim, who as a Jew had suffered greatly during the Second World War, 'could not accept Bowlby's view that a bad family was better than a good institution' (Singer 1992: 101). Behaviourist theorists (see Part 4) could not accept such intangible terms as 'mother love' and persisted in their 'belief in the superiority of expert upbringing and applied science outside the family' (Singer 1992: 101). By this means they sought to increase children's learning ability.

This argument has of course not gone away. Throughout the 1980s there was a great shortage of nursery places but with expansion (related once again to economic need) has come renewed challenges. Jay Belsky (see for example Belsky 2008) continues to argue that much of the expansion includes poor quality provision and that poor quality provision has long-term detrimental effects not only for children but for society (see Pound 2009).

Criticisms of methodology

Despite the fact that Bowlby's theories 'chimed with the times' there was a great deal of criticism (Riley 1983). Singer (1992) outlines some of the grounds for the criticism of Bowlby's research findings:

- numbers of children involved were small;
- control groups were not comparable;
- inherited factors were not known;
- standards of care in the institutions in which children were placed were poor;
- children were not only suffering from maternal deprivation but faced the loss of their whole family;
- the separation experiences of the children were often extreme and extended and should not be compared with day care provision or short separations.

Ainsworth's *strange situation* experiments have also been widely criticised, along with many other experiments in developmental psychology as being based on the measurement of 'strange behaviour of children in strange situations with strange adults for the briefest possible periods of time' (Bronfenbrenner 1979: 19). Her theories are also widely criticised for failing to take account of cultural differences. Cole (1998) highlights some of the anomalies in findings from this work. If the test were culture free one has to wonder why in Germany there are more than twice as many insecurely attached children as there are in the United States. In her work in Uganda, Ainsworth took her presence as in itself the strange situation – yet as Cole (1998: 25) comments:

> The only way to obtain functional equivalence of Strange Situation in different cultures ... would be to create a different assessment instrument for each culture.... However, using a different observational setting for each cultural group would immediately undermine the equivalence of procedures which is the foundation of standardization needed by those who seek to establish the universal validity of the Strange Situation.

Serious omissions

In his writing, Bowlby emphasised the support that families ought to be given in order to raise psychologically sound children. He wrote, for example, that 'if a community values its children it must cherish their parents' (Bowlby, 1951: 84). However Singer (1992: 98–9) suggests that 'Bowlby was so preoccupied with separation from the mother that, in 1983, he was forced to confess that he had not noticed child abuse in families' he was working with. This, despite the fact that later research (Singer 1992: 99 citing Draijer 1988) indicates that it is likely that a significant 'number of the children he examined in institutions ... had quite probably been abused within their families'.

The legacy of attachment theories

Perversely some of the criticisms of Bowlby's theories may also be regarded as part of the legacy. The shortage of nursery places led to the setting up of the playgroup movement and to a diversified (if inadequate) range of provision. Increased understanding of and interest in attachment has led to some exciting work in the field of child development.

Despite some later criticisms (see Part 5) interest in child development – together with the growth of technology – has supported some invaluable insights into children's learning and development. Perhaps the most immediate and far-reaching effect was the the work of the Robertsons (outlined above). It radically changed attitudes amongst parents and professionals towards the hospitalisation of children and their institutional care. Similarly, Daniel Stern, whose 'work was informed by the framework of "attachment theory" first established by the psychoanalyst John Bowlby and the psychologist Mary Ainsworth' (Gerhardt 2004: 4), filmed interactions between mothers and babies and analysed them frame by frame. In so doing Stern created 'a more complete understanding of early development than had been available before' (Gerhardt 2004: 4).

While Freud believed that attachment sprang from being fed by the mother or main carer, Bowlby emphasised the range of behaviours found in infants which ensure their survival. For him the key was *proximity* – smiles and cries draw adults to babies, ensuring their safety. It was this insight which highlighted the social and communicative aspects of mother or carer and child relationships. Keenan and Evans (2009: 250) write that:

> attachment theory extends the study of emotional development into the social realm, breaking down traditional barriers that focus solely on the individual as opposed to the individual as situated in relationships with other people.

It is this sense of the two-way process involved in bonding and attachment which was to pave the way for the subsequent work of theorists and researchers such as Colwyn Trevarthen and Daniel Stern who have emphasised the active role that the baby plays in maintaining adults' interest and care. Technological advances have also supported similar conclusions in neuroscientific enquiry. Dan Siegel (1999) for example writes of the importance of the 'meeting of minds' which attachment affords and the cognitive benefits which this bestows.

Reflective questions

1. Reflect on the importance to young babies of familiar adults as carers.
2. What evidence have you seen of communication between young babies and their carers?
3. What do you think the impact of day care is on very young children? How can it be made as secure and comfortable for them as possible?
4. What support do parents need to raise psychologically sound children?

Further reading

Elfer, P., Goldschmeid, E. and Selleck, D. (2003) *Key Persons in the Nursery.* London: David Fulton Publishers.

Singer, E. (1998) Shared care for children. In M. Woodhead, D. Faulkner and K. Littleton (eds) *Cultural Worlds of Early Childhood.* London: Routledge/The Open University.

Slater, L. (2004) *Opening Skinner's Box.* London: Bloomsbury Publishing. (See Chapter 6 which discusses the work of Harlow in relation to monkeys and attachment.)

10 Emotion and cognition

It is important to keep in mind the chronology of understandings around the mind or psyche during the first half of the twentieth century. In putting this book together decisions have inevitably had to be made about the order in which to present events and approaches which were in reality, if not happening simultaneously, at least were overlapping. As the list of key dates at the beginning of each section shows, progressive approaches to education, psychoanalytic, constructivist and behaviourist theories were all emerging during a similar period. In some cases there was a strong direct link between these developments. Susan Isaacs was for example a trained psychotherapist but she was also an educationalist with a very strong interest in another newly emerging field of study – namely child development.

Carl Rogers (1902–1987), together with Charlotte Buhler and Abraham Maslow, developed a movement in psychology which came to be known as the third force (see Pound 2008). The movement acknowledged the limitations of both behaviourism (which will be explored more fully in Part 4 of this book) and psychoanalytical approaches. Buhler has been described as the mother of humanistic psychology. Maslow is perhaps best known for his writing about what he termed a hierarchy of needs. He placed self-actualisation, which includes human characteristics such as tolerance and creativity, as highest level needs which could only be met if lower order needs were first satisfied. In this chapter, the work of Carl Rogers will show the links that he explored between behaviourism and psychoanalysis. Of the three figures at the centre of the third force – or humanistic psychology – it is Carl Rogers who is most closely bound up with both psychodynamics and with education.

The website of Rogers' daughter Natalie (Rogers nd) describes him as 'a model for compassion and democratic ideals in his own life, and in his work as an educator, writer, and therapist'. Early in his career (following a short period of interest in agriculture) Rogers' focus was on troubled children. This in turn led to an interest in child protection. Throughout this period he had been involved in psychotherapy and in 1956 he became the first president the American Academy of Psychotherapists.

The chapter will also examine the way in which the exploration of emotion, beginning with psychoanalysis, was to uncover links with cognition. This, in turn, has in the twenty-first century developed some interesting links with neuroscience.

Theories linking emotion and cognition

The work of the McMillan sisters focused on health which included well-being – a psychological concept. This focus was not simply identified with children's physical health – Margaret McMillan saw an 'atmosphere of love, joy and freedom' (Pound 2005: 25, citing McMillan [1904] 1923) as an essential preparation for future formal schooling. As we have seen, Steiner shared many of McMillan's ideals – not least in relation to imagination. For him the psychological well-being of the young child rested in adults 'holding back' while at the same time 'being present' (Drummond and Jenkinson 2009). The best preparation for successful learning at a later stage was seen as being for children to establish their will through play and physical action – focusing on hand rather than head. Montessori writes of the emotional impact of cognitive achievement, describing children's:

> mental explosions which delight the child so intensely when he makes discoveries in the world about him, when he, at the same time, ponders over and glories in the new things which are revealed to him in the outside world, and in the exquisite emotions of his own growing consciousness.
>
> (Montessori 1912: 232)

Susan Isaacs, working with children with a very different life experience, clearly identified in her direct practice with children and in her writings for parents the importance to learning and education of emotional health. She was a great advocate of play which she saw as having value for all aspects of development and education. In short she saw play as being 'the means by which he in his turn will lay hold of knowledge and skill' (Isaacs 1929: 11). She writes too of the emotional benefits of play:

> The discharge in play of . . . inward tensions makes it easier for little children to temper their behaviour in real life. This is one of the chief functions of play. . . . And sad it is for those children whose anxiety is so great that they cannot play. We may look upon the inability to join with other children in imaginative and creative play as one of the surest signs of grave inner difficulties that will sooner or later seriously disturb the mental life – no matter how well-behaved and controlled the child otherwise now seems to be.
>
> (Isaacs 1929: 99)

For Winnicott, the beginnings of symbolic understanding, which are of such importance in cognitive theories (see Part 4), lie in the mother and child relationship. Wright (2001: 6) comments on Winnicott's view that 'in the infant's early relationship to the mother's changing facial configurations, there is prefigured and inherited potential for symbolic understanding'. This is closely related to Bowlby's internal working model (see Chapter 9). More recent writers and theorists such as Siegel (1999) and Hobson (2002) have underlined the importance of these early and emotional attachments for the growth of cognition. Siegel (1999: 143) links the emotional interactions involved in successful attachment to the adaptive, flexible thinking needed to support cognition:

> intimate, reciprocal human communication may directly activate the neural circuitry responsible by giving meaning, integrating the capacity for flexible responses, and shaping the subjective experience of living an emotionally vibrant life.

Carl Rogers' theories

Carl Rogers' theories begin with the person. (Kramer [1961] 1995: x) describes Rogers' unique vision as threefold, namely 'acceptance, reciprocity and altruism'. He regards these as fundamental to all interactions including education (and therefore care). His reason for rejecting behaviourism was that it underplays or even ignores human motives and feelings. He had two main reasons for rejecting Freudian psychoanalysis. First, he believed that while Freud interpreted his clients' dreams, actions and anxieties for them, it was important for clients to see the subjective nature of their perceptions for themselves. Secondly, although Freud often described his clients in derogatory terms, central to Rogers' belief was the notion of what he described as *unconditional positive regard*. This meant that clients (and later in his work, students) should not be viewed in a negative light.

While Maslow referred to self-actualisation, Rogers referred to the fully-functioning person. Both concepts require mental health and psychological well-being. Growth for Rogers meant progress towards greater 'self-esteem, flexibility, respect for self and others' (Kramer 1995: ix). The aim of teaching Rogers suggests is to support the development of fully-functioning people – whose qualities will include dependability, realism, sociability, constant self-discovery and an alertness to newness. He focused on the role of teachers in facilitating learning through empathy and through creating a climate which allowed *freedom to learn* (Curzon 2003). He favoured experiential learning over direct instruction. For him experiential education included:

- the personal involvement of the learner
- an excitement which stimulated both feeling and cognition
- self-initiated learning
- learning based on meaning

(based on Curzon 2003: 117).

Linking theory and practice

The pioneers of early childhood education, while not all benefitting from the impact of Freud's theories and writing, understood from their direct knowledge of children the importance of children's feelings in promoting their well-being. For Froebel, Steiner and

McMillan this was closely linked to spirituality. Isaacs, on the other hand, a confirmed agnostic, if not atheist, sought to understand children's feelings in a different way. She turned to psychoanalytic theory and became aware that children's emotional state played a large part in determining their future. The way in which they were treated would determine how they acted in the world.

Rogers' theories concerning nondirective parenting and teaching which suggest that an assessment of process is key to the work of parents and educators (Kramer 1995) are readily understood by many early childhood educators. This may be because they chime with many other, more familiar, theories. In addition, for many, Rogers' words articulated their own views of children and education and enabled them to identify with his views. Many people working in the early years will readily say that they do not teach but that they do facilitate learning. This resistance to being seen to teach is a pity since it leaves the impression that practitioners are not concerned with learning. Jones and Pound (2008: 115) have identified five broad categories of teaching (and learning) strategies:

1 stimulating, sustaining and extending interests
2 modelling
3 direct teaching
4 interacting and communicating
5 playing.

Within these, Rogers' stress on the need for empathy and on the importance of supporting learning through young children's interests and building on the meanings they are constructing through experience remain difficult tasks. If they are to achieve these things, those who are educating young children have to be highly skilled and reflective. Direct teaching (the third of the strategies listed above) is not the same as Rogers' direct instruction. He probably had in mind images of what is often called 'chalk and talk' – a teacher standing in front of a blackboard. In terms of early years practice direct teaching might include describing what a child is doing, singing songs to support memory or express ideas, providing constructive feedback in order to help children build on what they are already able to do, breaking tasks down into relevant and accessible steps where appropriate, demonstrating so that children can learn through imitation, as well as questioning and where appropriate intervening. Facilitation means much more than simply providing an environment.

The impact of beginning to understand the relationship between maternal deprivation and later success has many important links to practice. Pugh (2002) has underlined the importance of identifying children and families at risk and the implications for society. Similarly Camila Batmangheldijh, a psychotherapist who works with severely disturbed children and young people, relies on her belief that when children have been loved they are more resilient than those who in being neglected, become 'marooned' by an 'inability to express (their) own hurt, or to understand the hurt of others' (Orr 2010: 9).

A critique of theories linking cognition and emotion

Those who resist a link between emotions and cognition often regard learner-centred theory and practice as well intentioned but lacking rigour. Many blame Rogers' theories for the rise in individualism and insufficient emphasis on the importance of collaboration. Others suggest that that they have led to too much emphasis on self-esteem and insufficient on facing up to failure, competition and perseverance.

Critics from within the ranks of psychoanalysts believe that Rogers demands too much of therapists. Similar criticisms may be made of his work in relation to education. Therapists, he suggests, should demonstrate honesty, empathy and respect for those they work with. Sonia Nieto (1999: 100) suggests that:

> The climate for learning ... cannot be separated from a climate in which care, concern, and love are central. By 'love' I do not mean a mawkish or sentimental demonstration of concern for students. Rather, I am suggesting that love is at the core of good teaching because it is predicated on high standards, rigorous demands, and respect for students, their identities and their families.

She continues by referring to the work of a colleague, Mary Ginley, who

> spoke in class about the absolute necessity to love all her students; without love, she maintained, she couldn't really teach them. Some she confessed were harder to love than others, but in all her years of teaching she had never failed to love any of her students.

Inevitably any mention of 'love' raises concerns about inappropriate shows of affection between children and practitioners. Of course children must be protected from harm, but by attempting to rule out the physical reassurance that many young children need – a cuddle or an opportunity to sit on a comfortable lap – we may be invoking a different kind of harm. Tobin (2004) refers to this as 'moral panic' and decries the rise of what he terms disembodied education. He argues that a wish for increased control and risk-avoidance have together contributed to this disembodiment with 'the unfortunate, unintended side-effect of reducing physical movement and contact in early childhood educational settings' (Tobin 2004: 124).

Bruer (1999) has criticised those who regard the early years as having particular significance in lifelong development. He rejects a link between attachment and brain development and suggests that parents should ignore warnings to the contrary. He suggests that damage is reversible – a view shared by others. However most theorists warn that although there are very few critical periods – periods of time when if children fail to develop in particular ways it will be difficult or impossible for them to do so later – failure to meet those that may be found to exist may have serious implications. Siegel (1999) for example suggests that if attachment fails to take place in the first year, it will be difficult to replace at a later stage. Bruer (1999: 209)) concludes that 'parents should realize that children thrive in a wide variety of physical and cultural environments and learn and benefit from experiences throughout their lives'.

The legacy of theories linking cognition and emotion

The linking of emotion and cognition has greatly extended and developed our understanding of social interaction in its earliest stages. The acknowledgement of a world of human development and growth which is not readily accessible to observation – namely the mind and its efforts to make sense or create meanings – has sparked an interest in babies. Notable psychologists have enriched our understanding. Daniel Stern, for example, whose psychoanalytical background gave him a particular interest in what he termed the interpersonal world of the infant (Stern 1985) has drawn attention to sensitive periods in a baby's earliest months as the emergent, core, subjective and verbal self develop. Colwyn Trevarthen has also used as his starting point the relationship between mother and baby but has highlighted intersubjectivity – a phrase which Stern suggests was devised by Trevarthen himself (see Pound 2009). Using video footage Trevarthen has analysed protoconversations between mothers and babies and writes about motherese (now often referred to as infant directed speech/IDS or parentese). Murray, Trevarthen's student, has studied the impact of a mother's depression on intersubjectivity in babies (see for example Murray and Andrews 2000).

There is too an undoubted influence within education itself (although the continuing focus on a product based approach to education may show that Rogers has had little influence. The jury is still out!) The focus on the emotional side of human life which psychoanalysis precipitated paved the way for Rogers' interest in a learner-centred approach – built on his client-centred psychotherapeutic work. This in turn coincided with the thinking of Gardner (1983; 1999) in developing interpersonal and intrapersonal intelligences – the ability to interact with others and the ability to look inwards on ourselves. Gardner himself attributes his work on personal intelligences to the writings of Sigmund Freud and William James (Gardner 1993). By the 1990s the neuroscientific work of Joseph LeDoux (1998) and the popular writing of Daniel Goleman (1996) on emotional intelligence placed emotional well-being firmly on the educational map.

Rogers' work continues to have influence. The introduction of individualised lessons at secondary school and the growing involvement of parents owes something to Rogers. Rogers' influence and that of humanistic psychology may be seen in early years curriculum documents. The emphasis on *being* and *becoming* found in the titles of Rogers' books *On Becoming a Person* (1961) and *A Way of Being* (1980) are reflected in strands of the New Zealand early years curriculum Te Whariki, for example.

In 1980 Rogers (1980: 263) wrote about holistic education:

> I deplore the manner in which, from early years, the child's education splits him or her; the *mind* can come to school, and the body is permitted,

peripherally, to tag along, but the feelings and emotions can live freely and expressively only outside of school.

... it is not only feasible to permit the whole child to come to school, with feelings as well as intellect, but that learning is enhanced.

Reflective questions

1. What can you do to help children express their feelings?
2. What do you think the differences between learner-centred and child-centred practice is?
3. What do you think Sonia Nieto means when she says practitioners must love those that they work with?
4. What can you do to ensure that children are seen in school as having feelings and intellect?

Further reading

Goleman, D. (1996) *Emotional Intelligence*. London: Fontana.
Rogers, C. (1983) *Freedom to Learn for the 80s*. New York: Merril.

Part 4
Constructivism and behaviourism

As indicated in Part 3, theories do not simply arise and replace one another. Theories overlap, merging in places – sometimes giving way in popularity to one another or falling out of favour, but rarely completely displaced in the human mind. This section will examine the rise of two distinctly opposing points of view – both of which, despite many contradictions, continue to impact on the care and education of young children. The concerns of nineteenth-century theorists and thinkers – whether dealing primarily with children from the working class as Owen was doing – or from more affluent classes as Froebel was doing – had an impact on the twentieth-century progressive educational thinkers and theorists such as those whose work is outlined in Part 2 of this book. Their work drew – as we have seen – on the psychoanalytical thinking that was emerging in the first half of the twentieth century. Even where the influence was not direct it was inexorable – a growing understanding of the importance of not just actions but thinking and feelings. As Gardner et al. (1996: 97) point out 'great psychologists put forth complex and intricate theories, but they are often remembered best for a striking demonstration'. They suggest that 'the striking demonstration' which is held in mind by the public of Freud's work is 'that unconscious wishes – for power, for sexual satisfaction – are reflected in ordinary dreams or slips of the tongue' (Gardner et al. 1996: 97).

Gardner et al. (1996) go on to highlight 'the striking demonstrations' of Pavlov and Piaget – key figures in behaviourism and constructivism respectively. Pavlov is, in the popular imagination, remembered for dogs salivating at the sound of a bell. Piaget, they suggest, is best known for his work on the conservation of quantities. It is for example striking that, as Piaget demonstrated, children can watch water being poured from one container into another and appear to believe that the amount of water has changed – simply because the shape of the container into which it is poured is different. In this part of the book, the diverse impact of behaviourism and constructivism as a whole will be explored – an impact which goes way beyond drooling dogs or tall thin beakers.

Talay-Ongan (1998) suggests that the development of the study of children can be categorised in five main ways, namely:

- psychodynamic theories
- behaviourist theories
- cognitive-developmental models

- contextual-cultural theories, and
- neurobiological or neuroscientific models.

Any categorisation is inevitably both far from perfect and less than total since there is so much overlap between theories. Moreover, what seem to the outsider apparently small differences in theory can cause theorists to dissociate themselves from other theorists. The theories explored in Part 3 (which examined psychodynamic theories) offer examples of both overlap and conflict.

The development of humanistic psychology in which Carl Rogers was closely involved is said to have grown out of dissatisfaction with both behaviourist and psychoanalytic theories. However, as we have seen in Chapter 10 it would seem that humanistic psychology has more in common with psychodynamic approaches than with behaviourism. The former is concerned with human growth, with what goes on inside the head while the latter is concerned only with actions. What cannot be seen, behaviourists argue, cannot be studied.

Behaviourism and constructivism

It may seem odd to group these two highly divergent approaches in the same section of this book. The significant differences on which they are based – their view of the child, their view of knowledge and their view of the role of adults – make them arguably more interesting when placed in juxtaposition than when separated. For behaviourists, knowledge is given to children by adults in bite size chunks, while for constructivists, knowledge is created as we experience life. The behaviourist child is malleable, mouldable, a form that can be shaped at will – entirely a product of the environment in which he or she grows up. The constructivist child is curious, seeking – with a pre-programmed process of development which need not be slavishly opened up but which may be tempered by experience. In the three chapters that follow, behaviourist theories, cognitive developmental theories, and contextual-cultural theories will be considered.

Reflective questions

1. Try to identify what you regard as the striking demonstrations of the theories you have read about so far.
2. What do you regard as the most significant similarities and differences between the theories considered so far?

Key dates

1849–1936   Ivan Pavlov
1874–1949   Edward Thorndike

1878–1954   **John Watson**
1896–1934   **Lev Vygotsky**
1896–1980   **Jean Piaget**
1904–1990   **Burrhus Skinner**
1925–   **Albert Bandura**

Further reading

Cohen, D. (2002) *How the Child's Mind Develops*. Hove, E. Sussex: Routledge. (See Chapters 2 and 3.)

11 Burrhus Skinner (1904–1990), behaviourist theories and approaches

Behaviourism began with the work of Ivan Pavlov in Russia but has perhaps been most widely developed in the United States of America. Burrhus Skinner is the name probably most commonly associated with the approach but Edward Thorndike and John Watson were also key to the development of the theories and undoubtedly influenced Skinner. Behaviourism is sometimes referred to in the literature as Learning Theory. In the nature-nurture debate, behaviourism is a theory which at its most extreme regards development and learning as entirely due to nurture. Despite many criticisms, which will be examined later in this chapter, behaviourist theories continue to be widely used in practice.

Behaviourist theories

Ivan Pavlov (1849–1936), a Russian, was initially interested in the gastric function of dogs but as he worked with them he became more interested in what came to be called their conditioned response to the feeding regime he used with them. Pavlov's version of behaviourist theory is generally referred to as *classical conditioning*. Pavlov noticed that if a bell was rung when food appeared, dogs learnt to associate the bell with food – eventually salivating when they heard the bell even when no food was available. Salivating is an unconditioned response – dogs do not have to learn how to do it in response to food. However, salivating when a bell is heard is a learnt or conditioned response. Pavlov's dogs learnt to associate a bell with food.

In the United States of America, Edward Thorndike (1874–1949) and John Watson (1878–1954) were also working on behaviourist experiments. Thorndike's work led to a theory known as the 'Law of Effect', which suggests that any behaviour which has a positive consequence will be repeated. Moreover, he theorised that repetition improves problem-solving. Watson, like Skinner, focused on operant, rather than classical conditioning (see below). His theory suggested that conditioning comes about when rewards follow an action. A child given a sweet when they have finished their meal is more likely, his theory suggests, to eat everything on their plate.

Skinner read, and was impressed by, Pavlov's work but as Slater (2004: 11) describes it – 'he wanted to go beyond a small mucous membrane, he wanted the whole entire organism'. In other words he wanted not simply to be able to shape the reaction of salivary glands but to find out how to modify the larger actions of animals and humans. This view is reinforced by Kohn (1993: 281) who describes a conversation with Skinner in which he outlines his efforts during the Second World War to train pigeons to steer missiles. Skinner's enthusiasm for his project, though not perhaps shared by others (including Kohn), is highlighted when he exclaims 'What a fascinating thing! Total control of a living organism!'

In particular, Skinner wondered whether behaviour which was not associated with reflex actions, as behaviour in Pavlov's experiments had been, could be similarly shaped or modified. He termed these actions which were not reflexes, 'operants' and his approach is termed *operant conditioning,* as opposed to classical conditioning. It may also be referred to in the relevant literature as *instrumental conditioning.* Skinner's work began with rats. Pressing a lever produced food – by frequently changing the number of times the lever had to be pressed he maintained the animals' interest. His experimental work included teaching pigeons to play ping-pong, a rabbit to pick up coins and put them in a money box, a cat to play the piano and a pig to use a vacuum cleaner (Slater 2004).

From these experiments he derived theories which included the following elements:

- *Positive reinforcement* describes the way in which pleasant consequences are used to reinforce behaviour.
- *Negative reinforcement* is the cessation of something unpleasant. If, for example, avoidance of electric shock is used as a reinforcer – the action that stops the electric current is a negative reinforcer. Kohn (1993: 52) adds that 'contrary to common usage, it is...closer to positive reinforcement (making a good thing happen) than it is to punishment'.
- *Punishment.* Skinner did not use punishment – only withdrawal of positive reinforcers (Slater 2004).
- *Intermittent reinforcement* is connected to *variable schedules of reinforcement* described below. Undesirable behaviour is less rapidly extinguished if reinforcement is intermittent rather than consistent.
- *Extinction.* In some experiments Skinner removed the reinforcer. Unsurprisingly, the learned behaviour (or conditioned response) ceased. Skinner experimented with and recorded how long it took to extinguish learned responses.
- *Variable schedules of reinforcement.* Slater (2004) suggests that this is perhaps Skinner's most significant discovery. He found that if animals were not always rewarded after completing the required task but only at irregular intervals the learned behaviour was even harder to extinguish. This finding is frequently cited as the reason why compulsive gambling, for example, is so hard to change.

Behaviourist theories in practice

Classical conditioning can be seen to be prevalent in infants. They learn to associate their hunger and the arrival of milk with a number of sensory experiences – perhaps touch as the mother holds the baby in a particular way in order to breastfeed; perhaps the smell associated with the mother or a particular room in the house; sights and sound may become conditioned responses associated with the reflex actions arising from the need for food or warmth or comfort. As adults such conditioned responses continue to evoke pleasure or fear – the smell of baking, the sight of a hypodermic syringe and so on.

Skinner's brand of behaviourism – operant or instrumental conditioning – is often referred to in the relevant literature as Learning Theory. This should not be confused with learning theories or theories of learning which refer to the full range of ideas about learning – not simply the behavioural. MacNaughton (2003: 26) reminds us that:

> Behaviourism has had a powerful influence on many early childhood educa-tors' view of learning. The ideas that we conform to our culture as we learn, and that praise, positive rewards such as 'gold stars' or a special role in the classroom can reinforce positive behaviours and assist children's learning are widespread.

It is clear that behaviourist ideas are particularly widespread in relation to the edu-cation of children with special educational needs. The Portage programme for example, (Bishop 1986) is based on creating a series of small steps which can be readily identified and rewarded when each is successfully completed. Over time, this can enable children, some of whom have severe disabilities, to learn to undertake tasks such as drinking from a cup.

What is perhaps less readily apparent is the aspect of behaviourism which MacNaughton (2003) refers to as teaching children to 'conform to a culture'. She identi-fies four distinct ways in which educators use behaviourism to get children to conform. She highlights as behaviourism in practice the way in which practitioners:

- decide who we want the child to become or what we want the child to learn ...
- choose reinforcers most appropriate to the child's learning goals ...
- actively teach the child what we want them to learn ...
- construct an environment that directly and indirectly reinforces what we want the child to learn.

(MacNaughton 2003, based on page 27)

Throughout his life, Skinner attempted to put all his ideas into practice. In a book entitled *Particulars of my Life* (Skinner 1976), Skinner describes a number of inventions. His animals were trained in what have become known as Skinner's Boxes and he in-vented what were called teaching machines. These were popular in some schools – as children were set tasks – the machine raising questions and students being rewarded if they got the right answer.

A critique of behaviourist theories

The fundamental criticism of behaviourism is that human behaviour is too complex to be explained by such a simple theory. This view can be summed up in a humorous quotation from the philosopher Arthur Koestler (cited by Kohn 1993: 3): 'for the anthropomorphic view of the rat, American psychology substituted a rattomorphic view of man'. The criticism is also exemplified by accounts of what is known as an air-crib (Slater 2004) although it is suggested that her account of the shaping of young babies has been exaggerated (Kohn 1993).

In his book entitled *Punished by Rewards*, Kohn (1993) sets out a strong argument against the use of gold stars and indeed even praise as an incentive or reward. Praise, he claims, 'is often favoured by those whose style of dealing with children is conspicuously controlling or autocratic' (Kohn 1993: 51). Kohn (1993) further suggests that there is 'irrefutable evidence that people who are trying to earn a reward end up doing a poorer job on many tasks than people who are not' (Kohn 1993: 49). He puts forward five reasons why this might be:

1. *Rewards punish*. Kohn (1993) contends that, although Skinner preferred the former to the latter, rewards and punishments have the same effect. Kohn continues by suggesting that:

   > the long-term use of either tactic describes the very same pattern; eventually we will need to raise the stakes and offer more and more treats or threaten more and more sanctions to get people to continue acting the way we want (1993: 50).

   Punishments and rewards leave people with the feeling of being controlled or manipulated and these feelings are 'impediments to working or learning effectively' (Kohn 1993: 54)

2. *Rewards rupture relationships*.

   > The presence or absence of rewards is, of course, only one factor among many that affect the quality of our relationships. But it is a factor too often overlooked in its tendency to cause flattery to be emphasized in place of trust and to create a feeling of being evaluated rather than supported. This, combined with its impact on the relationships among those seeking the goodies, goes a long way toward explaining how rewards often reduce achievement.
   >
   > (Kohn 1993: 59)

3. *Rewards ignore reasons*. Behaviourist strategies are frequently used with small children. A common example of this is in getting children to sleep, or as they get older, at least to stay in bed. Kohn (1993) suggests that whether we threaten (unless you stay in bed you won't get...), or bribe (if you stay in bed I'll

buy you a...) we are failing to understand what the child's motive is. Are they scared? Are they hungry? Are they too excited? Each possible explanation might indicate a different solution – a solution which unlike rewards, 'look(s) below the surface' (Kohn 1993: 60).

This particular aspect of Kohn's argument highlights other important factors. Behaviourism is often criticised for ignoring human qualities such as feelings, morality and emotion (see for example Gardner 1993). Slater (2004) outlines a related but slightly different criticism of behaviourism. After visiting Skinner's daughter, Slater describes her feelings as she attempts to get her own 2-year-old to sleep through the night. The parents have not ignored the reasons for her sleeplessness – nightmares and then gradually over time an habituation to the cuddles – but they are tired. After some debate they decide to as they term it 'Skinnerize' her. After just five nights in which they systematically reduce the amount of time they comfort her when she cries, the child sleeps contentedly for ten hours without waking. But Slater is left with an uneasy feeling – despite quiet nights she can't help but feel that her baby 'has been eerily gagged' (2004: 21). This highlights the sinister edge of behaviourism – its ability (whether actively used or not) to shape people in sometimes unethical ways.

4. *Rewards discourage risk-taking.* Most early childhood practitioners are in agreement that children are born problem-solvers and that humans learn from their errors. The problem with rewards is that they undermine this natural approach to learning. Why take risks by trying something innovative or creative when it might undermine your chance of gaining a reward for successfully completing something? Kohn offers the example of a reading programme that rewards children on the basis of the number of books they have read. Anyone who is reward oriented will inevitably choose short unchallenging books. The outcome is not that which was initially desired.

5. *Rewards change the way people feel about what they do.* Finally Kohn (1993) identifies a criticism which should be taken very seriously by everyone who works with young children. He argues that 'extrinsic rewards reduce intrinsic motivation' (Kohn 1993: 71). In other words 'what rewards do ... is smother people's enthusiasm for activities they might otherwise enjoy' (Kohn 1993: 74). He cites studies which show that

    •   Children who were paid to do drawings ceased doing them when payment ceased;
    •   Children who were encouraged to drink a particular milk product either through praise for finishing the drink or by being offered bribes, after a week liked the drink less than they had initially. By contrast, the group of children who merely drank the product, continued to like it at least as much and often more than they had at first.
    •   Programmes designed to offer incentives to increase children's reading encouraged children to read shorter books; made them less able to answer questions about what they had read; and meant that most children read less outside school.

Finally, a criticism which might be made by many reflective practitioners is that although behaviourist approaches are widely used and often seem to work – at least in the short term – they do not explain all learning. Skinner's experiments were conducted mainly on animals but his theoretical writing is about people. In turn these theories became largely applied to children (Pound 2005). Nowhere is this oversimplification of human behaviour more true than in Skinner's explanation of language learning. We have all wondered from time to time how children have taken on new vocabulary which they can rarely have heard. Moreover every child makes use of language forms which they will not have heard at all, such as overgeneralisations of grammar rules (for example 'I wented to the shops'); or made up words. It is in this area that behaviourism has led to the creation of an enormous legacy.

The legacy of behaviourist theories

Slater (2004: 11) reminds us that, although to us in the twenty-first century, Pavlov's findings appear mundane, this was not the case when he published his findings in 1927. Her idiosyncratic style of writing conveys this difference in perception as she writes:

> Back then this was huge. This was as hot as the spliced atom or the singular position of the sun. Never, ever before in all of human history had people understood how *physiological* were our supposed mental associations. Never before had people understood the sheer malleability of the immutable animal form. Pavlov's dogs drooled and the world tipped over twice.

Views of language learning

Although not in the ways that might have been expected, an equally huge impact, it may be argued, came from Skinner's views on language development. These drew a response from Noam Chomsky which was to lead to an explosion of interest in the whole field of language learning and development. In 1957, Skinner published a book entitled *Verbal Behaviour* in which he set out a behaviourist theory of language learning. He suggested that, like all other learning in his view, language was learnt from parents – a view that Pinker (1994) now describes as folklore. Two years later, Noam Chomsky (1959) published a review of Skinner's work which strongly challenged the view that language learning was a result of nurture.

Chomsky proposed a theory of language learning as an innate process. He argued that the complex and abstract nature of the rules a speaker follows are learnt so rapidly in early childhood that they could not be learnt in the way that behaviourists suggest. As an alternative view, Chomsky suggested that each of us is born with a language acquisition device (LAD) which gives us an inbuilt understanding of language structures. The debate that raged was to stimulate interest in language development for the remainder of the century. Nicholls and Wells (1985) suggest that this interest initially focused on grammar – an interest which was increased by the development of audio recording techniques. These made it possible for researchers to listen to and analyse samples of speech in a way that had not been possible before.

Chomsky's writing triggered a huge amount of interest in language which was subsequently taken up by cognitive psychology. Some questioned the idea of a specific LAD. All, including Piaget and Vygotsky, examined the link between language and thinking – described by Nicholls and Wells (1985: 4) as 'the transformation of pre-linguistic sensori-motor intelligence into the kind of symbolic thinking that language demands'. From the 1970s, like cognitive and developmental psychology, this interest in language was (like other areas of learning) to come to focus more on the social and cultural aspects of development. This included what Bruner (1983) was to call, linking his work to that of Chomsky, a LASS (language acquisition support system). More recently this interest has been taken up by neuroscience. The legacy – albeit an unintended or unforeseen consequence of Skinner's work – has been immense.

Programmed learning

Kohn (1993) suggests that Skinner's teaching machines led the way to programmed learning. He suggests that Skinner was proud to have been such a pioneer but disappointed that more schools had not seen the advantages of what he regarded as an individualised approach to learning. It should be noted here that such a legacy is itself not without critics. MacNaughton (2003, citing Crain 1995) suggests that the notion of independence in such approaches is a fallacy – every element of the programmes is devised and structured by adults.

Research methods

A further facet of Skinner's legacy has been his methodology. Skinner's experiments:

> yielded quantifiable data on how organisms learn and on how we can predict and control the learning outcome. With the achievement of predictability and control, a true science of behaviour was born, with bell curves and bar graphs and plot points and math, and Skinner was the first one to do it to such a nuanced and multileveled extent.
>
> (Slater 2004: 13)

This ties in with Kohn's (1993: 280) description of Skinner as:

> less a theorist than a technician. The man was fascinated – indeed, almost obsessed – with practical problems of design.... Everything, as Skinner saw it, was a problem to be solved, and his most famous and infamous pronouncements can be understood in that context. 'Designing a culture is like designing an experiment', he once wrote.

Social learning theory

It would be wrong to leave behaviourist theories without mentioning Albert Bandura (1925–). He is responsible for social learning theory – a theory which builds on behaviourist theories. While agreeing that stimulus and response were important elements of learning, Bandura's theories suggest that the reinforcement of learning occurs as we imitate or model ourselves on others we want to be like. As such, social learning theory has come to be regarded as the bridge between behaviourism and constructivism. Unlike behaviourism social learning theory takes account of mental processes, recognising that learning may occur even though reward (or reinforcement) is not immediate or obvious. Perhaps best known for his experiments known as the 'bobo doll studies', Bandura suggests that aggressive behaviour is learnt through imitation. We seek reward, he claims, by imitating and becoming more like those we admire.

Reflective questions

1. To what extent do you think that the criticisms of programmed learning apply to the way in which technology is used?
2. Bandura's conclusions have been criticised as ignoring some of the human aspects of interaction – hitting a bobo doll is not the same as hitting a person. What is your view?
3. Review the criticisms that Kohn makes of behaviourist theories. To what extent do you agree with him?
4. Reflect on the moral dilemma which faces Slater when she writes of 'skinnerizing' her child. What are your views?

Further reading

Slater, L. (2004) *Opening Skinner's Box*. London: Bloomsbury Publishing. (See Chapter 1.)

12 Jean Piaget (1896–1980) and constructivism

In the introduction to Part 3 the development of humanistic psychology was discussed as arising out of a rejection of both behaviourism and psychoanalysis. Despite this third way, behaviourism and psychoanalytical theory flourished for some time. Neither theoretical approaches were to be really challenged until the 1960s. The work of Piaget and Vygotsky (to be explored in the next chapter) was ignored for an extended period. Gopnik et al. (1999: 19) write that:

> The theories that did dominate psychology, especially in America, were Freudianism and the behaviorism of psychologists like B. F. Skinner. Both theories had lots of things to say about young children. But . . . neither Freud nor Skinner took the step of doing systematic experiments with children or babies. Freud largely relied on inferences from the behavior of neurotic adults, and Skinner on inferences from the behavior of only slightly less neurotic rats. . . . Freud saw children as the apotheosis of passion, creatures so driven by lusts and hungers that their most basic perceptions of the world were deeply distorted fantasies. Skinner's view was that children were the ultimate blank tablets, passively waiting to be inscribed by reinforcement schedules.

Piaget is the name most commonly associated with constructivism although as MacNaughton (2003) reminds us it was not – even when Piaget began developing his theories – a totally new concept. She suggests that Giambatista Vico, writing in the early part of the eighteenth century, was perhaps the first constructivist – although a philosopher rather than a psychologist. She further suggests that the philosopher Immanual Kant, also writing in the eighteenth century, believed that knowledge is not passively received but interpreted in the light of the learner's experience. Egan (1983) goes one better by describing Plato in similar terms.

It would probably be no exaggeration to say that Piaget's theories and writing have had an immeasurable influence on all subsequent thinking about children's learning and development. Talay-Ongan (1998) suggests that all frameworks, or groups of theories have a grand theorist. She describes Piaget as the grand theorist of what she terms cognitive-developmental approaches. She contrasts cognitive-developmental approaches with behaviourism since unlike behaviourism they give a key role to the mind and to cognition. She also likens cognitive-developmental approaches to psychodynamic theory as both place a strong emphasis on the active process of constructing knowledge through internal representations of people and objects and 'through interactions with events, and relations' (Talay-Ongan 1998: 14). Although Talay-Ongan (1998) has grouped them together it may be helpful to identify some distinct roots.

Developmental psychology

Keenan and Evans (2009: 5) suggest that Darwin 'was an early pioneer in the study of children', using records of his own son's development 'to understand human development in light of the theory of evolution by natural selection'. *Baby biographies*, as these records came to be known, were produced by many eminent theorists and became:

- 'the source of many modern ideas about children's development';
- 'criticized for their emotional and biased descriptions of children'; but
- praised for the 'extremely high standards they set for observing and recording behaviour accurately'.

(based on Keenan and Evans 2009: 5)

Some key landmarks in the rise of developmental psychology may be outlined as follows:

- Stanley Hall was amongst the first to be recognised as a developmental psychologist. His research included a study (entitled *Studies on Children* and published in 1893) which was based on questionnaires and interviews about what children know on entry to school.
- James Mark Baldwin was a pioneer, in Canada, of children's mental development – appointed to the University of Toronto in 1889. He studied imitation and intentionality – an area of research which was to lead later to an understanding of theory of mind (see for example Hobson 2002).
- Watson, the behavioural psychologist, believed that all development arises out of learning. He famously boasted that he could, given the opportunity, shape any child into becoming 'any type of specialist ... regardless of his talents, penchants, tendencies, abilities, vocations, and race of his ancestors' (Watson 1934: 104).
- In contrast, Arnold Gesell 'believed that development is the result of our genetic endowment, a view that is known as maturation' (Keenan and Evans 2009: 6). His research led him to look for 'norms' of development. Amongst his best known work is his study of twins. Typically one twin would be trained to perform a new skill such as climbing stairs and his studies tended to show that 'the untrained twin tended to acquire the behaviour just as quickly as the trained twin' (Keenan and Evans 2009: 16). As indicated in Part 3, Gesell set up a Child Study Centre in 1911.

- The St George's School for Child Study was established in Canada in 1926. The centre was made famous in the 1930s for its study of the Dionne Quintuplets (Keenan and Evans 2009).
- Susan Isaacs became the first head of the Department of Child Development in London in 1933.

The cognitive revolution

Less well known than developmental psychology are the theories that have emerged from what has come to be known as the cognitive revolution. These grew out of wartime interests in computers and artificial intelligence and ways of enhancing human performance. These theories as Talay-Ongan (1998) suggests have also been influential in shaping the views of practitioners although the psychologists associated with these theories are probably much less well known to early childhood specialists. Cognitive psychology has long been associated with information processing (see also Part 6). Keenan and Evans (2009: 7) suggest that the link between developmental and cognitive psychologies lies in efforts to understand children's thinking:

> Information processing psychologists most often focus on how children take in or encode information from their environment, how they represent it to themselves, and how they operate on the representations of knowledge to create outputs of products . . . like the solution to a math problem or an answer to a question about what Winnie the Pooh will do next.

Cognitive psychology was defined by Neisser as 'the study of how people learn, structure, store and use knowledge' (Sternberg 2009: 12). Neisser's seminal text (1967) – seen as of fundamental importance within the cognitive revolution – focuses on perception, attention language processing, memory and thought. The *Journal of Cognitive Psychology* which was established in 1970 sees its role as highlighting research connected with memory, language processing, perception, problem-solving and thinking – all of which can be seen as having some links with developmental psychology.

Steven Pinker (2002: 34) has written about the cognitive revolution. Regarded as an evolutionary psychologist, Pinker refutes the notion of the mind as a blank slate. He writes that:

> *The mind cannot be a blank slate, because blank slates don't do anything.* As long as people had only the haziest idea of what a mind was or how it might work, the metaphor of a blank slate inscribed by the environment did not seem too outrageous. But as soon as one starts to think seriously about what kind of computation enables a system to seen, think, speak, and plan, the problem with blank slates becomes all too obvious: they don't do anything. . . . This argument against the Blank Slate was stated pithily by Leibniz . . . . 'There is nothing in the intellect that was not first in the senses . . . except the intellect itself'. *Something* in the mind must be innate, if it is only the mechanisms that do the learning. Something has to see a world of objects rather than a kaleidoscope of shimmering pixels. Something has to infer the content of a

sentence rather than parrot back the exact wording. Something has to interpret other people's behavior as their attempts to achieve goals rather than as
trajectories or jerking arms and legs.

(Pinker 2002: 34–5, original emphasis)

Pinker (2002: 35) goes on to argue that even 'mundane challenges like walking around
furniture . . . or guessing someone's intentions are formidable engineering problems that
are at or beyond the frontiers of artificial intelligence'. However despite this agreement,
cognitive psychologists are far from agreed on the extent to which nature or nurture
drives our learning.

Bruner (1990: 2) also highlights the role of cognitive psychology in interpreting
actions. He regards cognitive psychology as:

> an all-out effort to establish *meaning* as the central concept of psychology. . . . It
> was not a revolution against behaviorism with the aim of transforming behav-
> iorism into a better way of pursuing psychology by adding a little mentalism
> to it. Its aim was to discover and to describe formally the meaning that human
> beings created out of their encounters with the world and then to propose
> hypotheses about what meaning-making processes were implicated.

Making meaning is a familiar concept to most early childhood practitioners since it
is again a term that is reflected in many early childhood curricula. Halliday published
a book in 1975 entitled *Learning How to Mean*. In 1985 Wells published another entitled *The Meaning Makers: children learning language and using language to learn*. Making
meaning is central to constructivist theories and approaches – in everything we do,
they argue, we seek to make meaning, make sense of our world.

Jean Piaget (1896–1980)

Piaget was born in Switzerland in 1896, co-incidentally in the same year as Vygotsky.
By the age of 22, Piaget had become a Doctor of Natural Sciences, his first degree subject
being zoology. Even before entering his degree studies, Piaget's interest in animals was
well established. At the age of 10 he had written a paper about an albino sparrow he had
discovered near his home and before entering university he wrote a series of articles
about molluscs.

After gaining his doctorate Piaget became interested in psychology which, as was
seen in Part 3, was still a relatively new subject at this time. He went first to Zurich
where he studied under Carl Jung (see Part 3) and then to Paris where he worked with
Alfred Binet (see Part 2). His work there apparently involved administering reading tests
as part of Binet's intelligence testing. In fact Piaget became interested in why it should
be that the wrong answers given by children should so often be the same. It was this
that led him to what was to become his life's work.

In 1921 Piaget became the Director of the Jean Jacques Rousseau Institute in
Geneva. The institute had been set up in 1912 with the express aim of turning
educational theory into a science but Piaget stayed only a short time. In 1923 he was
made professor of psychology, sociology and philosophical sciences at Neuchatel. Much

of Piaget's work at this stage was philosophical – his prime interest being epistemology, that is the study of the nature of knowledge. In 1929 he became a professor of child psychology in Geneva – the university where he was to spend most of the reminder of his working life.

Piagetian theories

Piaget's theories are complex – made no less so by the fact that his theories were developed over time and therefore may sometimes appear contradictory and by the fact that they have been translated from French. A further factor contributing to this complexity is his style of writing and use of vocabulary – said by Callaway (2001) to be a deliberate strategy on the part of Piaget. In this section some of the key elements of Piaget's ideas are outlined.

Stages of development

This is a central plank of Piaget's theories. He believed that development and learning followed a series of qualitatively different stages which were primarily linked to the age of the child. Freud too identified stages of development but while his were linked to emotional and sexual development, Piaget's interest was intellectual development.

> Piaget saw the child as constantly constructing and reconstructing reality – achieving increased understanding by integrating simple concepts into more complex ones at each stage. He argued that there was a natural sequence for the development of thought governed by what he termed 'genetic epistemology' . . .
>
> (Pound 2005: 37)

Piaget identified four stages beginning in babyhood and ending as adulthood was achieved. He believed that the order in which the stages develop is invariant – stages are not missed out. Secondly he regarded the stages as universal – applying to all children and not affected by social or cultural factors. Piaget also believed that 'development occurred as a result of our predispositions to organize and adapt to new experiences'. The stages, as described by Piaget, were as follows:

- *Sensorimotor stage*. This stage covers the period from birth to 2 years of age. During this stage, understanding (or knowledge) is drawn from physical action and from sensory experience. Piaget argued that the greatest achievement of this stage was the development of object permanence (see below). He postulated six sub-stages which were namely:
  - Reflexive schemes – the basis of development during the first month of life when babies, through practice, gain control of reflex actions.
  - Primary circular reactions – seen from about 1 to 4 months of age. During this stage chance actions such as thumb-sucking which prove pleasurable

are repeated. In addition babies begin to show some ability to anticipate events – perhaps making different mouth shapes when presented with a teat or nipple and a spoon.

- Secondary circular reactions – from 4 to 8 months of age babies begin to manipulate objects outside their own bodies. They are able for example to repeatedly shake a rattle – using more than one schema or module of action at a time. Shaking a rattle requires both grasping and shaking movements. Piaget did not regard these actions as intentional.

- Coordination of secondary circular reactions – from 8 to 12 months. At this stage, Piaget suggests, babies begin to combine actions with intentionality. For example in order to retrieve an object from beneath a cloth, they are able to remove the cloth and grasp the object. This is referred to as means-end behaviour – removing the cloth is the means, retrieving the object is the end or goal. This suggests some idea of object permanence since there would be no point in removing the cloth if the baby did not think there was something underneath it. However Piaget claimed that object permanence was not fully established at this stage since babies will often look in the first place in which an object was hidden 'revealing that they do not view the object as existing independent of their actions on it' (Keenan and Evans 2009: 161). Piaget also suggests that this is the stage at which babies tend to imitate.

- Tertiary circular reactions – occur from 12 to 18 months of age. Babies repeat and expand actions, challenging themselves. They imitate more complex behaviours and engage in repeated schemas – such as banging two objects together or repeatedly dropping objects. Piaget also suggested that this is the stage at which a sense of self begins to emerge. (See also Chapter 8.)

- Invention of new means through mental combinations. From 18 to 24 months of age, children begin to think symbolically. Their imitations may be of events or words first seen or heard up to a week beforehand. Pretend play begins to emerge.

(based on Keenan and Evans 2009: 160–2)

- *Preoperational stage*. This stage lasts from around 2 to 7 years of age. Talay-Ongan (1998) describes this stage as involving magical thinking – and as being prelogical. In addition, 'areas of play, moral awareness and social functioning reflect the manipulation of symbolic or representational functioning' (Talay-Ongan 1998: 14). Attempts at logic are often based on incomplete knowledge as when children suggest that the wind comes from trees waving.

- *Concrete operational stage*. This stage is said to last from 7 to 11 years of age and is the stage at which logical thought develops. There is often an emphasis on classification focusing on similarities and differences.

- *Formal operations stage*. This stage runs from about 12 years of age through into adulthood. For Piaget this stage involved orderly and logical thought processes. At this stage learners 'can manipulate abstract ideas, make hypotheses' (Pound 2005: 37) and understand the implications of their own thinking as well as that of others.

Key processes in constructing knowledge

Active exploration is the mechanism by which organisms come to adapt to their environment (Piaget 1970, cited by Talay-Ongan 1998). As the organism explores it develops theories about the world and thus begins to *construct* knowledge. Three processes are involved in the construction of knowledge, namely assimilation, accommodation and equilibrium. New knowledge or experience is assimilated by the mind or brain, it simply rests alongside existing knowledge. At some point this causes some doubt or discomfort so in order to re-establish a sense of equilibrium we (or the organism) have to rethink (or accommodate) the idea. Pound (2005: 37) offers the following example:

> A young child picks up a piece of paper and the toy which was wrapped inside it falls out, making a sound. The baby will at first assimilate the idea that paper makes a clunking sound – testing out the idea on several pieces of paper. Over time he or she begins to realise that not all paper makes that sound, disequilibrium follows and will lead to an accommodation that paper can only make that particular sound in certain circumstances.

Keenan and Evans (2009: 158–9) offer an alternative description:

> an infant sees a circular ring – she can assimilate this new object into her experience, applying her grasping scheme. The infant then encounters a much smaller object such as a plastic token. The child cannot grasp it using her standard grip. She is forced to accommodate to the object, altering her grip so as to pick up the token and continue her exploration . . .
>
>   . . . Piaget argued that when we can assimilate changes in the environment we are in a state of cognitive equilibrium, a 'steady state' which our system aims for. However, when we are forced to accommodate we enter into a state of disequilibrium. States of disequilibrium force us to modify our cognitive structures so that we can assimilate changes and regain equilibrium. Piaget referred to this continual balance between achieving states of equilibrium and disequilibrium as equilibration . . . (which) leads to the development of more efficient cognitive structures.

Limiting characteristics of the preoperational stage

Singer and Singer (1990: 66) suggest that

> This delightful period in a child's life, the preoperational stage from birth to age seven, the early years before school, is characterized in Piaget's terms by distortions of time and space, by number confusion, by egocentric behaviour, and by such concepts as animism, transduction, juxtaposition reasoning, artificialism, literalism, and a failure to conserve.

To Singer and Singer's list, Piaget's concept of egocentrism has been added since it too is seen as a limiting characteristic of this age group. The terms may be defined as follows (Singer and Singer 1990, citing Piaget 1962):

- *Animism* refers to the belief that young children often hold that things that move, such as a flickering candle or a moving bike, are alive. An unlit candle or a stationary bike are therefore dead.
- *Transduction* refers to the idea that linked events are cause and effect. This might involve the idea that trees waving cause the wind, or a whistle blowing starts the train.
- *Juxtaposition reasoning* may be demonstrated when children are asked to group a set of objects. Singer and Singer (1990: 66) write that:

    > When Piaget asked a five-year-old to group together objects that were alike, the child placed a woman next to a fir tree, a bench against a house, and a church together with a small tree and a motorcycle but with no idea of why he had put these particular objects together.

    Similar thinking may be observed when young children are asked for example to think of something that rhymes with cat. Their suggestions may include dog or tabby. Here there is a link (but not a rhyme) and it is entirely possible that the child interviewed by Piaget also had reasons not apparent to him.
- *Artificialism* refers to the idea that superhuman figures create natural phenomena. Singer and Singer (1990) cite the example of a child who believed there were three taps in the sky – one for rain, one for snow and one for hail.
- *Literalism* is that common feature of young children's understanding of language. Phrases like 'Daddy will be late – he's tied up at the moment' or 'I've got a frog in my throat' are, quite understandably, often interpreted literally by young children.
- *Conservation* As reported in the opening to this section of the book, Gardner et al. (1996) have claimed that it is Piaget's theories about conservation for which he is best known. Singer and Singer (1990: 67) suggest that:

    > Before the age of six-and-a-half or seven the child depends more on appearance than on logical reasoning, and as a result, responds more in terms of what looks like 'more'.

Thus faced with juice in a long thin glass rather a short fat one will be seen as more; as will clay shaped like a ball or a sausage; or a row of ten pennies spread out rather than clustered. Even though the pre-operational child will have watched the transformation they are unable to say that they are the same. Keenan and Evans (2009) link this failure to conserve quantity with Piaget's notion of centration. At this stage of development, he argued, children can only focus (or centre) on one aspect at a time. In the case of the clay either sausage-shaped or round like a ball, their focus is on length.

- *Egocentrism*. Piaget characterised the pre-operational child as egocentric – unable to see things from another's point of view or perspective – and regarded this as a further characteristic which limited their thinking. He devised a test which is known as the three mountain task (Piaget and Inhelder 1956). Keenan and Evans (2009: 164–5) describe the task as it was carried out by Piaget:

  > the child sits on one side of a table upon which is a three-dimensional model of a number of mountains and some distinctive landmarks such as a cross and a house. Importantly, some of the landmarks can only be seen from certain perspectives and children are allowed to experience this for themselves by walking around the entire table. The child is then seated on one side of the table and a doll is placed on the opposite side. The child's task is to choose from a set of photographs which best describes what the doll can see. Before the age of 6 or 7, children will have great difficulty with this task and will often respond by picking the photograph which is consistent with their own point of view.

Moral development

It is interesting to note that although Piaget did not write much about emotions and feelings he did develop theories about moral development. He links morality to children's rule-bound play. He refers to children under the age of 6 who are happy to play without rules and will happily flout those that are introduced. Six-year-olds on the other hand apply make and apply rules rigidly while 10-year-olds are characterised as realising that rules can be manipulated. He developed stories outlining moral dilemmas and analysed children's responses. First, he believed, came moral realism – naughtiness measured by the amount of damage done. This was followed by moral relativism – a stage at which children are able to take account of factors other than the damage in assessing the morality.

Linking theory and practice

Egan (1983: 123) argues that Piaget's theories cannot be linked into practice because they do not constitute an educational theory. He writes:

> The function of an educational theory is to tell us how to design a curriculum which will produce educated people, or rather, to lay out such a curriculum. Such a theory must tell us what content we should teach to produce such people. The content can never be merely instrumental to achieving other goals . . . because the educated person is in part constituted of the content learned. The theory must tell us how we should teach such content because in education the medium forms some part of the message, and because learning that best promotes educational development requires that the learner be interested in the content being taught.

Such a theory would also set out when and how content should be taught, the content should be engaging and meaningful. Since curricula are inevitably 'culture-bound and value-saturated' educational theories also have both political and social implications. Since, Egan continues, Piaget's theories do not set out these things, nor are they based on any 'falsifiable empirical claim' which would enable them to be tested or researched – they cannot be said to have educational application.

Nonetheless, Piaget's interest was not primarily about practice. It was perhaps not until after he had visited Susan Isaacs' school, the Malting House, in 1927 that he began to consider the educational implications of his work (Graham 2009). Isaacs' emphasis on children's spontaneous activity contrasted with Piaget's work with children, which was largely conducted in tightly structured experimental contexts. Piaget learnt from his visit that observations of spontaneous activity 'allowed the adults to learn that the children could do more if left to explore for themselves, though with adult support' (Graham 2009: 114). In what has been described as the second phase of his writing (Hunt 1969), Piaget wrote up the observations of his own children and the way in which they directed his experiments and thinking. Much of Piaget's thinking about both learning and education arose from these detailed observations.

Although Piaget did write something about education (see for example Piaget 1976), it would be difficult to claim that he himself put his theoretical ideas into practice. He was aware of the significance of his work for educationalists but was himself more interested in developing understanding of children's conceptual development and understanding. He is described as an epistemologist – his interest is the nature of knowledge.

However, Smith (2001) suggests that Piaget identified diagnosis, processes and outcomes as key to education. His experimental tasks were regarded as contributing to diagnostic assessment – and 'Piaget recommended that teachers should be investigative in carrying out their assessments' (Smith 2001: 41, citing Piaget 1932) since knowledge of human learning is incomplete. Processes of learning need to involve both group and individual learning in order to allow for the development of autonomy which 'is not anarchy such that learners do what they want; rather, learners should want to do what they do' (Smith 2001: 41). Thirdly, the outcomes need to be matched to the learner since if it is too difficult it is likely to produce mere parroting of facts.

Of teaching, Smith (2001: 41) interprets Piaget as believing that 'teaching is necessary but insufficient, something else is required as well'. The something else is equilibration (or complex learning). For teaching to be effective:

> what is required is the creative design of learning tasks which are normatively empowering rather than causally disabling. This occurs in the triggering of transformations required for novel learning.
>
> (Smith 2001: 42)

Despite the fact that Piaget's work is hard to understand and frequently opaque (Callaway 2001), it has been widely used to inform practice. The publication of the Plowden Report (CACE 1967) drew heavily on Piaget's work. There is some irony in this (especially as Nathan Isaacs, Susan Isaacs' widower, sat on the committee). Graham (2009: 313) points out that:

> The Plowden Report cited Piaget as the source of the view that children needed active experience in handling materials if they were to learn effectively, but in fact Susan Isaacs, following John Dewey, had made this a central feature of her educational philosophy well before Piaget considered the educational implications of his work.

The following ideas drawn from Piagetian theory may be seen to have some implications for practice (based on Pound 2005: 38):

- New ideas and knowledge should be presented at a level and style consistent with the child's current mode of thought. Piaget suggested that there were limitations to the logical thought of young children.
- Teaching should be matched to the needs of individuals. Children should be presented with moderately novel situations or experiences to trigger assimilation and accommodation. Open-ended questions can support this process.
- Learning is supported by action. Children need to experiment actively with materials and to experience things in the real world (in order) to develop thought.
- Children need to have control over their learning – learning how to find out and constructing knowledge for themselves. This requires open-ended activities.
- Children require long, uninterrupted periods of play and exploration. Piaget (1962) believed that the first imitations were children's repetitions of their own actions. These he suggested were followed by imitation of the familiar actions of another and then new actions performed by someone else. For Piaget, imitation became symbolic when there was an element of deferment. If the child is able to immediately imitate a new action rather than going through a process of trial and error; if he or she can imitate a model which is no longer present, Piaget would regard that as deferred imitation – a precursor of symbolic representation.
- Observation of what children do and say can and should inform understanding of children's intellectual development – this will tell (the practitioner) where they need support.

Shayer and Adey (2002) have described a process by which they sought to put the theoretical insights of Piaget and Vygotsky into practice in teaching science and mathematics at secondary level and this will be explored in more detail in Chapter 13. The most well-known of early years curricula to be based on Piagetian theory is HighScope which will be considered more fully in Chapter 18. However throughout the 1960s and 1970s aspects of Piagetian theory such as active learning were a firm part of the rhetoric and practice of early childhood care and education. De Vries and Kohlberg (1987) outline and evaluate a range of Piagetian programmes or curricula.

A critique of Piagetian theories

For a thinker and theorist so widely revered, so widely quoted and so often mentioned, Piaget has received enormous amounts of criticism. Perhaps the first of his critics was Susan Isaacs. Graham (2009: xi) comments:

> Who knows that it was (Susan Isaacs) who first formulated serious criticisms of the studies of Jean Piaget, the foremost child psychologist of his time, forcing him to reconsider his approach? It was not until the nineteen seventies, over forty years later that developmental psychologists re-discovered the objectives she had been the first to raise.

While praising Piaget's contribution to what she termed genetic (now more generally known as developmental) psychology, Isaacs criticised his experimental methods and suggested that his conclusions were over-generalised. Moreover she believed that his somewhat artificial methods had led to a significant under-estimation of what children can and do achieve in everyday life. His theory of staged development was also a target for her criticism:

> In place of the rigidly defined stages of growth he proposed, she saw children's minds as having the basic equipment for logical thought much earlier on in their lives and the improvement in their competence as attributable not to any acquisition of new mental structures, but very largely to their exposure to a wide range of experiences and their gradually increasing ability to handle more and more complex tasks.
>
> (Graham 2009: 156)

Susan's husband, Nathan Isaacs, also specifically criticised Piaget for his method of investigating children's 'why' questions. Isaacs believed that the most effective way of examining children's thinking would be to observe and analyse their use of such questions, rather than, as Piaget himself did, to ask 'why' questions. Although as Cohen (2002) points out after the 1930s there were relatively few critics of Piaget until the 1970s, Isaacs' criticisms have since been taken up by many others. Bruner (1972) regards Piaget's work as artificial. With its emphasis on logic it ignores all the other kinds of thought that children engage in. Gardner (1999) also challenges Piaget's focus on logico-mathematical thinking – stating that the social and emotional aspects of learning are given insufficient consideration. Gardner (1993) has also argued against stage theory, as has Siegler (1996). The latter suggests that children use a far wider range of strategies than Piaget's work indicated either was (or could be) the case.

Criticisms of stage theory

Stage theory is a good example of the way in which theories are developed as a story which best explains the available data – the construction of meaning, the making of meaning (Wells 1985). For Piaget the best story was discrete stages but others claim that this view depends on the way in which data is collected (see for example Freud's comment in Chapter 7) and analysed. Siegler (1996) favours an explanation which consists of overlapping waves of development but suggests that:

> If you assess children's competence every few months, then sudden changes in their level of reasoning will appear abrupt and stage-like. If you assess development on a smaller time scale, development may look more contin-uous.
>
> (Keenan and Evans 2009: 171, citing Siegler)

Believing in a staged approach led Piaget to believe that certain behaviours dis-appeared. Play offers an excellent example of this. His emphasis on the internal and symbolic representations, which play offers, played a part in overcoming the supremacy of behaviourist thinking since it emphasised the role of the mind – rather than just ob-servable action. However, Piaget himself did not see the full value of play, suggesting that symbolic play disappears around the age of 4. As Singer and Singer (1990) re-peatedly point out this appears to owe more to opportunity given by adults than to the nature of play itself. In current thinking about creativity for example, play has an important role in opening up possibility thinking. Singer and Singer (1990: 40–1) go on to remind us that since Piaget believed that mature thought depended on logical thinking:

> play emerges as a critical, if passing, feature in early childhood, where it takes the form of sensory-motor play, symbolic or pretend play, and games with rules. According to Piaget all play serves a mastery function; he rarely dis-cusses its affective function... mature thought was chiefly limited to formal, sequential processes such as the shaping and reshaping of organized verbal meanings.... He saw no role for it in... seriation, classification and conserva-tion – that are the means by which we represent the 'real' world in organized, ongoing thought.

An aspect of staged theory which has been widely criticised is the notion that it car-ries of 'readiness'. Gesell's studies appeared to show that early training was not helpful – that indeed when children were 'ready' or at an appropriate stage of development they would learn and develop. Social constructivists, on the other hand, argue that children become ready by doing things – learn to read by reading, learn to talk by talking and so on. For them the cultural opportunities and expectations make children ready for learning. This is an argument which finds resonance in Britain today (and is alluded to in Chapter 4). On one hand, some policy makers (see Parts 1 and 2) argue that an early start to formal learning will make children more successful in formal learning. Others argue that children are not ready for formal learning – that their conceptual development requires firmer foundations.

Criticisms of experimental methods

Like Isaacs, a number of writers and thinkers have challenged Piaget's experimental methods. The opacity of his writing has also been criticised – perhaps nowhere as aggressively as Callaway (2001: 2). He suggests that Piaget employed an 'extremely deceitful double use of words (which) is unique in all the professional literature'. He goes on to quote the words of two researchers (Callaway 2001: 48, citing Brown and Thampy):

> (Piaget) was a great thinker but an inconsiderate if not downright awful writer.... We do not know the reason. We have only felt the pain his prose inflicted.

A very wide range of experiments building on and challenging Piaget's results have been undertaken. Some of these and other experiments will be considered in the following section of this chapter, which explores the legacy of Piaget's work. However Cohen (2002: 53) writes that:

> critical studies suggest Piaget wasn't operating in the logically perfect manner he demanded of others. He blinded himself to possible alternative explanations for some of his results.

Feminist criticisms

In common with Freud, Piaget is criticised for his focus on boys. Likening children's learning to that of a scientist, they argue that girls are marginalised since the behaviour of a scientist is generally thought of as male. Piaget's child is regarded as masculine but it should be remembered that every theorist is a product of their own time.

While moral development is more readily associated with the super-ego of psychoanalytical theory (see Chapter 7) and with social learning theory (see Chapter 11) Piaget's identifies four stages. The first three are pre-conventional; conventional and postconventional. It is not until the final stage that 'universal, moral principles are adhered to' (Pound 2009: 79) even where this brings conflict with those around you. This work and the work of Kohlberg which built upon it has been criticised by Cannella (1997) focusing as it does only on male perspectives.

The legacy of Piagetian theories

Like that of Freud, it would be difficult to over-estimate Piaget's legacy to psychology and education. He too changed the way in which we view children – while critics claim that his stage theory of development may put a ceiling on expectations, it is also true that his theories and experiments taught us not only to see but to respect the logical, reasoning, competent beings that young children are.

At the beginning of this chapter the rise of developmental psychology was discussed and the role of baby biographies was outlined. Gopnik et al. (1999:15) outline the importance of the diaries which Piaget (and his wife) kept of their own three children's development:

> In the thirties Piaget began to record the lives of his own three infant children, Jacqueline, Lucienne and Laurent. There have been baby diaries before and since, but there is nothing like the Piaget diaries. They record in minute, crystalline detail the significant patterns of the apparently formless behaviour of very young babies. Moreover, they do so day by day and even moment by moment, so that each observation becomes part of a larger unfolding history. By reading Piaget's books we know Jacqueline's, Lucienne's and Laurent's babyhood more intimately than we know those of our own children.... The observations of the babies are embedded in an alternately impenetrable and brilliantly insightful theoretical apparatus. When we remember that all this was done without any recording devices other than keen observation, pen, and paper, in the intervals of a demanding academic job, it becomes almost inconceivable that one man could have accomplished it. And, as a matter of fact we now know that one man didn't accomplish it. Valentine Piaget, Piaget's wife and the children's mother and herself a psychologist, was actually responsible for much of the observations. It's a pretty impressive accomplishment.

Despite Egan's (1984) assertion that Piaget did not have an educational theory, Piaget's theories have continued to influence subsequent educational theories. The successful HighScope programme was developed with Piaget's concept of an active, curious child at its heart (Epstein et al. 2011). The world-famed early years provision of Reggio Emilia also identifies Piaget's constructivist approach as being fundamental to its work (Edwards et al. 1995). The development of the Te Whariki programme acknowledges the contribution of Piaget, but Carr (2001: 14) identifies the shifts in thinking that post-Piagetian theories have brought about. She suggests that the assumption that:

> learning is about individuals acquiring knowledge and skills of an increasingly general, abstract, symbolic and logical nature: treading the path towards a much later endpoint called 'formal operations' ... has given way to alternatives. Stages have in effect been tipped on their side and described as different and equally valuable modes of making sense of the world. The notion of multiple ways of thinking and knowing has (given) ... renewed value to the 'here and now', originally seen in Piagetian terms as an immature stage of development.

Piagetian research

Research which has made a strong contribution to the work of many practitioners in Britain was conducted by Chris Athey (1990) (see also Chapter 2). Her research, widely known as the means by which practitioners and parents could be helped to identify schemas in young children, was based strongly on Piagetian theory. Athey (1990: 37) defined a schema as 'a pattern of repeatable behaviour into which experiences are assimilated and that are gradually co-ordinated. Co-ordinations lead to higher-level and more powerful schemas'. The basis for her research was that enriching experiences enriched schemas and thus enriched thinking. Chris Athey's research (for a full account see Athey 2007) builds on Piaget's theory and suggests that physical action precedes abstract thinking. She identifies three levels of symbolic behaviour – beginning with the physical, moving to the symbolic (making one thing stand for another) and what she terms a level of functional dependency which emerges from children's growing understanding of cause and effect – which leads children to abstract thought.

Post-Piagetian theories

Perhaps Piaget's greatest legacy is the rise of rich and diverse neo-Piagetian or post-Piagetian thinking. During the 1970s a range of criticisms arose of many aspects of Piagetian theory (see for example Donaldson 1978). But on the whole these criticisms were to enhance understanding of Piagetian theory and to add greatly to our under-standing of the thinking and learning of children (and perhaps adults too). Cohen (2002: 51) for example describes experiments undertaken by Bryant whom he suggests is 'an ardent supporter of Piaget'. He also draws attention to the work of Bower (1973) who undertook a number of experiments with very young babies – which demonstrated their problem-solving abilities and others which challenged Piaget's view of their in-ability to have a sense of object permanence.

Cohen describes a series of experiments which challenge the idea that mature adults necessarily think logically. Cohen reports the findings of a range of studies which appear to show that:

- 'Patients with particular kinds of brain damage often did better than fine-brained students' (2002: 53)
- 'Adults are constantly fooled by logical questions because we have "tunnel vision", focusing all too easily on one aspect of a problem' (2002: 53)
- 'Only 4% of 18 year olds who were studying humanities and 18% of those who were studying experimental sciences reached the formal operations stage' (2002: 54)
- 'A majority of students of mathematics (60%) were in the formal stage' (2002: 54)

Cohen (2002: 54) concludes:

> It is not wholly clear what the implications of these findings are. Does it mean that only the mathematically skilled ever become really intellectually mature? Or does it mean that many people can perform very well in other kinds of disciplines – English, writing, art – without having reached the final stage Piaget identified as the pinnacle of cognitive achievement?

Perhaps the most influential of the post-Piagetians is Margaret Donaldson. Her seminal text published in 1978 includes accounts of a number of studies which set out to build on Piaget's findings. Piaget's findings on egocentrism in the three mountain task are clarified by setting a task which offered a simplified activity. This involves children in finding a place in which a small boy doll cannot be seen by police dolls. In a range of studies involving conservation of quantity children were able to identify two quantities as remaining the same – despite a changed appearance – by giving an explanation for the change. In some studies a naughty teddy makes the apparently confusing change. In another the researcher explains that the container is chipped and that therefore the liquid should be transferred to another vessel. In these kinds of situations children were not confused, but were able to state that materials remained the same, unchanged by the alteration in their appearance. Donaldson (1978) concludes that where the studies make 'human sense' children are able to think at a higher level than Piaget predicted. Donaldson's later work (undoubtedly influenced by the time she spent working with Bruner) suggests two modes of development in thinking – intellectual and emotional. In the latter imagination is central to learning and understanding (Donaldson 1992).

Cohen (2002: 105) describes Case as 'the most influential of the neo-Piagetians'. One of the very common criticisms of Piaget is that he appears to ignore the affective, social and emotional sides of human nature. However, Case and some colleagues (see for example Case and Yakamoto 1996) have attempted 'to marry Piaget's ideas with those of advocates of social and emotional intelligence' (Cohen 2002: 103). Case (1995) proposes four stages of cognition which encompass social, spatial and logical skills and suggests that problem-solving lies at the heart of children's competences. Moreover he suggests that his theories are an integration of those of Piaget and Vygotsky, emphasising the role of culture and adults in supporting cognition.

Another area of work drawing on the work of Piaget but in a very different field is personal construct theory developed by George Kelly (Raskin 2002). This, like the work of Case, deals with emotions – exploring ways in which humans construct their social realities. Kelly's work has been highly influential in psychotherapy. His techniques are often used in research methodologies and as such may be seen as part of the legacy of constructivism. Raskin (2002: 24) describes constructivism as of being of 'critical importance (in the understanding) of human making-meaning processes'. The repertory grid technique used by Kelly was, for example, used as a means of understanding the personal constructs of students in the CASE and CAME projects (Robertson 2002; see Chapter 13).

Reflective questions

1. Do you think Piaget's findings are still relevant?
2. What difference did it make, if any, that Piaget and Kohlberg focused their experiments on moral development on boys?
3. Do you think there are distinct stages of development – or does the way of collecting data influence the researcher's view?
4. The research indicated above seems to suggest that intellect depends on more than mathematical logic? What is your view on this?

Further reading

Athey, C. (2007) (2nd edn) *Extending Thought in Young Children.* London: Paul Chapman Publishing.

Cohen, D. (2002) *How the Child's Mind Develops.* Hove, E. Sussex: Routledge. (See Chapter 4.)

13 Lev Vygotsky (1896–1934) and social constructivism

Lev Vygotsky was born in the same year as Jean Piaget, 1896. Another coincidence is that, like Piaget, early in his career, Vygotsky was engaged in administering intelligence tests. However, unlike Piaget who lived to be more than 80, Vygotsky died of tuberculosis in his thirties – having been ill since the age of 23 when he was teaching in a provincial school. He did not enjoy this role and soon after began to lecture in psychology at a teachers' training college. By the age of 28 he had been invited to become a research fellow at the Moscow Institute of Psychology. Vygotsky was a very prolific writer and although his work was not well known outside Russia until some time after his death, he was familiar with the work of both Freud and Piaget.

The Russian Revolution in 1917 which deposed the royal family impacted on Vygotsky. Like many other young intellectuals of the time in Russia, he was attracted to Marxist ideology which emphasised the social aspect of human nature – privileging cooperation over individualism. However when Stalin came to power in 1928, despite his public denials of anti-semitic feelings, Jews were persecuted. As a Jew himself, this would have had some impact on Vygotsky before his death in 1934.

It is popular to contrast the work of Piaget and Vygotsky but Smith (1996) suggests that there are many similarities in their thinking and writing. In fact he paraphrases the closing part of Orwell's *Animal Farm:* 'they looked from Vygotsky to Piaget, and from Piaget to Vygotsky, and from Vygotsky to Piaget again; but already it was impossible to say which was which'. In order to prove his point, he goes so far as to produce a self-test which asks participants to decide whether quotations come from Piaget or Vygotsky. For example the quotation 'there is a wealth of manifestations of egocentric speech by the child. We already know that difficult situations evoke excessive egocentric speech' (Vygotsky [1934] 1994: 118) with its focus on egocentric speech sounds like something Piaget might have written – but he did not.

In their editors' introduction to the same book, (which incidentally was compiled in 1996 to mark the centenary of the birth of both Piaget and Vygotsky), Tryphon and Vonèche (1996) compare the two men's views of each other. We know that the two never met but Vygotsky had read some of Piaget's work and Piaget did know a number of Russian psychologists and that his tasks were used on several hundred children in Soviet Russia in the 1930s. Here are some of the key features of the analysis of the links between the two constructivists:

- New government in Russia lend people to think about new thinking about humanity – which Piaget's work promoted.
- The publication of Piaget's *The Language and Thought of the Child* ([1923] 2002) was enthusiastically taken up by Russian psychologists because it emphasised communication amongst children in an active learning context.
- Piaget's work also offered Russian psychologists new methodologies. Piaget's 'free conversations' with children were not dissimilar to Freud's 'talking-cure'.
- When *The Language and Thought of the Child* (Piaget 2002) was translated into Russian, Piaget wrote a preface to it (printed in full in Tryphon and Vonèche 1996: 3) in which he emphasised 'the structure of individual thought (which) depends on the social surroundings'.
- While for Piaget, egocentric speech was a passing developmental marker, for Vygotsky it remained as a cognitive tool. However, since it was increasingly internalised as children grew older it was less easy to observe.
- Vygotsky, like Isaacs, challenged the idea that the stages discovered by Piaget were universal – applying to all children. Piaget's view was later to be much more widely challenged (see Part 5).
- When Vygotsky's book *Thought and Language* was first translated into English (1962) Piaget acknowledged the links between their theoretical perspectives. He wrote in the preface:

  > It is not without sadness that an author discovers, twenty five years after its publication, the work of a colleague who has died in the meantime, when the work contains so many points of immediate interest to him which should have been discussed personally and in detail.

- Piaget acknowledged but disagreed with Vygotsky's criticisms of his views on egocentrism and egocentric language.
- 'For Piaget development is a stage-like biological evolution, a succession of "events" . . . , whereas for Vygotsky, development is a meaningful human generalisation' (Tryphon and Vonèche 1996: 8).
- In 1932, in the Russian translation of *The Language and Thought of the Child* (2002), Piaget suggested that individual thinking is dependent on the social context. However by 1960 he suggested that Bruner and colleagues were 'too sensitive to the role of the environment' (Tryphon and Vonèche 1996: 8). Tryphon and Vonèche (1996) question what his stance would be today as America seems gripped by the role of genes in learning and development. Would he, they ask, be 'putting the emphasis back into the environment' (1996: 8) with a focus on the natural and spontaneous nature of equilibriation?

Social constructivist theories

While Piaget was writing about the ways in which infants react to objects, Vygotsky was interested in studying children in their social context, in order to understand development. As Cohen suggests (2002: 59) the child in Vygotsky's theories was neither egocentric (as Piaget's envisioned child has been characterised) 'logical or illogical but social and communicative'. Talay-Ongan (1998: 15) describes Vygotsky as 'a product of a culture that valued the collective rather than the individual' and argues that this produced his focus on 'contextual and societal influences'.

Socio-cultural influences

Cooperation through discussion and reasoning, for Vygotsky, shaped thinking and learning. He wrote that 'the very mechanism underlying higher mental functions is a copy from social interaction; all higher mental functions are internalised social relationships' (Vygotsky 1988: 74). The development of concepts, language, memory and attention all have their roots in culture and the culture itself throws up 'tools for thinking' such as language and number and a range of symbol systems. The learner becomes aware of these tools through interaction with family, community and peers. Egan (1991) has identified tools for learning appropriate to young (and therefore by definition illiterate) learners as including story, song, rhyme and rhythm. The work of Barbara Rogoff is strongly influenced by that of Vygotsky and she has written extensively about cultural tools for thinking. Her work will be explored more fully later in this chapter.

Development, he believed, was first interpersonal – demonstrated in interactions with others and only later becoming intrapersonal and internalised. Vygotsky (1981: 163) expressed this as follows:

> Any function of the child's cultural development appears twice, or on two planes. First it appears on the social plane, and then on the psychological plane.

Keenan and Evans (2009) offer as an example of internalisation, the way in which young children use language and actions they have observed in others in order to solve problems – talking to themselves. Eventually this becomes internalised and no longer needs to be said out loud or acted out – it can simply be thought about. It was Vygotsky's belief in the importance of the social context that led to the development of his theory about proximal development.

Play

Vygotsky (1962) believed that fantasy play had immense value in helping children to identify solutions to real-life problems. He famously suggested (see for example Bruce 2005) that in their play children acted at a higher stage than that at which they operate in real life. Play is structured by rules – some self-imposed – but others emanating from the character being played. For example, if a child is being mum they generally act within the rules that apply to mums – telling babies what to do, cooking or whatever children's experience has led them to expect that mothers do. Research (Elias and Berk 2002) suggests that children who employ complex rules in their socio-dramatic play are better able to follow rules imposed by the teacher when they enter formal education.

Language and thinking

As discussed in Chapter 11, Chomsky's challenge to Skinner triggered a wide interest in language and thought. Vygotsky's writings pre-empted this interest in the west. Arguably his two best known books, *Thought and Language* (1962) and *Mind in Society* (1978) were widely read by cognitive and developmental psychologists as well as practitioners at the time of the burgeoning interest in language and thinking.

While Piaget saw language as developing out of experience and cognitive growth, Vygotsky believed that the symbolic function of language enabled the learner to use it as a tool for developing understanding or cognition. What Piaget termed egocentric speech, Vygotsky saw as private speech. He regarded this self-talk as a means of problem-solving and of modifying behaviour. (Watching a toddler tempted to do something which they already know to be frowned upon will often reveal language used for self-regulation. As the hand moves towards the plant from which the child can barely resist pulling off a flower, the action may often be accompanied by 'no' said repeatedly and by violent shaking of the head.) He suggested that private speech preceded language for social interaction. Finally in Vygotskian theory, inner speech develops 'where language goes underground and becomes thought, which is essential to all higher mental functions, including memory, reasoning, planning and evaluating' (Talay-Ongan 1998: 109).

Zone of Proximal Development (ZPD)

While Piaget suggested that children worked independently to solve cognitive problems, ZPD is the aspect of Vygotsky's work known by everyone – though the term is frequently misused. Contrary to the belief of one practitioner (who shall be nameless) ZPD is not, as she claimed, a worksheet! The term describes the gap between what a child knows or can achieve alone and what they can do or achieve with the help of someone more experienced. That might be an adult but it could also be an older or even a peer child with more experience in a particular area. If during the interaction which occurs between the learner and the more competent person – often described as scaffolding – new information is introduced which fits the learner's understanding, growth will occur.

There are two important considerations in thinking about ZPD. First it means working with the child at a higher level than that at which the child has been observed working. Secondly, it reflects Vygotsky's interest in understanding the child's potential for learning. Keenan and Evans (2009: 174) add:

> Given his belief in the study of developmental processes rather than endpoints, Vygotsky's emphasis on the child's potential being the state we should be concerned with in assessment is extremely appealing.

Linking theory and practice

Vygotsky's belief in the ZPD was borne out by language studies conducted in the 1980s. Gordon Wells undertook a longitudinal research study which examined the language used between children and their carers. He found that parents spontaneously structured the way in which they spoke to their children – only introducing more complex sentences when either they heard their child use them and therefore knew that they would be understood; or by accident (Wells 1985b). This sounds remarkably similar to Vygotsky's view of effective parent-child interaction:

> Parents tend to adjust their level of interaction dynamically, by responding to the child's level of ability and trying to pitch their teaching at a level which is just beyond what the child can do on their own, but is still at a level which is within the child's ability to do with help. Vygotsky believed that parents and teachers worked at a level that was optimal for stimulating children's development.
>
> (Keenan and Evans 2009: 45)

ZPD has had a strong influence of practice. Vygotsky himself did not use the term scaffolding to describe what adults do to support learning but it has been extensively used by Bruner (1983) and by Wood et al. (1976). Nor did Vygotsky discuss how ZPD would be achieved other than by the spontaneous or intuitive activity described above. Successful scaffolding can only be achieved where adults are tuned in to children's thinking. Where it is successfully achieved in problem-solving tasks, it enables children to act more successfully on their own in similar situations (Berk and Spuhl 1995).

The shared understandings that arise in social interaction have been called inter-subjectivity. This again is not a term devised by Vygotsky, but generally credited to Trevarthen (see Pound 2009). As child and adults work out how to communicate they gain an understanding of each other's minds. This is a vital aspect of the way in which children are drawn into the culture which will shape their thinking and learning.

Keenan and Evans (2009) believe that Vygotsky's theories have impacted on practice in schools and early childhood settings. They write about the role of reciprocal teaching and cooperative learning in schools. However to early childhood practitioners terms such as apprenticeship learning will often imply interaction between adult and child, but it seems likely that Vygotsky also regarded ZPD as relating to peer support with the more experienced and competent partner supporting the learning of the novice or inexperienced partner.

CASE and CAME projects

Adey and Shayer (2002) describe a research project undertaken in classrooms as part of the Cognitive Acceleration through Science Education (CASE) and the Cognitive

Acceleration through Mathematics Education (CAME) projects. For the purpose of the study, they identified six pillars drawn from the theories of both Piaget and Vygotsky. Concrete preparation and bridging are not specific to either theorist but have more to do with the manner of teaching. The remaining four pillars are:

- *Schema theory.* As we saw in Chapter 12, this is drawn from Piagetian theory. The researchers identified concepts appropriate to secondary school science and mathematics (for that is where their study began). These included things like control of variables and probability.
- *Cognitive conflict.* This pillar draws on Piaget's theories about equalibriation and Vygotsky's thinking about ZPD. It requires teachers to scaffold children's learning, describing it as 'working in the construction zone'. They also use the term 'challenge and support' which is reminiscent of Ball's reminder (1994) to early childhood practitioners that parents should act as 'warm demanders' in their children's learning.
- *Social construction.* Adey and Shayer (2002: 6) sought to ensure in their project that the social aspects of constructing knowledge were supported through 'talking around new ideas, exploring them through group discussion, and asking for explanations and justifications'. Teachers were also required to 'encourage students to describe and explain their ideas, to feel unafraid of getting things wrong, and to engage in group polylogue (or discussion) with colleagues while teasing out a group understanding'.
- *Metacognition.* Vygotsky's work highlights the role of language in supporting thinking but also in learning to think about thinking – that is to engage in metacognition. Reviewing and discussing what has gone on after the event supports metacognition. Piaget believed that what he termed 'reflective abstraction' was only apparent in late adolescence.

Of particular interest to early childhood practitioners is Shayer's analysis (2002) of the findings of these studies. He describes the 'jumps in performance' achieved when ZPD is used in supporting their development.

A critique of social constructivist theories

Because Vygotsky died young, and because his writing was not widely circulated until sometime after his death, some writers feel that he has escaped the level of criticism which Piaget faced (Keenan and Evans 2009). Indeed Burman (1994) suggests that his early and wasting death has given him heroic qualities, unsuited to his actual contribution to thinking about early childhood learning and development.

Nonetheless like Piaget, Vygotsky's experimental methods have been criticised. Unlike Piaget, he did not seek to research carefully but often used untested anecdotes and hypotheses. Cohen (2002: 59) writes that 'Vygotsky was more of a theoretician than a careful experimenter and many of his writings are more brilliant sketches than they are fully developed research'.

Some critics suggest that in emphasising the role of culture and the child's social context insufficient emphasis is given to the nature side of the nature-nurture debate. This would include the developmental aspects of learning and the child's own contribution to his or her learning. He wrote about a natural and cultural line of development but little detail about the former exists (Keenan and Evans 2009).

Rogoff (2003), a writer who has embraced much of Vygotskian theory, is critical of his ethnocentric view. Much of Rogoff's work has been undertaken in many parts of the world, but being of his time, Vygotsky's work is essentially European in its viewpoint. Language is not considered as central to communication in some cultures – where for example patterns of social interaction might be considered more important.

The legacy of social constructivist theories

Vygotskian theories have inspired a huge amount of research and thinking. But perhaps the greatest legacy is the work of eminent psychologists who have been inspired by and built upon the work of Vygotsky. Three psychologists who have contributed a great deal to social constructionist theories have been selected below.

Jerome Bruner (1915–)

Gardner (2001) suggests that many influential psychologists around the world have been drawn to work in education after reading Bruner's book entitled *The Process of Education* (1960). In it and in subsequent writing, Bruner emphasised some key thoughts about education and learning:

- that the process of learning is more important than facts – in his words 'knowing how something is put together is worth a thousand facts about it' (Bruner 1983: 183);
- that children are active problem-solvers;
- that learning is not confined to what is consciously taught, but occurs anywhere and everywhere, all the time;
- that 'any subject can be taught effectively in some intellectually honest form to any child at any stage of development' (Bruner 1960: 33).

In a later publication, written at a time when he was already over 80 years of age, Bruner (1996: 43) defined education as follows:

> Education is not simply a technical business of well-managed information processing, not even simply a matter of applying 'learning theories' to the classroom or using the results of subject-centred 'achievement testing'. It is a

complex pursuit of fitting a culture to the needs of its members and their ways of knowing to the needs of the culture.

Bruner is a developmental psychologist, a cognitive psychologist and a social constructivist whose work brings together Vygotsky, Freud and Piaget. He bestows the title of 'modern titans of developmental theory' on these three men (Bruner 1986: 136). However, one of the many impressive things about Bruner and his work is that throughout his long life he has continued to develop his thinking. To key figures in current psychological and educational circles he too remains a titan. Those who have worked with and been influenced by him include Kathy Sylva, Howard Gardner and Margaret Donaldson. Bruner has played a significant part in thinking about the development of language (1983), in research on play (Bruner et al. 1976) and in 'under-explored issues such as motivation, affect, creativity and intuition' (Gardner 2001: 93).

He has been at the forefront of many aspects of thinking about development and cognition. He built on Piaget's theory of staged development and, in Carr's words (2001: 14), (quoted in Chapter 12) 'in effect . . . tipped [the stages] on their side and described [them] as different and equally valuable modes of making sense of the world'. Bruner (1966) defines three modes of thought or representation. The first he defines as enactive, not very different from Piaget's sensori-motor stage of cognition – involving action. The second is described as iconic representation in which images stand for something. The third is symbolic representation – similar to the abstract mode of thinking which Piaget saw as the pinnacle of cognitive behaviour – but which as we saw in Chapter 12 is not consistently achieved by all. This could include a wide range of symbol systems – a factor which was to influence Gardner's work on Multiple Intelligence Theory (MIT) (Gardner 1983).

Piaget's model of the development of thinking appeared to imply that the development of thinking is a one-way street. In his theory once sensori-motor modes of symbolic behaviour are left behind, it is generally assumed that everything we do is at the next stage of development. Bruner (1990) however emphasises the way in which physical modes of representation and symbolisation are not left behind as we move towards abstract thinking. For him, enactive, iconic and symbolic modes of thinking overlap – suggesting a horizontal rather than a vertical pattern. These three modes, he suggests, enable 'children to transform experiences into knowledge: through action, through imagery and, eventually, through a range of symbol systems' (Gardner 2001: 93).

Vivian Gussin Paley (1981) uses a good example of the way in which children shift between modes of representation, when she describes giving children change. The children in her group each had to bring 25 cents (a quarter) to school. She tapes each coin against the child's name but when change is needed the children are uncomfortable with the idea that a single dollar bill is the same as four of their separate coins. They need the enactive element of handling their own coin and can cope with the iconic element in seeing their coin against their name. Although some at least can talk in the abstract – Kim for example states 'they're all the same quarters' – two weeks later the same confusion is evident. This reminds us of Paley's assertion that young children are often only in temporary custody of concepts. It also underlines the shifting nature of modes of representation and thinking.

Bruner's interest in modes of thinking was linked to an interest in education. Gardner (2001: 93) writes 'much of education involves a negotiation, and sometimes a conflict among these modes of representation'. He was dissatisfied with his own attempts at creating a curriculum (Bruner 1960) but maintained an interest in schooling. He led a research group in the 1980s. The Oxford Pre-school Research Group as it was known was one of a number of publications and projects critical of preschool provision at that time. Bruner's words (1980: 199) at that time sadly still have some relevance today, thirty years on:

> If preschool experience – even in its present imperfect form – helps children develop, and helps them fare better in school later, how much more so would it do that given an improvement in the present provisions. But this is putting the case far too abstractly. We know a good deal about how to improve preschool provision, how to make it more interesting and challenging and humane.... We are going through hard times economically. Yet,... this may be the seed time for working out ways to give young children a better start and their families more heart in the future. It would not be costly. The return in kindling human hope for the future would be great.

Barbara Rogoff

Barbara Rogoff has been described as 'the guardian of Vygotsky's theories' (Pound 2009). She has built on his theory of ZPD and developed a theory of guided participation. She suggests that guided participation involves the mutual bridging of meanings in interactions – a process Trevarthen would term as intersubjectivity. Learning (or cognitive development) occurs as children and adults share and engage in conversation, recounting, elaborating, listening, practising and playing. These interactions may take the form of instruction or they may be spontaneous or part of daily routine (Robson 2006). Rogoff (2003: 237) states that:

> Cognitive development consists of individuals changing their ways of understanding, perceiving, noticing, thinking, remembering, classifying, reflecting, problem setting and solving, planning and so on – in shared endeavors with other people building on the cultural practices and traditions of communities.

The notion of individuals changing their thinking is related to the concept of transformation which is key to Vygotskian theory (see for example Pahl 1999). This concept is also central to ideas of creativity and imagination. Although Rogoff highlights the role of communities of learners, she, like Vygotsky, believes that human biological development works together with cultural influences in shaping learning. She suggests that innate, inherited factors enable us to learn from social contexts – of which tools for thinking such as language are a vital part. As the work of Bruner and Trevarthen has shown, for example, adults innately understand the importance of musicality and imitation in their interactions with babies (see for example Malloch and Trevarthen 2008). Babies naturally babble. However the particular uses of language depend on the culture – as before birth babies begin to take in the sounds of their mother's first language and tune into the cultural patterns of that language.

Like Bruner, Rogoff (2002) is interested in the applications of social constructivism to education. Critical of the assumptions that underpin most education systems, she highlights (Rogoff nd) the possible impact of a school system which focuses on:

- collaboration;
- learning through observation, children's interest and the world around them;
- adults as guides; and
- opportunities to break out of the age segregated aspects of schooling and bring children into normal cultural activities.

Urie Bronfenbrenner (1917–2005)

It seems a pity that Rogoff's work is not better known since she has much to say that is of vital importance to practitioners. However, Urie Bronfenbrenner's name is probably not much better known, if at all, and yet his theories have had an immense impact on thinking and practice in the early years. Primarily described as a developmental psychologist, Bronfenbrenner developed a model which demonstrates the cultural factors which impact on learning and development, a model which he claimed to belong to a discipline called human ecology. Human ecology draws on a wide range of disciplines including geography, psychology, anthropology and economics.

Bronfenbrenner's ecological systems theory (1979) suggests that children are influenced by four rings or layers of systems. The inner ring, which Bronfenbrenner terms the *microsystem*, includes the child, 'the objects to which he responds or the people with whom he interacts on a face-to-face basis' (1979: 7). Next comes the *mesosystem* – consisting of the contexts in which the child participates. These might include school, extended family, place of worship or other aspects of the child's own community. The *exosystem* includes people and places with whom the child may not interact but which have some influence on his or her life. Bronfenbrenner suggested that this may be a two-way process. He offers the example of children with disabilities. Their exosystem may include organisations which campaign for the rights of children with disabilities. This will impact on the child's life – but the child's needs will also influence the organisation. The outer ring of Bronfenbrenner's model is called the *macrosystem* and represents the larger socio-cultural context. He includes in this the attitudes and ideologies of the culture. In his later work (Bronfenbrenner 2005) he also considered the global or intersocietal similarities and differences which affected children's lives. Also at a later stage Bronfenbrenner (2005) added to his model the concept of a *chronosystem*. This is not represented as an additional ring but as the passage of time impacting on the child. Here he gives the example of the impact of divorce – effects may not be seen immediately and may be greater for boys than for girls.

Reflective questions

1. Think about a child you know and consider how the mesosystem and the exosystem for that child are made up.
2. To what extent you are able to offer the approaches which Rogoff suggests would have a greater impact on learners?
3. What do you need to do or know in order to offer support in the zone of proximal development?
4. Reflect on the relationship between language and thought. Are you more in sympathy with the views of Piaget or Vygotsky?

Further reading

Burman, E. (1994) *Deconstructing Developmental Psychology.* London: Routledge.

Part 5
Challenging theories and practice in the twentieth century

Dissatisfaction with schools and schooling was not a new phenomenon in the twentieth century. The work of Owen and Froebel, Isaacs and Montessori was borne of a realisation that what was currently offered to children (as well as to parents and perhaps society) was in some way inadequate. But their response to what they regarded as unsatisfactory opportunities for care or education were not the only possible responses. In 1914 for example, Tom and Kitty Higdon set up what is known as the Burston strike school – a form of alternative schooling which was to last until 1939 (van der Eyken and Turner 1969). This was their response to what they felt to be an unsatisfactory learning environment, a view in which parents and children supported them. Part 5 deals with a range of alternative voices of those wishing to challenge theories and practice in relation to the care and education of children.

In many of the cases discussed earlier in this book, such as Susan Isaacs or Margaret McMillan, theories apparently developed from or grew out of practice. This would seem to contrast to Egan's view of educational theory (1984: 123) that practice should emerge from theory. He writes:

> every consideration relating to education – whether the organisation of furniture in the classroom or matters of local policy-making, so far as these educational rather than socializing matters – must be derived from an educational theory.

However, the work of the pioneers of early childhood care and education discussed so far began with an interest in education – a belief or philosophy which led them to have faith that nurturing young children had important societal outcomes. They began with a personal theory which was modified in the light of experience or when coming into contact with new ideas.

The theories explored in Parts 3 and 4 were on the whole not developed initially as educational theories but arose from various branches of psychology. Over time some psychologists themselves – such as Bruner and Rogoff became interested in education. Others such as Freud never entered the world of the care and education of young children, although their work was seen by practitioners as having strong practical applications.

Perhaps what all the theorists explored in this book have in common is that they challenged conventional or mainstream thinking about the way in which young children should be cared for and educated. Sometimes that challenge came from within the relevant professions and sometimes from outside. Carl Rogers' work, for example, was developed in the field of psychotherapy – but both he and practitioners saw the concerns and approaches they had in common.

In Part 5, the focus will be more recent and arguably more direct or forceful challenges to thinking about the care and education of young children. The source of these criticisms often had their roots in other disciplines such as philosophy and sociology. Other criticisms, such as those discussed in Chapter 14, often came from those within education and childcare. Responses and action (such as there have been) have had to come from the sector itself.

In this section the word 'school' will be firmly in evidence. This is in itself challenging to many early years practitioners who regard themselves as outside the school sector. However it is in line with practice in Reggio Emilia where even provision for children up to the age of 3 is described as schooling. The reason for maintaining that language within Part 5 may be seen as 'an attempt to hold the meaning of "school" open for interpretation and discussion' (Rinaldi 2007: xix). Rinaldi also comments on the agenda of Italian school reform which she says:

> puts the acquisition of abilities that are functional for the economy and the workplace before the construction of personalities capable of imagining and constructing futures, of shared common hopes and values. The reform does not reform, it confirms the role of schools as instruments and denies them the possibility of becoming 'motors for change'.

This contrasts with many of the theories outlined in this book which have changed and developed and which, despite different approaches have generally had the aim of creating 'shared hopes and values'. Berube (2004: 86), an American writer, reminds us that:

> The history of progressive education has largely been written in schools for young children – in kindergartens and early childhood centers and Head Start centers. Its spokespeople have been professionals who have studied and practiced their craft with the young, Maria Montessori, Jean Piaget, John Dewey, Lillian Weber and Barbara Biber and so many other teachers who have gone before. They created schools where what students studied was intimately connected to their lives and where people had a chance to work and learn side by side.

Although there is some important food for thought, there are also some inaccuracies in Berube's analysis. Dewey did not regard early childhood education as his priority. However there are aspects of his theory which fit well with many early childhood approaches – his focus on real experience; on the importance of reflection; the role of the environment and of interactions in learning together with a focus on education for democracy. Montessori, on the other hand, although best known for her work with young children, was interested in creating an education system not simply a nursery – an aim in which Steiner Waldorf education has been successful.

Reflective questions

As you read about the challenges (outlined in this part) to the accepted ways in which practitioners view children and childhood, consider the following questions (MacNaughton 2003: 3) addressed to 'those who reflect critically on their work and on the understandings that drive it':

- How have I come to do things this way?
- How have I come to understand things this way?
- Who benefits from how I do and understand this?
- Who is silenced in how I do and understand this?
- How many other ways are there to do and understand this?
- Which of those might lead to more equitable and fair ways of doing things and understanding things?

Key dates

1921–1997	**Paulo Freire**
1923–1985	**John Holt**
1926–1984	**Michel Foucault**
1926–2002	**Ivan Illich**
1929–	**Jurgen Haberman**
1943–	**Henry Giroux**

Further reading

Dahlberg, G., Moss, P. and Pence, A. (2007) (2nd edn) *Beyond Quality in Early Childhood Care and Education*. London: Routledge.

14 De(constructing) schooling

The period before the Second World War was, as we have seen, a period of progressivism and change. Amongst the progressives were those, such as Maria Montessori and the McMillan sisters, who wanted to improve the lot of the poor and believed that early care and education had a vital role to play in achieving that. There were others like Susan Isaacs who had a different but related vision. Fired up by the growth of psychology both in the field of psychoanalysis and of child development, she believed that she could change for the better the education of young children.

In the years immediately following the Second World War there was in Britain a period of immense optimism. Many believed that a more equal society would emerge from the period of shortages and ever-present danger that war-time conditions had brought. In Britain, radical changes were made to both the health and education services (Nicholls and Wells 1985) immediately after the war. While the health reforms were regarded as largely successful, there was less satisfaction about the state of education. By the late 1950s, in both Britain and the United States, education was being questioned. Concerns in Britain focused on the widespread failure of working-class children which led many people to reconsider 'the educational process (and) to question ... the way children learn and how teaching takes account of this' (Nicholls and Wells 1985). This concern is evidenced by the publication of the Crowther Report (CACE 1959) and the Newsom Report (CACE 1963) both of which considered the low achievement of working-class children and attributed it, at least in part, to linguistic disadvantage. In Britain, this

> beguiling explanation for failure in school has continued to influence educational thinking and practice ever since. Fortunately it has also stimulated an enormous amount of research and, because of this, the connection between language, social class and educational success is no longer seen in such simple, not to say insulting terms.
>
> (Nicholls and Wells 1985: 2)

In America, there was a similar sense of disillusionment but with arguably a different cause and different outcomes. Nicholls and Wells (1985: 1) suggest that:

there was growing concern that schools were not producing enough people equipped to contribute to the development of new technology – a concern exacerbated by the Russian success with Sputnik. The immediate effect
of this emphasis on educational product was to direct attention to the
curriculum . . . rather than on the learning process.

Interestingly, this coincides with the period when Bruner was developing his curriculum
framework *A Study of Man* (1960) discussed in Chapter 13 – which set out to offer both
new content with a focus on global matters and a distinct emphasis on the process
of learning. Penn (2005) has described Bruner as acting like a mirror – reflecting back
trends in thinking.

Deschooling theories and theorists

Whether or not you wholly agree with this analysis it is clear that a number of books
were published in the United States in the 1960s which called for deschooling. Some
deschoolers called for the abolition of compulsory schooling (Hern 1996) while others
proposed radical changes in the schooling system. Writers such as Jonathan Kozol and
Robert Coles (1967) and Neil Postman (with Charles Weingartner 1971) emphasised
the inadequacies of the school system in the United States. Other writers and thinkers
linked to the thinking of the deschoolers, such as Illich and Freire, shared concerns
about education, but focused on the situation in South America. The writings of peasant
children in Italy (School of Barbiana 1970) focused on similarly dissenting views in a
poor part of Europe.

The ideas of the deschoolers have not disappeared. They have continued to develop
and expand their theories which voice continuing dissatisfaction. In 1996, for example,
Postman published *The End of Education*, in which he condemns the emphasis American
schools place on consumerism and ethnic separatism. He suggests that these should
be replaced by a focus on global citizenship; a healthy intellectual scepticism and an
appreciation of diversity. These ideas are also linked to concerns about the way in
which young children are being brought up in the twenty-first century (see for example
Gerhardt 2004 and Palmer 2006).

Three of the better known 'deschoolers' and their thinking have been selected for
further discussion below.

Paulo Freire (1921–1997)

Freire was born in Brazil and worked in the field of adult education. He became known
for his work in the field of adult literacy. There was widespread adult illiteracy in Brazil
and his success in tackling it led to him being made responsible for a national programme to address the problem. Despite this, for political reasons Freire was exiled to
Chile in 1964. During his period in exile he worked throughout South America and for
both UNESCO and for the World Council of Churches.

In 1979 Freire was able to return to Brazil. His enthusiasm for tackling the plight of oppressed peoples was undiminished. He developed key elements of his theory of critical education which went far beyond adult education. Foundational to his thinking was the idea that:

> education can help us to understand the world we live in and can make us better prepared to transform it, but only if we deeply connect education to the larger realities in which people live, and to struggles to alter those realities
>
> (Apple et al. 2001: 130)

One of the larger realities with which Freire was faced was of course that of poverty and its accompanying sense of powerlessness. He quotes the words of a peasant (Freire 1972: 40), describing himself, like all other oppressed peoples, as emotionally dependent:

> He can't say what he wants. Before he discovers his dependence, he suffers. He lets off steam at home, where he shouts at his children, beats them and despairs. He complains about his wife and thinks everything is dreadful. He doesn't let off steam with the boss because he thinks the boss is a superior being. Lots of times, the peasant gives vent to his sorrows by drinking.

Citing Erich Fromm (see Part 3 of this book) Freire suggests that the solution to this destructive or necrophilic behaviour is critical dialogue, action and serious reflection which together form something called praxis. Freire (1972: 41) describes praxis thus 'true reflection leads to action... that action will constitute an authentic praxis only if its consequences become the object of critical reflection'. Freire sought to transform society in order to achieve social justice. For him this was no theoretical or abstract concept: it was his life's work. Apple et al. (2001: 128) describe Freire and his commitment to his work thus:

> His focus on the role of education in the struggles of oppressed people was characterized by a rare combination. His political statements and radical perspectives were combined with personal humbleness, a powerful ethical outlook and an impressive intellectual coherence.

Ivan Illich (1926–2002)

Although he was born in Vienna and spent time studying in Rome and Salzburg, it is with Latin America that Illich is most closely associated. In the1950s he served as a catholic priest in a New York community composed largely of Puerto Rican immigrants. He worked hard to integrate into and understand the community in which he worked – learning to speak Spanish fluently and spending extended periods of time in Puerto Rico.

Illich's success in working with Puerto Rican families in New York led to him being sent to establish a centre in Puerto Rico itself 'that would immerse American priests in Puerto Rican and Latin American culture' (Gabbard and Stuchal 2001: 183) and improve their command of the Spanish language. After five years, Illich was forced to leave the island because of his active stance in favour of contraception, against the teachings of the Catholic Church. Before settling in Mexico, Illich spent some time apparently walking (and hitchhiking) the considerable distance through the length of South America.

While in New York, Illich had become dissatisfied with the impact of education on the lives of his parishioners and decided that schools should be disestablished. The title of his second book, *Deschooling Society* (Illich 1970) was actually coined by the publisher, rather than by Illich himself (Gabbard and Stuchal 2001).

That book reflected a view that 'schools should be required to pay taxes so that schooling would come to be recognized as a luxury object' (Gabbard and Stuchal 2001: 185) in order to prevent discrimination against those who lacked schooling. Illich also believed that disestablishment or deschooling as it came to be known would:

> lead to an improvement in the quality of education. Because education would cease to be compulsory, the pursuit of learning could be pursued with more authentic purpose and without ulterior motive by those who sought it, and it could be provided as an act of leisure and a gift of love and mercy by those in possession of the knowledge being sought.
>
> (Gabbard and Stuchal 2001: 185)

In a book published in 1977, Illich, as a historian, outlined a new edge to his earlier theory. He wrote:

> By the early seventeenth century a new consensus began to arise; the idea that man was born incompetent for society and remained so unless he was provided with 'education'. Education came to mean the inverse of vital competence. It came to mean a process rather than the plain knowledge of the facts and the ability to use tools which shape a man's concrete life. Education came to mean an intangible commodity that had to be produced for the benefit of all, and imparted to them in the manner in which the visible Church formerly imparted invisible grace. Justification in the sight of society became the first necessity for a man born in original stupidity, analogous to original sin.
>
> (Illich 1977: 75–6)

John Holt (1923–1985)

John Holt, an American, has been described as the grandfather of deschooling (Pound 2008), although, as described above, it was Illich's publisher not Holt who was responsible for the term. Holt's specific interest came to be homeschooling and unschooling (see for example www.holtgws.com). Homeschooling is generally thought of as education which largely conforms to standard curricular expectations while unschooling is a more radical solution, described below more fully. Holt wrote a number of highly influential books in the1960s and 1970s, of which perhaps *How Children Learn*

(Holt 1967); *How Children Fail* (Holt 1964); and *Instead of Education* (1976) are the best known.

He believed that children are naturally curious and that schools fail to take account of their different needs and interests. Describing the thinking that led to *Instead of Education*, Holt (1996: 29) writes:

> This is a book about how we might make the societies we have slightly more useful and liveable . . . , about the resources that might help some people, at least, to lead more active and interesting lives – and, perhaps, to make some of the beginnings, or very small models of such a society. It is not a book about how to solve or deal with such urgent problems as poverty, idleness, discrimination, exploitation, waste and suffering. These are not education problems or school problems. They have not been and cannot and will not be solved by things done in compulsory schools, and they will not be solved by changing these schools (or even by doing away with them altogether). The most that may happen is that, once freed of the delusion that schools *can* solve these problems, we might begin to confront them directly, realistically and intelligently.

Linking theory and practice

For most deschoolers, theory arose out of dissatisfaction with practice. The need for change in practice was highlighted by experiences which demonstrated the inequalities that faced many disadvantaged groups around the world as well as in minority world and highly advantaged countries such as the United States. Although Holt began by writing about changes that should or could be made in school, Holt (1996: 28) later suggested that 'my concern is not to improve "education" but to do away with it, to end the ugly and antihuman business of people-shaping and let people shape themselves'.

Unschooling is a term invented by Holt and it is defined by one of his followers as follows:

> This is also known as interest driven, child-led, natural, organic, eclectic, or self-directed learning. Lately, the term 'unschooling' has come to be associated with the type of homeschooling that doesn't use a fixed curriculum. When pressed, I define unschooling as allowing children as much freedom to learn in the world, as their parents can comfortably bear. The advantage of this method is that it doesn't require you, the parent, to become someone else, i.e. a professional teacher pouring knowledge into child-vessels on a planned basis. Instead you live and learn together, pursuing questions and interests as they arise and using conventional schooling on an 'on demand' basis, if at all. This is the way we learn before going to school and the way we learn when we leave school and enter the world of work.
>
> (Farenga nd)

In England, Education Otherwise offers advice to parents wanting to educate their children at home. Their website (www.education-otherwise.org) reassures parents of their right to educate their child at home in line with their philosophical convictions (which should be worthy of respect in a democratic society). Parents are advised to prepare a statement setting out their beliefs, the resources involved and the way in which, giving examples, beliefs are translated into practice.

Home schooling is not generally the concern of parents of young children. However, the introduction of the Early Years Foundation Stage (QCA 2007) has brought different but related concerns. The introduction of a fixed curriculum has been described as 'a joyless shoehorning of children's young lives to fit a rigid curriculum' (Monahan 2009).

Education for democracy is a philosophical or theoretical standpoint but deschoolers have sought to find ways to build it into practice. Berube (2004: 86) suggests that:

> Democratic educators seek not simply to lessen the harshness of social inequalities in school, but to change the conditions that create them. For this reason they tie their understanding of undemocratic practices inside the school to larger conditions on the outside.

He goes on to suggest that education for democracy requires steps all of which have many implications for practice:

- an open flow of ideas;
- a belief in children's problem-solving abilities;
- procedures for critical reflection and evaluation;
- a recognition of the dignity and rights of individuals and minority groups;
- an understanding of democratic values.

MacNaughton (2003) describes Freire's philosophy (and by implication the work of other deschoolers) as one which sets out to transform society. The implications for practitioners are, she suggests:

- changing any aspect of practice which reinforces society's inequalities;
- ensuring full involvement in education for everyone;
- encouraging children to examine fairness and unfairness; and
- enabling children to become articulate advocates, able to take social action.

A critique of deschooling

One critique of the work of this group of theorists must be that far from shaping children for the needs of contemporary society as Holt suggests, schools, it is argued, do *not* currently meet the needs of society. There is a complex argument here, the answer to which depends on philosophy. Should schools meet the needs of children or society?

In maintaining a standard curriculum, are schools denying children the opportunities they need to develop the characteristics or skills which society will need in the future? Gatto (1996: 45) explores this point:

> Bertrand Russell once observed that American schooling was among the most radical experiments in human history, that America was deliberately denying its children the tools of critical thinking. When you want to teach children to think, you begin by treating them seriously when they are little, giving them responsibilities, talking to them candidly, providing privacy and solitude for them, and making them readers and thinkers of significant thoughts from the beginning. That's if you want to teach them to think. There is no evidence that this has been a stated purpose since the start of compulsory schooling.

A number of criticisms may be levelled at theories and approaches which promote deschooling. Some critics feel that if children do not attend school they may miss out on opportunities that mixing with peers offers. Others feel that without a defined curriculum children may miss out on important areas of learning or opportunities to achieve the qualifications they may need at a later stage of education. Some people feel that if children are withdrawn from schooling because of bullying or for other social reasons this may prevent them from learning to deal with challenging social conditions. Critics cite difficulties that children may have in taking direction if they have not been exposed to formal education. Sadly, there is also a thankfully small number of incidents where withdrawal from school is used to mask neglect or abuse (Shepherd 2010). In addition to questions about their emotional or psychological suitability to teach their children at home, some criticisms relate to parents' level of expertise and their ability to teach or facilitate learning in areas of the curriculum where they themselves lack competence.

A rather more esoteric but still concerning criticism has to be that despite the heavy analysis and deconstruction that has gone on, politicians continue to use the care and education of young children as a political football. As discussed in Chapter 9 on Bowlby's work, there is a long history of political interference in the provision of day care (Riley 1983). However, even today political parties continue to intervene in pedagogical matters sometimes with scant understanding or respect for what educators are trying to achieve (Curtis 2009).

The legacy of deschooling

Perhaps the greatest legacy of the deschoolers has been the broader recognition or awareness that education is a political tool. Some theorists have been accused of deliberately setting out to make it political but as Shaull (1972: 13) in his foreword to *Pedagogy of the Oppressed* points out:

> There is no such thing as a *neutral* education process. Education either functions as an instrument which is used to facilitate the integration of the younger

generation into the logic of the present system and bring about conformity to it, or it becomes 'the practice of freedom', the means by which men and women deal critically and creatively with reality and discover how to participate in the transformation of their world. The development of an educational methodology that facilitates this process will inevitably lead to tension and conflict within our society. But it could also contribute to the formation of a new man and mark the beginning of a new era in Western history.

Although in almost forty years this new era has not emerged, a further legacy has been the increased debate about the role of schools and of home schooling. It would be uplifting to think that the trend in England towards academies is a shift towards the democratisation of schools. However, since these schools will be answerable only to central government it is difficult to believe that this is anything other than a move designed to strengthen the hand of political control (Millar 2010).

Alternative curricula

Dissatisfaction with schooling has not evaporated. There is a tension between government policies which on one hand argue for more creativity and on the other for more strongly imposed structures; for individualised approaches and for greater uniformity. Some schools (particularly in Australia and the United States) have responded by placing greater emphasis on aspects of the curriculum highlighted by Gardner's multiple intelligence theory (1993). In Britain there has been widespread interest in schools (including some early years settings) in an approach devised by Claxton, which he calls Building Learning Power (BLP) (www.buildinglearningpower.co.uk). He suggests that instead of the traditional 3Rs, children in the twenty-first century need 4Rs – resilience, resourcefulness, reflection and reciprocity (the term he uses for making relationships).

Deschooling and early childhood

Although thinking about deschooling does not overtly include early childhood settings, there is a connection between the thinking and policy. By and large, the childcare responsibilities demanded by the presence of young children together with the fact that many are not 'schooled' have generally precluded such discussions. However, nurseries have not been exempt from the general criticism of educational institutions. In the United States, the dissatisfaction with the levels of achievement of children from poor backgrounds led to the setting up of the Head Start programmes. The most famous of these was HighScope which began in the early 1960s. All Head Start programmes were designed to enable disadvantaged groups of young children to gain greater advantage from their schooling. Of all the programmes developed at that time, HighScope has maintained its profile. Longitudinal studies have demonstrated its effectiveness (see Epstein et al. 2011).

In Britain, critical reflection on the role and effectiveness of the care and education of young children came later. In 1980, Bruner and colleagues published a series of books detailing their findings from the Oxford Pre-school Research project. At the time, practitioners supported the finding that provision was limited (see Chapter 13) but were shocked at the level of criticism contained within the study. Both curriculum content and pedagogy were challenged. In 1984, Barbara Tizard and Martin Hughes (who, as was discussed in Chapter 12, later worked with Margaret Donaldson) published a book entitled *Young Children Learning*. It was highly critical of practice in nursery schools – comparing children's use of language there unfavourably with their use of language at home.

Reflective questions

1. Does the curriculum you work to allow children to develop skills and attributes they will need in the future?
2. Does it meet their present needs?
3. Do you agree with Holt (and others) that schools are failing children?
4. Reflect on Cannella's view that power plays a part in whose constructs are valued or heard. What is your view?

Further reading

Epstein, A., Johnson S. and Lafferty, P. (2011) The HighScope approach. In L. Miller and L. Pound (eds) *Theories and Approaches to Learning in the Early Years*. London: Sage.

15 Deconstructing early childhood

In common with many early childhood practitioners, Cannella describes the reflective journey she took in coming to terms with relevant theories:

> my first interests as a professional have been for the care and education of children ... was repelled by the apparent control imposed on human beings by the use of behaviourism and profoundly influenced by Piagetian genetic structuralism ...
>
> (Cannella 1997: 3)

In the introduction to Cannella's book, Kincheloe goes on to explain that over time Cannella came to an

> understanding that the backgrounds and cultural expectations of all observers, scholars in particular, inform their perceptions, [which led her to assert] that social, cultural and political factors influence the complex constructivist process.
>
> (Kincheloe 1997: vii)

However, Cannella's thinking (or perhaps deconstruction of her own ideas) did not stop there. She goes on to suggest (1997: 4) that through her reading of writers such as Vivian Gussin Paley, Erica Burman and Jonathan Kozol she became dissatisfied with constructivist thinking. She came to recognise her own evolving 'postmodern philosophy' which included:

- the view that knowledge is created, but that power plays a part in whose construct is valued and heard;
- a belief that knowledge has therefore to be deconstructed – that is questioned or 'problematized';
- a desire for increased social equality for children and adults.

Postmodern is a term that will feature a great deal in this chapter. It is a theoretical position which is more widely linked to art and architecture, literature and politics – and less commonly applied to the theory and practice of early childhood care and education. In order to understand postmodernism, it will be necessary to explore what is meant by modernism. MacNaughton (2003: 71–2) suggests that the characteristics of *modernist* thinking are the use of:

- reason as a means to create a better world;
- scientific ways to explain, predict, and thus control the world through building universal truths about how it works.

This, she argues, has been challenged by postmodernist thinkers since it is clear that reason has not brought a better world – war, disadvantage and poverty may appear to have increased. The use of science has most often benefitted those already advantaged. Finally she adopts Foucault's argument that there are no absolute truths – something to which we will return later in this chapter.

In this chapter, postmodern will be used as something of an umbrella term covering a broad range of theories, while to the outsider these perspectives often seem to be similar if not indistinguishable with only slightly differently nuanced meanings. However, while recognising that these differences are often crucial to adherents to a particular viewpoint, this chapter can do no more than give a flavour of their arguments.

Transforming theories

Postmodern theories, as they relate to early childhood, reject the use of the term 'child-centred'. Although not exclusively used by practitioners coming from a constructivist viewpoint, 'child-centred' is a term widely associated with Piagetian thinking. Dahlberg et al. (2007: 43) challenge the notion of a child-centred pedagogy preferring to take a postmodern view and to *decentre* the child 'viewing the child as existing through its relations with others and always in a particular context'. They regard the view of the child being at the centre as representing 'a particular modernist understanding of the child as a unified, reified and essentialized subject'. In short they reject any idea of a single truth about children and childhood, a theme which will be taken up in Chapter 16. Moreover they underline the idea that all of us, including children, are different in different contexts and with different people. MacNaughton (2003: 74) reflects similar thinking:

> both Piaget and Vygotsky looked for theories of language and cognition that can be applied at any place and time. In contrast, poststructuralist theorists believe that no one universal theory of children, of learning, or of human development can explain and predict development across cultures and across time. This is because the process of becoming human is a complex web of interactions between historical, social, linguistic, emotional, communicative, political and cultural dynamics in our particular world.

Transformation, as discussed in Chapter 13, is key to Vygotskian thinking. MacNaughton (2003: 70) uses the term 'transforming' to consider postmodern theories and theorists. She describes postmodern theories as leading to curricula which transform society rather than leading to reform or conformity. She writes that:

> Several broad schools of thought believe we can both transform and are transformed by nature and culture and that our capacity to be transformative holds the key to maximizing young children's learning.

The group of theories, which MacNaughton (2003) terms as transforming, mean many different things to different people. The simplest starting point is that these theories are an attempt to replace earlier thinking (thus the use of the term 'post-'). In almost all cases what they seek to replace or even subvert is a sense of order, of rationality or predictability – and to reject the idea that there could be one right way of doing things. Some definitions of the most common forms of postmodern thinking are described below.

Postmodernism

Dahlberg et al. (2007: 23) are amongst the best known and well-respected of postmodern writers in the field of early childhood. They describe their view of postmodernism as follows:

> From a postmodern perspective, there is no absolute knowledge, no absolute reality waiting 'out there' to be discovered ... the world and our knowledge of it are seen as *socially constructed* and all of us, as human beings, are active participants in this process ... engaged in relationships with others in meaning making rather than truth finding

Social constructionism

As Dahlberg et al. (2007: 55) make clear, another related term *social constuctionism* ought not to be confused with the *social constructivism* arising from Vygotsky's theories.

> There is much discussion about 'constructivist' and 'social constructivist' teaching, and the different approaches and concepts covered by these terms. ... From our perspective, it is different understandings of knowledge that distinguish our postmodern *social constructionist* perspective from the *constructivist* movement which has had a revival in educational reforms in recent years. Both view the child as active and flexible and expect the pedagogue to start from the child's everyday understanding and construction of the surrounding world. But from the constructivist perspective knowledge seems to be seen as something absolute and unchangeable, as facts to be transmitted to the child, and thus as separate from the child, independent of experience and existing in a cultural, institutional and historical vacuum...

By contrast, a pedagogue working with a social constructionist perspective would give the child the possibility to produce alternative constructions before encountering scientifically accepted constructions. The child can then place constructions in relation to scientific constructions, and make choices and meanings.... This is understood to be a learning process not only for the child but also for the pedagogue, if he or she is able to encounter the child's ideas, theories and hypotheses with respect, curiosity and wonder.

Post-structuralism

Post-structuralists share the view of postmodernists that our world is 'incoherent and discontinuous' but differ from postmodernists in that they 'focus on individuals' while postmodernists 'focus on society' (MacNaughton 2003: 72). MacNaughton (2003: 72) further suggests that 'for post-structuralists, everything and everyone can – and does – shift and change all the time'.

Post-fordism

Albon (2011, citing Brown and Lauder, 1992) highlights this term drawn from the 'late modern period of industrialisation'. She links fordism and modernism, post-fordism and postmodernism:

> fordist ideas are akin to the manufacturing practice of the Ford car industry. Fordist modes of production can be likened to modernism as they emphasise standardization of product (as opposed to niche markets), order and certainty. In addition, fordist modes of production can be related to large scale organisations overseen by hierarchical management systems.

Postcolonialism

Viruru (2005: 140) suggests that 'postcolonial theory is not a simple concept to define or to limit' and that 'getting too involved in questions such as what postcolonialism really means can distract one from some of the real possibilities that have been raised through it' (Viruru 2005: 141). Essentially it seeks to challenge the colonialism where 'through the direct or indirect use of power, individuals or groups of people have been constrained to behave in ways that are alien to their cultural ways of being, and that violate and contradict their view of the world' (Viruru 2005: 142).

Key elements of postmodern thinking

A key figure in postmodern theorising is Michel Foucault (1926–1984). He is described by Habermas as (like the theories themselves), difficult to define, since 'not only did he change the direction and emphasis of his thought over his lifetime but also he did not fit into any of the normal academic categories' (Habermas 1986: 107). Foucault was French and is said to have 'revolutionized much Western philosophical, social and political thinking' (MacNaughton 2003: 83–4). His work is based on the premise that we constantly seek truth rather than knowledge. For him the 'will to know' goes beyond truth, and requires us to question how we should think, feel, act – moving beyond the safety of the assumptions which truth allows us to hide behind. Many of the key ideas of postmodernism and related theories take Foucault's work as their starting point.

Key concepts associated with postmodern and related theories

- *Othering*:

  > is a concept to describe how we position ourselves in relation to other groups of people as being different and distinct from us. This can oc- cur in many situations including the parents-teacher relationship or the teacher-child relationship. We may construct ourselves as superior, or more expert, and simultaneously construct the 'other' as deficit in the relationship.
  >
  > (MacNaughton 2003: 306)

  This term is generally applied to situations in which dominant groups – middle class, male or white, for example, treat others not simply as different but as inferior in some way. It carries with it connotations of power. Othering is felt to contribute to low achievement amongst particular groups such as girls or women. Piaget's work is criticised as creating an image of the child as scientist – a stereotypically male image, which leads to the othering of girls.
- *Discourse* is more than conversation. It refers to the way in which symbolic lan- guages act as a template for the way in which we view the world. MacNaughton (2003: 81) suggests that the term discourse 'describes the ideas, feelings, words, images, practices, actions and looks that we use to build our social world'. We all operate within a range of discourses, constantly making decisions about which one we will operate within at any point in time. This covers all aspects of our lives – shall I be the efficient boss; the loving mother; the respectful daughter; the dynamic leader? Key to this concept is the idea that the way in which we represent ideas to ourselves and others determines how they are viewed. Dahlberg et al. (2007) argue that construction replaces representation since there be no single truth or image of reality. Closely linked to discourse therefore are knowledge and power (Foucault 1980).
- *Questioning certainty*. A key aspect of postmodernism is 'questioning the cer- tainty of truths that have underpinned modernist thinking' (Sumsion 2005: 195). This questioning can have the effect of making what has been invisible, visible – of helping us to see things in a new light once we have taken the step of abandoning the 'fixed referents and traditional anchoring points' (Sumsion 2005: 195) that our earlier modernist thinking offers. The metaphor which is frequently used is that postmodernism enables us to see from a variety of perspectives – using a range of lenses rather than simply one way of looking at things.
- *Co-construction of knowledge* goes beyond the Piagetian or Vygotskian theory of the construction of knowledge. It identifies children (and other relatively

powerless groups) as knowledgeable and able to co-construct knowledge and culture alongside both adults and peers. This view of knowledge rejects the idea of 'linear progress towards an agreed set of facts. Different people know different truths' (Pound 2009a: 82). It also rejects the idea of the truth of knowledge being determined by more powerful groups. Moreover, science should no longer be viewed as the only source of knowledge.

- *Border crossing*. This phrase or concept is attributed to Henry Giroux (1992), an American, born in 1943, whose work is associated with critical pedagogy – a topic explored later in this chapter. The term 'border crossing' refers to the boundaries between different 'cultures, languages, literacies, histories, sexualities and identities' (Giroux 1992: 2). He argues that identifying the boundaries:

> allows one to critically engage in the struggle over those territories, spaces and contact zones where power operates to either expand or to shrink the distance and connectedness among individuals, groups and places.

McArdle (2005: 90) suggests that 'boundaries cannot be transgressed until they are made visible'. She argues that it is fun, drama, humour and play which make us aware of these boundaries or borders.

- *Metanarratives*. This term, sometimes referred to as 'grand narratives' (Lyotard 1984) is attributed to Jean-Francois Lyotard (1924–1988). In line with thinking about there being no single truth, he rejects the idea of grand narratives in favour of the 'little narratives' or 'forms of local knowledge, which are internal to the communities within which they occur' and 'self-legitimating in that they determine their own criteria of competence' (Dahlberg et al. 2007: 25). Lyotard (1984: 163) also refers to '"counternarratives" – the little stories of marginalized groups, whose voices had been traditionally unheard'.

Linking theory and practice

Since postmodern theory may be termed 'nihilistic' (Pound 2009), it should come as no surprise that the link between theory and practice is not highly developed. Peters (2001: 174) suggests that 'educationalists are only at the beginning of exploring the relevance and promise of Foucault's thoughts to their own field'. Rinaldi suggests that in schools (and therefore within her definition early years settings) and within postmodern theory, change becomes:

> the essential feature of schools. The transformational change, which comes from deep learning processes and knowledge building. A 'school which changes'... means that the transformational essence, the ability, the pleasure, the fatigue and the joy of change are intrinsic to the identity of the school as a place of 'dialogue'.

> (Rinaldi 2007: xxiii)

Dahlberg et al. (2007) identify early years provision in Reggio Emilia as an example of postmodern theories being put into practice – with a focus on democracy, on creating listening cultures and on pedagogical documentation. It is perhaps the latter for which Reggio Emilia is particularly well known where it is regarded as a teaching tool which supports the process of the co-construction of knowledge and of transformational change through detailed discussion. Dahlberg et al. (2007) refer to a Swedish practitioner developing pedagogical documentation who describes herself as 'swimming in observations'. Carla Rinaldi, a senior and respected figure in Reggio Children gives her view that documentation contributes to change not simply for those within the school but within the 'political and social context'. She adds that observation is not synonymous with pedagogical documentation:

> Child observation has as its centre of interest not so much the learning processes of a given child, but rather the aim of classifying and categorising children with reference to a general scheme based on levels and phases of development. Pedagogical documentation, on the other hand, is fundamentally related to the attempt to see and to understand what happens during the pedagogical experience and seeks to do this without reference to a rigid framework of schema of pre-defined expectations.
>
> (Rinaldi 2007: xxv)

Dahlberg et al. (2007: 156) link the process of gathering pedagogical documentation to the acts of listening and seeing.

> The art of listening and hearing what the Other is saying, and taking it seriously is related to the ethics of an encounter. So too is seeing – but what do we mean by seeing? It is all too easy to separate human relationships from their moral significance. As Bauman observes 'taking pictures becomes a substitute for seeing ... looking is not seeing. Seeing is a human function, one of the greatest gifts with which man is endowed; it requires activity, inner openness, interest, patience, concentration. Today a snapshot ... means essentially to transform the act of seeing into an object'.

Perhaps the area of practice in which postmodernist thinking has been harnessed to change and develop practice is in relation to inclusion and equalities. The concept of Otherness has been critical in developing thinking. Giroux (1991) suggests that postmodern thinking has brought challenges to stereotyping. He challenges, for example, multiculturalism – indicating that only an anti-racist pedagogy can decentre whiteness. While multiculturalism, he declares, celebrates Otherness, anti-racism requires a recognition of the way in which prejudice is politically and socially shaped. In the United States, Louise Derman-Sparks (1989) has developed an anti-bias curriculum for early childhood settings while in England, Babette Brown (1998) writes about an anti-discriminatory curriculum for which she makes use of Persona dolls.

MacNaughton (2003: 191) cites some of Derman-Sparks' (1989: 40) work on disability. It is interesting to note the inclusion of the phrase *developmentally appropriate,* a topic which will be explored further in Chapter 16. Included in a list of curriculum goals are the following items:

- to provide all children with accurate, developmentally appropriate information about their own and others' disabilities and to foster understanding that a person with a disability is different in one respect but similar in many others;
- to teach children with disabilities how to handle and challenge name-calling, stereotypical attitudes and physical barriers;
- to teach non-disabled children how to resist and challenge stereotyping, name-calling and physical barriers directed against people with disabilities.

A critique of transforming theories

Practice in Reggio Emilia celebrates the rights of children (Reggio Children 1995) and in many ways addresses the issues raised by postmodernism (Dahlberg et al. 2007). However, the absence of anti-discriminatory practice has been commented on by Browne (2004: 49). She writes:

> A major issue that the 'Reggio approach' is silent about is the notion that an individual's identity develops as a result of the interactions of gender, class and 'race'. . . . This is one issue that will need to be grappled with . . . to facilitate gender equity.

Browne (2004: 48) also questions the stance of Reggio children personnel to visiting professionals:

> Although one of the tenets of the 'Reggio approach' is that children are encouraged to 'question what we have constructed as adults'. . . . And are not encouraged to accept truths passively . . . the same cannot be said for educators who are attempting to understand the 'Reggio approach'.

Probably the greatest criticism of postmodernist thinking must be that there is a constant danger of arguing itself into an untenable position. If there can be no one right way, post-modernist theories rarely offer solutions, merely identify problems. Cannella (1997: 2) alludes to this when she states that 'deconstruction without reconstruction is an act or irresponsibility. . . . No decisions would be made, no actions taken, if we simply deconstruct.'

Another, related criticism of postmodernism is that it involves a slippery use of language. As an example of the this consider the words of Sumsion (2005: 194–5):

> Many writers caution that the term 'postmodern' defies definition or simplistic explanation. Indeed, they argues that trying to define postmodern subjects it to a modernist of 'scientific' way of thinking that is incompatible with post-modern understandings.

Similarly this extract from the highly respected work of Dahlberg et al. (2007: 27) gives a further flavour of postmodernism's slipperiness. They cite Flax (1990: 188) and they agree that even speaking of postmodernism risks 'violating some of its central values – heterogeneity, multiplicity and difference'. They continue by questioning the use of the term postmodern suggesting that already it has ceased to be sufficiently questioning.

The slipperiness together with the absence of any assumptions can make it very difficult to engage with postmodernism. Pound (2009a) cites babies' smiling as an example of the impact of changing theories. What Bower (1973) refers to as classical theory held that babies did not smile until a particular stage of maturation. With the advent of video cameras it became apparent that even newborn babies did indeed smile in response to someone smiling at them. This puzzled scientists until mirror neurons were identified in the brain (Rizzolatti and Craighero 2004). However, postmodernists suggest that what we interpret as smiling is not smiling at all but an adult's construction (Burman 1994)!

It will probably come as no surprise to find that some criticisms of postmodernism are of the theorists themselves. Christmas (1998) suggests, for example, that the great weakness in Foucault's argument is that his assertions were in themselves a play for power – no different or more truthful than those of any other theorist. Above all, too often postmodern theorists leave practitioners with nowhere to go, no indication of what practice should or could look like. There is also a danger that since no absolutes or bottom lines are defined which may mean that young vulnerable children are left without protection. Critics argue that there are clearly some elements of quality, a term rejected by Dahlberg et al. (2007), which are not negotiable.

The legacy of transforming theories

Albon (2011) argues that:

> the key contribution postmodernist thinking has made to early childhood education and care, is in disrupting commonly held 'truths' about our understandings of children and how they develop and learn and consequently, the curricula and pedagogical approaches practitioners employ in early childhood settings.

Some of these commonly held truths will be explored further in the next chapter. In addition, Janzen (2008: 288) asserts that postmodernism supports our understanding of the need to respect children's voices. It reminds researchers to consider the way in which they are constructing the children they are researching. Moreover it ensures that children are positioned as 'subjects within the project as opposed to objects of the project'. This is an important element of ethnographic research (Mukherji and Albon 2010).

In addition to the issues of equality explored above, there are two, not unrelated, major areas of impact arising out of postmodernist thinking. The first relates to critical pedagogy or reflective practice and the second to the issue of quality. While the first is having a significant impact of practitioners and practice, changes in the way we judge quality are far removed from what is suggested below. Nonetheless it is included as an aspirational part of the legacy! Targets are being challenged; perhaps there is a growing understanding that not everything of value can be measured.

Critical pedagogy

In Chapter 13, the term metacognition was highlighted and seen as part of the process of evaluation and review. Throughout this part of the book, there has been reference to the fundamental importance and application of critical and reflexive thinking, problematising and deconstruction to the thinkers and theorists. This underlines the pivotal role of questioning, critical reflection and reflective practice – terms which are widely used (see for example Paige-Smith and Craft 2008) in early childhood care and education; and in related professions (Bolton 2005). Current moves to intensify inter-agency and multi-professional working in children's centres are part of this focus.

While pedagogical documentation is a term mainly associated with Reggio Emilia, a number of postmodern thinkers – among them Giroux and Freire are regarded as having developed critical pedagogy. Whatever the term used, it is clear that in practice the questioning and resistance to dogma have been driven by postmodern thinking.

MacNaughton (2003: 2) suggests that 'critical reflection is an intellectually engaged activity geared to changing practices by transforming knowledge'. Citing a range of writers and researchers she argues that critical reflection may be seen as:

- 'a way to discover and transform an individual's understanding and practices' (MacNaughton 2003: 2, citing Bleakley 1999);
- 'the collective examination of the social and political factors that produce knowledge and practices' and 'the use of this knowledge to strategically transform education in socially progressive directions' (MacNaughton 2003: 3, citing Giroux 1991 and Darder 2002).

The role of postmodern thinking on critical reflection is characterised as:

- troubling (giving a hard time) to the 'big ideas' (truths) we take for granted;
- exploring where our 'big ideas' or 'truths' about how the world works come from, who has generated them and whose interests they serve;
- seeking many perspectives on our 'truths';
- giving preference to ways of understanding the world that come from those groups who are consistently marginalized or silenced.

(MacNaughton 2003: 3)

Jurgen Habermas (1929–) is widely regarded as a key figure in challenges to educational theory and practice. As a philosopher and cultural critic (Morrison 2001)

Habermas was another of those who developed 'critical pedagogy' which demands in the interests of equality that practitioners develop 'a critical ideology critique' (Morrison 2001: 219) of their entire educational theory and practice – its aims, curriculum design, evaluation and so on. In addition, Peters writes that:

> Critical pedagogy argues that educators must work with, and on, the lived experience that students bring to the pedagogical encounter rather than imposing a curriculum that reproduces social inequality.... Students' everyday experiences of oppression, of being silenced, of having their culture and voices excluded from education and decision-making are to be interrogated for the ideological messages that are contained in such acts. Raising awareness of such inequalities is an important step to overcoming them.
>
> (Morrison 2001: 218)

Re-assessing quality

One of the major impacts which the work of Dahlberg et al. (2007) has had is in asking practitioners to renew thinking on the issue of quality. They suggest that:

> The language of quality is not only a technology of normalisation, establishing norms against which performance should be assessed, so shaping policy and practice. It is also a technology of distance, claiming to be able to compare performance anywhere in the world, irrespective of context. And it is a technology of regulation, providing a powerful tool for management to govern at a distance through the setting and measurement of norms of performance...
>
> (Dahlberg et al. 2007: ix)

This is contrasted with their suggested alternative to quality frameworks – namely the language of meaning making, an idea which emerged from constructivism but which is also to be found at the heart of constructionism:

> The language of meaning making opens up to evaluation as a democratic process of interpretation, a process that involves making practice visible and thus subject to reflection, dialogue and argumentation, leading to a judgment of value, contextualised and provisional because it is always subject to contestation.
>
> (Dahlberg et al. 2007: ix)

Dahlberg et al. (2007: ix) continue by contrasting the way in which the two approaches arrive at a view. Practitioners will be familiar with the rating scales, inspections frameworks and checklists through which quality is judged. However,

> meaning making takes quite a different approach: it works with pedagogical documentation and reflections, and through listening.... It is greatly facilitated by certain conditions: commitment to particular values such as

uncertainty, subjectivity, democracy, creativity, curiosity and a desire to experiment and border cross; a reflective, researching and socially valued workforce,
and sustained support from critical friends.

(Dahlberg et al. 2007: xii)

Dahlberg et al. (2007: 115–16) describe targets as 'the tail of evaluation wagging
the dog of pedagogical practice'. They go on to suggest that meaning making should be
something for which we, not 'grandmasters', take responsibility, namely the future of
the children with whom we work. The questions that follow are designed to make you
question your practice and with colleagues make more meanings. Reggio practitioners
regard it as a priority to collect pedagogical documentation and to discuss, discuss,
discuss it (Rinaldi 2007).

Reflective questions

In the spirit of postmodernism, ask yourself and discuss with others:
- In my work with children am I aware of the ways in which my use
  of discourse can all too easily lead to bias?
- Do I make use of the range of perspectives offered to me when I
  work with other professionals?
- Do I monitor and reflect on my own practice to ensure that I really
  listen to and take account of children's views?
- Do I talk and think about practice with colleagues to ensure that we
  do not fall into the trap of thinking that there is 'one right way'?

(Pound 2009a: 18)

Further reading

Albon, D. (2011) Postmodern and post structuralist perspectives on early childhood education. In L. Miller, and L. Pound, (eds) *Theories and Approaches to Learning in the Early
Years*. London: Sage.

16 Deconstructing development

Critical pedagogy is seen as key to the process of deconstruction. While the immediate interest of theorists such as Freire and Giroux was not early childhood, this chapter will focus on the way in which the transformational process which they envisaged (MacNaughton 2003) may be seen as highly applicable to practices of caring for and educating young children.

Piaget's work on developmental stages (see Chapter 12) is widely challenged by postmodern theorists, as is that of Vygotsky in general. In postmodern terms the notion of universal stages allows children to be 'objectified' and 'othered'. The knowledge which emerged from Piaget's research methods is presented as official knowledge. It has impacted on research and on approaches to learning and to teaching.

Kieran Egan (2002: 80) who is not widely identified as a postmodern thinker, arrives at similar conclusions. He argues that developmental theories 'whose stages determine what knowledge the developing individual can understand' cannot adequately inform effective practice. He gives three reasons for rejecting the claim that they could possibly do so:

- We know relatively little about how the mind works. Early psychological theorists used the body as a metaphor for the mind. If the body needs food, their argument suggested, the mind needs nourishment in the form of knowledge. This, Egan argues, led to the belief that children's thinking was an embryonic stage of adults' thinking – a view supported by Penn (2005) who suggests that this view of children's development regards adults as the real thing and children as therefore subordinate.
- The notion of 'cognitive development is an illusion' (Egan 2002: 82). He suggests that there is no parallel between physical and cognitive development – the latter he believes 'might be better seen as the results of people's acquiring and using specific sets of cognitive tools in specific, logically constrained, sequences' (Egan 2002: 83).
- Ideas of developmental progress came from the modernist, highly structured views of nineteenth-century thinkers. Learning and development are viewed as a ladder-like structure – a model which ignores the costs of development. Egan offers examples such as the fact that skills of oral memory and visual imagery

are undermined by literacy. A 5-year-old's creative imagination far outstrips that of the average adult (Gardner 2006). Again Penn (2005) supports this view – rejecting a ladder-like view of development in favour of a recognition that development is patchy and uneven. She argues that, with very few exceptions, our brains are sufficiently flexible that critical periods can readily be overcome – we do not necessarily have to learn things in a particular order.

Theories deconstructing development

In this section challenges to theories of childhood, to the tenets or deeply held beliefs of early childhood practitioners, and to developmental theory (taken up more fully in the next chapter) and to developmentally appropriate practice will be examined.

Challenging constructs of children and childhood

Prout and James (1997) have explored the construction and reconstruction of childhood. It is widely suggested that Aries (1962) 'discovered childhood' (Prout and James 1997: 16) in that he suggested 'that the concept of childhood emerged in Europe between the fifteenth and eighteenth centuries, thus blasting a large hole in traditional assumptions about the universality of childhood'. He argued that the introduction of 'coddling' emphasised their need for care, while the growth of schooling separated increasing numbers of children from mainstream society. Although James and Prout (1997) raise counter arguments which suggest that the 'childhood' Aries was looking for may not have existed but that others did – 'even if children were regarded differently in the past, this does not mean that they were not regarded as children' (Pollock 1983: 263). They identify a new paradigm – a suggested framework – for thinking about childhood. Its key points are that:

- childhood is a social construction;
- it is a social variable (like class or gender) and cannot be thought of as 'a single and universal phenomenon' (Prout and James 1997: 8);
- children's culture is of interest, free from adult interpretations. They suggest that ethnographic study 'allows children a more direct voice and participation in the production of sociological data' (Prout and James 1997: 8) than more quantitative forms of research;
- their new paradigm is part of 'the process of reconstructing childhood in society' (Prout and James 1997: 8).

Dahlberg et al. (2007, the following section is based on pages 44–50) identify several social constructs of children and childhood:

- *the child as knowledge, identity and culture reproducer*: They refer to this as Locke's child – starting life as an empty vessel. The emphasis for education is on structured training. For society the aim is producing a workforce, which will offer long-term success as global markets began to open up.

- *the child as an innocent in the golden age of life.* Dahlberg et al. (2007) refer to this construct as Rousseau's child – seeking out virtue, truth and beauty. For the child the focus is on free play, For society, the emphasis is on protecting children from 'the corrupt surrounding world – violent, oppressive, commercialized and exploitative' (Dahlberg et al. 2007: 45). James et al. (1998) however remind us of the legacy of this construct – a recognition that parents must protect their innocence and the beginnings of the idea that children are society's concern.
- *the scientific child of biological stages.* 'Piaget's child' as Dahlberg et al. (2007: 46) name this construct is seen as an individual, without a cultural or social context 'who develops through natural and autonomous processes'. Progress through the stages will lead to a fully functioning human. James et al. (1998: 19) place a heavy burden of responsibility on Piaget's shoulders for:

> it is not just iniquitous comparison with their peers which children suffer through testing and league tables, but also a constant evaluation against 'a gold standard' of the normal child. For those who fail to meet that standard, whether in education, bodily development or welfare, the repercussions and sanctions are strong.

- *the child as labour market supply factor.* This child is quite definitely not Bowlby's child! With this child in mind, society funds:

> child care information and referral services . . . alongside a range of other occupational benefits all intended to attract and retain labour – until such time may come that labour is no longer required.
>
> (Dahlberg et al. 2007: 47–8)

In a period of threatening recession, following just such a period of relatively high spending, these words hold more than a hint of threat!
- *the child as a co-constructor of knowledge, identity and culture.* This is the postmodern child – in the terms of Reggio Emilia, a rich, strong child, capable and autonomous. This may seem to be at odds with the description by James et al. (1998: 27) of the *socially constructed child* – the product of social constructionism – within which 'there is no universal child with which to engage'.

James et al. (1998) also identify *the tribal child*, who is characterised by, for example, the work of the Opies who documented the 'world of the schoolyard, the playground, the club and the gang' (James et al. 1998: 29, citing Opie and Opie 1977). They suggest that this view of the child has fuelled our understanding of children's minds. They go on to highlight a further construct, *the minority group child*. This construct has obvious links with women studies (Oakley 2005) and with the growth of interest in children's rights (see for example www.crae.org.uk).

Challenging the tenets of early childhood

Alloway (1997) challenges what she regards as traditional or developmental views of early childhood care and education:

- *Early education is about developing the whole child.* Alloway (1997) feels that this, a central tenet of early education, is not beyond contention. While practitioners may feel, for example, that spiritual, cultural, sexual or religious matters are essential elements of early childhood care and education, parents may have other views. Against this view we may set neuroscientific views that all learning is inextricably linked, or a social constructivist view that elements cannot be left out – as they inevitably impinge on the child (see for example the outline of Bronfenbrenner's theory in Chapter 13). Penn (2005) suggests that some assumed aspects of development such as the social, emotional, intellectual or physical are themselves constructs and that this makes talk of holistic development problematic.

- *Individuals are the focus of early childhood care and education.* Alloway argues that since psychology (and in particular developmental psychology) has dominated early childhood provision there is an overemphasis on the individual. She argues for a sociological perspective that takes account of gender, class, race and ethnicity – focusing on socially and culturally appropriate practice rather than developmentally appropriate practice. However Te Wharikii, the New Zealand early years curriculum document, is based very soundly on socially and culturally appropriate practice. In many parts of the world, (particularly the majority world) the curriculum favours collaboration and mutual support.

- *Progressive child-centred practice is best practice for young children.* Child-centred practice was discussed in Chapter 15. Grieshaber and Ryan (2005: 9) describe child-centred practice as 'an enduring and fixed entity in early childhood education. In fact it could be said that it is a revered concept'. For Alloway (1997) it is characterised by learning through play, an absence of direct instruction and a constructivist approach – encouraging children to explore and construct knowledge for themselves. She argues that some communities would argue for more instructional approaches and that there should not be thought to be one right way. For Singer (1992: 113) child development theories offer no practical help in working with children. Citing the example of the many failed Head Start programmes in the United States, she argues that 'schools cannot compensate for society. Education cannot abolish society's injustice and discrimination'.

  Burman (1994: 164–5) offers an additional criticism of child-centredness. She identifies five elements namely – 'readiness, choice, needs, play and discovery' all of which she critiques. Again Bronfenbrenner's theory (1979) offers an alternative view of child-centredness – each child within his or her own micro-, meso-, exo- and macrosystems. Postmodernists argue that middle-class children do better in school because the dominant discourse of educational settings favours them. There are other possible explanations which may still of course be open to postmodern interpretation. For example do middle-class families do better because they enjoy socio-economic benefits? Do these enable their children to have more opportunity to make choices and decisions (Walkerdine 1989), widely regarded as a key factor in effective learning? Or do they do better because their health is better (Ramesh 2010)?

- *Independence and autonomy should be the goals of emotional development for young children.* 'Theorists like Erikson have been highly influential in convincing us that separation, autonomy and independence are the emotional goals for children's early growth and maturation. Development that waivers from these goals can be defined in terms of developmental delay, emotional immaturity or dysfunction' (Alloway 1997: 2). Alloway's argument that such ideas are Western in origin and that they may not be shared by majority world cultures cannot be disputed. Ainsworth's views (see Chapter 9) on patterns of attachment have been criticised as focusing on western interpretations of children's behaviour. It is however unclear why Alloway has highlighted just emotional development. For many early childhood practitioners there is an even greater urgency about the marginalisation of physical development (Tobin 2004). In many cultures physical autonomy or agency is much more highly valued that in many western cultures (Walsh 2004). Alloway suggests that women may value community and interdependence but this is in itself an assumption which generalises both in terms of culture and gender. Collaboration (or interdependence) is, for example, highly valued across Japanese culture – for boys and girls (Boaler 2009).
- *Terms such as the child and childhood or mother, father, parent, family are an essential part of practice.* These are socially and historically constructed terms and concepts. Culture, medical and technological developments all impact on our assumptions about what the words mean. Alloway's argument that there is no one true view of children or childhood is certainly true (see for example James et al. 1998). This is also true of family related words. Such disparate factors as the use of IVF or the language use of terms like cousin or auntie impact on their meanings.

(based on Alloway 1997: 2–4)

Deconstructing developmental theory

Many theorists argue against developmental psychology and the 'normalcy' that it imposes. Cannella (1997: 63) suggests for example that it has identified development as a linear process; marginalised children who do not fit the norms produced by developmental theories; and privileged particular forms of thought such as logic. Younger children are characterised as being most inferior and children in general are thought of as lacking something – mainly of course maturity.

One of the foremost critics of developmental theory has been Erica Burman (1994). She identifies the key elements of her argument as follows:

- *Developmental psychology arose out of societies' demands for measurement.* This cannot be denied – both Piaget and Vygotsky were involved in intelligence testing early in their careers. This was a popular field of research – Gardner (1999) highlights the role of Darwin, Galton and Binet in this process. Woodhead (2003) supports Burman's argument when he suggests that a concept of development is closely linked in western cultures with age, not only in research but in everyday thinking and that this focus arose from the introduction of mass schooling when there was a desire to set standards. He cites cultures where age is not exact, and where expectations are linked to status – such as being orphaned or being middle class. He offers a number of very different models of development – including a Navajo one which suggests that it is not until 6 to 9 years of age that the child begins to think and not until the age of 30 that one can 'think ahead in all things' (2003: 91).

- *Developmental psychology seeks to regulate the adequacy of mothers*. In pursuing this theme Burman's criticism goes far beyond Piaget and Vygotsky and falls upon such notables as Bowlby, Trevarthen and Bruner. In particular she challenges their interpretation of children's intentions – the researchers' attempts to make meaning.
- *'Developmental psychology makes claims to be scientific'* (Burman 1994: 4) but uses its ability to classify and categorise 'to maintain class, gender and racial oppression'. Singer (1992) strongly criticises developmental psychologists citing for example descriptions of mothers as 'the providing genius'; or 'the psychic organiser'.
- *Psychoanalyis as a resource to critique developmental psychology*. Burman sees this as a good thing suggesting that 'a psychoanalytic reading of developmental psychology offers glimpses into the repressed themes of fear that underlie the scientific demand for control and prediction' (Burman 1994: 4).
- *Condemnation of 'individualistic interpretations of socially structured phenomena'* (Burman 1994: 4). This places failure on the shoulders of the child (or the mother) whereas consideration of the structural aspects and impact of bias or poverty, for example, highlights other explanations.

Deconstructing developmentally appropriate practice

Rejecting developmental theories, inevitably demands a rejection of developmentally appropriate practice (DAP). It is interesting to note that Derman-Sparks (1989) mentions developmentally appropriate anti-bias practice (see Chapter 15) since on the whole postmodern thinkers reject the notion of developmental stages and developmental appropriateness. Indeed Grieshaber and Ryan (2005) do identify the limitations of her work – suggesting that it results in tokenism. MacNaughton (2003) on the other hand presents Derman-Sparks's work as a contribution to transformational practice.

Widely taken up by a range of writers and thinkers (see for example Hurst and Joseph 1998: xi), DAP was developed in the 1980s (Bredekamp 1987). It contains statements that can easily be seen to be counter to postmodern, deconstructive thinking. The two excerpts below offer examples:

- 'human development research indicates that there are universal, predictable sequences of growth and change that occur.... In all domains of development – physical, emotional, social and cognitive' (Bredekamp 1987: 2)
- 'play enables children to progress along the developmental sequence from the sensorimotor intelligence of infancy to preoperational thought in the preschool years to the concrete operational thinking exhibited by primary children' (Bredekamp 1987: 3).

Despite more recent revisions (Bredekamp and Copple 1997) to acknowledge the impact of social and cultural influences of learning and development, Cannella (1997) continues to reject the approach. She (1997: 131) suggests that DAP is 'potentially dangerous for those whose cultural values are different from those imposed by the method'. She further comments that it has been 'disseminated all over the world as the guide for the education of young children' and that 'the statements and the actions generated (by DAP) represent an extreme form of pedagogical determinism' (Cannella 1997: 131).

Theory into practice

As with so many aspects of postmodern thinking it is easier to identify what is being deconstructed than what is being put in its place. (Grieshaber and Ryan 2005: 5) illustrate this point:

> as progressive and traditional teaching approaches are not enough, this new kind of early childhood teacher requires a different set of knowledge and curricular approaches. The critique of child development . . . and developmentally appropriate practice. . . . Point out the difference between curricula based on psychological theories and those that attend to factors such as race, ethnicity, and socio-economic issues, placing greater demands on the field to respond to the characteristics of a globalized world. In other words, the social facts of mobile, heterogeneous, multilingual and multicultural populations are calling into question conventional models of child development and their normative models of childcare, schooling and early education.

They go on to acknowledge this, commenting on the fact that early attempts to replace 'progressive and traditional teaching approaches' have, for example, resisted technology, banned superhero play or attempted to maintain a construct of children as vulnerable. They do however offer some examples.

Te Whariki

Ritchie (2005: 112) comments on the importance in developing culturally relevant curricula or pedagogy of embracing 'difference, complexity, uncertainty and even confusion .... as part of the process'. She highlights the little narratives (see Chapter 15) and the dangers of 'attempts to speak for others' (Ritchie 2005: 113, citing McLaren

1995). She refers to Te Whariki as a bicultural curriculum which represents an attempt to restore the legitimacy of Maori knowledge and learning – following colonial marginalisation.

In order to achieve this it has been necessary to foreground Maori language and culture. But more importantly a reflexive approach has been adopted. Reflexivity is defined as 'an ability to reflectively critique prior and ongoing assumptions, knowledge, and understandings (Ritchie 2005: 115, citing Siraj-Blatchford and Siraj-Blatchford 1997). As discussed in Chapter 15, critical pedagogy in its many forms is a highly important element of postmodern thinking. There is consideration too of bicultural development – while postmodern critiques are noted it is explained that it is transformative change towards an equitable society that is being argued for.

The postmodern notion of multiple realities is addressed in the recognition of the need for metacultural and metalinguistic awareness amongst practitioners. This involves giving more opportunities for non-Maori practitioners to learn the language but if there is to be genuine co-construction there will also need to be a higher proportion of Maori educators in the field of early childhood.

The shifts in practice brought about by the introduction of Te Whariki have included a recognition that children's individual interests should not take precedence over 'project-type approaches involving sustained learning experiences around shared interests in the socio-cultural contexts of home, community and centre' (Ritchie 2005: 122, citing Anning et al. 2004). Ritchie also describes the work of a practitioner seeking to use mealtimes as a learning experience – reflecting and building on the differences between cultures. She had noted that while within Polynesian culture food sharing was the norm, in the nursery it was not allowed. Ritchie (2005: 131) concludes that:

> As Maori knowledges and practices are incorporated inclusively within the everyday environment, resources, and interactions of early childhood settings, children (and adults) present have opportunities for enrichment through enhanced metacultural and metalinguistic awareness and respect for different ways of knowing and being in the world, co-creating the potential for new collectively co-constructed world views.

Reinventing Vygotsky

Lobman (2005: 247) reminds us that Vygotsky (see Chapter 13) is on the whole firmly rejected by postmodern thinkers. Morss (1996) describes him as refining but not challenging developmental theory. Lobman also suggests that his emphasis on the cultural is imported into early childhood education (see for example Bredekamp and Copple 1997) but does not seriously challenge underlying beliefs.

However, Lobman (2005) admires Vygotsky's emphasis on dialogue or discussion and his understanding of play. She takes these and uses them to develop improvisation as a pedagogical tool. Citing Holzman (2000), she suggests that 'what is important to human development in general and early childhood in particular is the characterization of people as changers and creators of new circumstances' (Lobman 2005: 249). Using her own improvisational skills she begins to use improvisation as a way of engaging with children's play. She writes:

> From inside play I could challenge some of the children's assumptions about the way things are; I could be a mommy who hated to cook, or a superhero who cried, not as an imposition of a lesson but as a creative choice that challenged them to keep making creative choices. I showed them that we could continuously play with, and create with, the meanings we see in the world.
>
> (Lobman 2005: 253)

Vivian Gussin Paley

Lobman (2005) refers to play in an entirely academic discourse. Paley writes reflectively and engagingly about play with barely an explicit word of accepted theory. Yet her work is both thought-provoking and reflexive. Her extensive writing is based entirely on her desire to make meaning – to make sense of the work she was doing with children. From her first book *White Teacher* (1979) to her latest book *Boy on the Beach* (2010), Paley documents what she sees and hears, analyses and interrogates her thinking and that of the children. Her interactions with children are authentic. She co-constructs meanings, in her earliest books largely with the children, in her later books with practitioners. Paley would not categorise herself as a postmodern thinker yet in the 'little narratives' she relates she shows herself to be so. She looks at the world through a range of lenses, particularly those of children.

A critique of deconstruction theories

In considering the deconstruction of development, there are two major critiques. The first relates to the work of Burman (1994) in particular, although not exclusively. The criticism relates to what others raised in Chapter 15. What is this work for? Where does it take us? Since children's development – however that is defined – and pedagogy are real foci of real people in the real world, a straightforward deconstruction takes us nowhere. It can leave people without a sense of what practice might look like.

Secondly, as many of the theorists whose work has been examined in this chapter make clear (see for example Graue 2005), development does happen. Morss (1990) has suggested that those deconstructing development (including himself) are in danger of being seen to make nonsensical claims since it is clear that development does happen. Babies grow and develop. Adults continue to grow and develop (Rogers 1969). Some deconstructivists suggest that they are deconstructing only cognitive development. Others refer to the process of development as the lifelong dynamic process of change and transformation – clearly not something that happens in neatly and hierarchically arranged stages.

The legacy of deconstructive theories

The deconstruction of development has taught professionals that pedagogy is not the same as child development. In the introduction to this book the words of Alexander et al. that 'teaching is not applied child development' were quoted. They also (1992: 18) wrote that:

> To teach well, teachers must take account of how children learn. We do not, however, believe that it is possible to construct a model of primary education from evidence about children's development alone: the nature of the curriculum followed by the pupil and the range of teaching strategies employed by the teacher are also of critical importance.

Dahlberg et al. (2007: 101) claim that the over-reliance of developmental psychology or child development has left the field of early childhood 'the poorer for its dependency on one discipline and its neglect by others'. This view is supported by Egan (2002) who believes that developmental theories cannot help since we do not have a clear enough view of how minds work and how people actually learn. His remedy is to offer the opportunity to 'make their minds most abundant by acquiring the fullest array of the cultural tools that can, through learning, be made into cognitive tools' (Egan 2002: 184). He claims to draw on Vygotsky because 'he more than anyone seems to me to have had an understanding of the process whereby the cultural becomes cognitive'. Rogoff (2003) does this very well too and perhaps in a more contemporary form.

A rejection of developmental theories has led to a rethinking of the rhetoric of 'readiness' (see Chapter 12). Social constructivism (such as that developed by Rogoff) rejects it on the grounds that contexts make children ready or not for learning; while postmodern social constructionism argues that since there is no pre-determined development, readiness, in Piagetian terms, cannot exist either.

As discussed in Chapter 15, the whole notion of critical pedagogy and pedagogical documentation is a very important legacy of deconstructionist theories. Observing carefully and analysing obsessively are vital skills in coming to know and understand children's learning. There is an increasing recognition of the perspectives or lenses that deconstruction can bring to help us see children in a new light. McArdle (2005) uses a helpful metaphor – that of cubist painters who see and represent the whole, who take advantage of many perspectives at the same time. New insights can (and have) lead to a rejection of biases which harm children and society. Of course, these have not been eradicated but questioning assumptions and challenging ideas is making changes. Transformations take time!

Finally, perhaps the greatest legacy of all is the recognition that deconstruction and reflexivity together have brought to the field of early childhood care and education a new and improved vision of children – a full member of society who, like all of us, is both being and becoming a full member of humanity. The legacy teaches us that there are many children and childhoods and that children are a social attribute, a culture worthy of study in their own right with voices of their own.

Reflective questions

1. As suggested above, deconstruction theory makes it difficult to see what one can or should do. Try to identify an area of practice that you would like to question.
2. What does listening to children, in the sense implied above, mean for your practice?

Further reading

If you haven't read any of Vivian Gussin Paley's books choose one that appeals to you. It will give you a feel for the questioning approach that deconstructive theories demand. Paley does not however lose sight of her personal theory and beliefs

Woodhead, M. and Montgomery, H. (2003) *Understanding Childhood – an interdisciplinary approach.* Chichester: John Wiley and Sons Ltd. (See Chapter 3.)

Part 6
Weighing up the evidence

Postmodernism is not a dismissal of science but rather an understanding that there are alternative ways of understanding the complexity and multiplicity of the world.
(Janzen 2008: 288)

In Part 5, the rise of postmodernism can be seen to have been strongly related to a desire to move away from the structure and logic that is associated with science. It is argued that scientific ideas change – this means that the findings of research carried out at any time are likely to differ from current thinking (Penn 2005). At the same time the fact that ideas within early childhood care and education change slowly means that there is likely to be a time lag. Piaget's theories for example, initially developed in the 1930s, did not become popular in education until the 1960s and 1970s. Writing in the 1980s, Claxton et al. (1985) argue that although behaviourism had been repudiated within scientific circles it was (and still is) widely used in educational circles. Greenfield (2009) echoes this sentiment by highlighting the gap between science and education. She suggests that thinking in education rarely makes use of current scientific evidence.

Egan (2002: 183–4) reminds us that science is itself a cultural tool. When applied to the natural world they offer a reliable view of that world. However, when applied to our cultural world (of which he argues learning is a part) it is a much less impressive tool. He continues:

> They are good at exposing that nature of things but less good at exposing the culture of things – the human meanings of which so much of our consciousness consists. When they have been applied in trying to understand the processes involved in education, they seem less impressive still.

Alongside that thinking however were ideas that suggested that science does not need to be modernist in its viewpoint but may require intuition and imagination. Einstein (Isaacson 2007) regarded his use of imagination as a vital element in the development of his creative scientific thinking. In the twenty-first century a number of mathematicians have also been keen to demonstrate that maths is a creative and imaginative subject (see for example Devlin 2003; du Sautoy 2010).

Part 6 differs from the previous five parts in that it does not set out theories, philosophies or approaches as such but seeks to examine the nature of evidence and to invite the reader to consider a range of research perspectives. It also differs in that it has a different structure – there are no chapters but a series of sections which together invite the reader to critically reflect on:

- different sources of evidence;
- the extent to which these lead to theories or evidence-based practice; and
- the impact that different kinds of evidence have had, and continue to have, on early childhood theory and practice.

The nature of research

How many sentences, written or spoken, begin with the phrase 'research shows ...' or even 'research proves ...'? The purpose of this section is to review aspects of research methods and to invite reflection on what research can actually indicate, or not.

Paradigms

Mukherji and Albon (2010: based on page 11) cite a range of definitions of the word 'paradigm':

- a theoretical framework (Mackenzie and Knipe 2006);
- a loose collection of logically related assumptions and concepts and propositions that orient thinking and research (Bogdan and Biklen 1998: 22);
- a way of seeing the world that 'frames a research topic' and influences the way that we think about the topic (Hughes 2001: 31);
- a set of beliefs about the way in which particular problems exist and a set of agreements about how such problems can be investigated (Fraser and Robinson 2004: 59).

The authors (Mukherji and Albon 2010: 11) conclude that 'our choice of paradigm is important in influencing the methodology we choose, but it also shapes our perceptions of children and childhood'. In the introduction to this book, the notion that we all hold our own theories was raised. If, even at an unconscious level, we believe, as Owen did (Singer 1992), that children are inherently good – inevitably when identifying documenting incidents of aggressive behaviour, for example, our observations will look quite different from those of someone who holds a different philosophy. Psychology grew out of philosophy (see Part 1) and it cannot escape the link.

Similarly, in Chapter 13, Bruner's role in the Oxford Pre-school Research Project (Bruner 1980) was discussed. At that time, the research was widely interpreted as favouring structured tasks in early years provision – a concept which would be at odds with the views of many of the practitioners at that time but perhaps not the researchers. The paradigms and expectations of the two groups were not shared. In the thirty years since the Oxford Pre-school Research Project was carried out there has been a much greater emphasis on engaging the subjects of research whether they are children or adults. This is evidenced in ethnographic studies and in studies that seek to listen to the voice of children (Mukherji and Albon 2010). The other factor, explored in Part 5 of this book, is of course postmodernist views which promote questioning and challenge – or the problematising of ideas.

Positivist or quantitative research

When governments talk about evidence-based practice, they are generally thinking of qualitative (or positivist) research – research from which graphs and statistics can easily be gleaned. Such research rests on a number of assumptions, namely that 'behaviour is seen to be predictable and regular'; that the purpose of research is 'to explain and predict'; and that 'the researcher is interested in understanding general laws that apply to whole populations rather than particular groups' (Mukherji and Albon 2010: 14–15). This in turn means that efforts are made to minimise any variables; that researchers' attempt to be neutral or objective and that measurements are made in ways which are structured and therefore reliable, and which can be readily validated. At the heart of this approach to research lies the belief that there is a universal truth waiting to be discovered. As discussed in Chapter 15, this belief is not universally agreed or shared.

Interpretivist or qualitative research

Approaches of this sort are often regarded as 'soft'. The results are less generalisable but ethnographic researchers would argue – richer, providing 'thick descriptions' (Mukherji and Albon 2010, citing Ryle); statistics are not involved; and the context under which the research is conducted is naturalistic – familiar to the subjects. There is no attempt to be objective since the involvement of the researcher is seen as shaping the data, from understandings based on culture, language and the meanings that have been previously established within him or her.

Ethics

Every piece of research should pay due attention to the ethics of the situation. Lahmann refers to young children as 'competent but vulnerable' a description which pays attention to their rights yet acknowledges that their inexperience can lead them to be exploited. Approaches which focus on listening to children have ethics at their heart – practitioners and researchers are attempting to understand what children want to say. Does the research evidence we are exploring pay attention to the unequal power implicit in many situations? Does it take account of the need for informed consent? What does the informed consent of a pre-verbal child look like? Mukherji and Albon (2010) suggest that ethical considerations apply at every level of research.

Research and policy

The Labour government formed in 1997 claimed to place a strong emphasis on evidence-based policy (Davies 2004). However, 'doing what works' is not always straightforward. Two examples drawn from early years practice during the years of the Labour government demonstrate the limitations of this approach. Early evaluations of Sure Start were critical (NESS 2005) – a view that was heavily publicised in the press and media. Despite this the government continued to fund projects, believing the researchers' view that it was too early to evaluate the impact. Although a later evaluation (NESS 2008) showed improvements, the press continued to highlight the earlier adverse findings (Pound 2009a). What complicates these findings, the 'noisiness' of research (MacNaughton 2004), is the emotions which surround considerations of daycare for young children, and attendant beliefs about the role of mothers. In addition the aims of Sure Start initiatives are long term in nature and as such cannot be judged over such a short period.

Phonics is another highly charged political issue. In 2005, Jim Rose produced a report for the government suggesting, on the evidence of one study in Clackmannanshire, that synthetic phonics should be taught to all children, beginning at the foundation stage. In the same year, Torgerson et al., also commissioned by the DfES, produced a review of relevant research on the subject of phonics. Their findings were that there were no significant differences between children taught through synthetic phonics or those taught using analytic phonics. Was it dogma, media pressure or evidence-based policy that led the same government department to both fund research and commission a review that refuted or ignored the evidence provided? For more information on this fascinating topic see Pound (2008) and Wyse (2006 – full details given below in further reading section).

The role of longitudinal research

Longitudinal research is expensive and by its nature time consuming. It is, however, often seen as only way in which to understand what actually works. Early childhood care and education is littered with such studies. More than in any other sector, politicians have time and time again sought to justify their actions through (or as in the case of phonics cited above ignore) the findings of research. Two examples (based on Pound's work) are explored below.

1.   HighScope was one of many Head Start programmes developed in the 1960s in the United States of America. Its curriculum was influenced by the writings of Piaget with an emphasis on cognition – its eight key experiences are drawn from Piaget's areas of experience (MacNaughton 2003). An aspect of HighScope often overlooked is also its emphasis on training and development for staff and parents. The name HighScope derives from the notion of high aspirations and a broad vision for children (Pound 2005).

      While all Head Start programmes were required to include evaluations, HighScope undertook longitudinal research which continued to investigate research participants through their preschool experiences beyond the age of 40 (Schweinhart et al. 2005). Comparisons with people who had not been

HighScope participants were also made. Publications throughout that period demonstrated that:

- those who had been involved in HighScope were significantly more likely to be employed;
- by the age of 27 and beyond, HighScope 'graduates' earned significantly more than others;
- those who had been part of the HighScope experience were less likely to have been involved in crime or to have needed costly support such as support for special educational needs, teenage pregnancy or drug abuse;
- men who had been involved in HighScope were twice as likely as others to have raised their own children.

(based on Pound 2005)

These and other similar findings led the HighScope organisation to be able to claim that for every dollar invested in high quality early childhood education, seven dollars could be saved. This in turn engaged politicians and led in England to the creation of Sure Start.

2. *The Effective Provision of Pre-School Education (EPPE)* project (1997–2003) was initially established with the aim of identifying the characteristics of effective early childhood provision. It has been extended to include findings from children now in secondary school.

   The project has been regarded as highly reliable since it involved over 3,000 children and has been conducted by leading researchers including Kathy Sylva and Iram Siraj-Blatchford. Many important findings have been published including:

- evidence of the importance of sustained shared thinking on achievement;
- findings of the positive impact on learning and development of qualified teachers working with young children;
- findings on the role of parents, whatever their social class or level of education, in supporting their own children's learning.

(based on Pound 2008: 68)

These findings have not been without critics – nor have they been consistently used to support evidence-based practice. Discussion of the impact of EPPE includes:

- Funding has been provided to ensure a better level of qualifications for some of the people working with young children but in some cases this has been little more than token with many children receiving less input from well-qualified staff.
- While Sure Start does offer opportunities for parents to improve the quality of their interactions with children it has also been set up by government to promote mothers working.
- The emphasis on reading and writing represents a political agenda – a different perspective than that valued by significant numbers of practitioners and parents.

The nature of intelligence

Interest in intelligence was heightened by the work of Charles Darwin. His theories of evolution heightened interest in the development of psychological aspects of development including intelligence. Darwin's cousin Francis Galton was the first to collect data on the intellectual differences between groups. He was also the first to identify what is termed 'regression to the mean' – his explanation for the fact he identified that exceptionally tall or intelligent people tend to have children whose measurements are closer to the average (Gardner 1999). He also began to develop some testing procedures for what he regarded as aspects of intelligence such as reaction times and sensory discrimination.

Alfred Binet's name is associated with a number of the theorists discussed in this book. Both he and Freud studied with Charcot, who developed work on hypnosis. Both Montessori and Piaget were involved in the administration of the tests he developed. Montessori worked with Binet himself while Piaget worked with his colleague Simon. The underlying motive for this work was to identify those amongst disabled children who had sufficient intelligence to benefit from mainstream schooling. As we saw in Chapter 11, Piaget became more interested in why so many children giving incorrect responses gave the same incorrect response.

Binet is credited with developing the first, more comprehensive intelligence tests. Their reliance on verbal memory, verbal reasoning, numerical reasoning and logical sequencing were to remain largely unchallenged until the 1980s, with the development of Gardner's Multiple Intelligence Theory (MIT) (1983). However, Gardner (1999) suggests that three questions have remained critical to thinking about intelligence:

Is there just a general intelligence or do we have many intelligences?

A number of theorists have explored this issue. In 1902, Spearman suggested that intelligence could be defined as having two factors. By the 1930s Thurstone suggested that there were seven aspects of intelligence; and in 1967 Guilford identified well over one hundred 'factors of the intellect' (Pound 2008). In articulating MIT, Gardner has suggested seven or eight areas of intelligence – the exact number changing as Gardner's thinking has developed and changed (1999). Gardner maintains that by and large those who favour psychometrics, the measurement of intelligence, believe it to be generalised.

Is intelligence inherited?

Galton, in common with many people at that time, believed intelligence to be an inherited trait. Interestingly, Darwin did not agree. Writing to Galton he declares 'I have always maintained that, excepting for fools, men did not differ much in intelligence, only in zeal and hard work' (cited by Gardner 1999: 14). Studies of identical twins have been widely used to support the notion of inherited intelligence. Cyril Burt was responsible for a number of such studies but in the 1970s his work was discredited, amidst claims that he had falsified data in order to give support to his belief that intelligence was inherited. Despite this, many studies do show an inherited element but as Gardner points out (1999) a number of other factors could account for that – such as being comprised of an essentially white, middle-class set of subjects; and similar appearance eliciting similar responses from others. This view is supported by Kagan (1998) who suggests that culture and temperament all play a part in intelligence. Being intelligent may look very different in one culture than another. Similarly he asserts that only 10 per cent of measured IQ is associated with vocational success in Europe and America – although the picture is different in societies where social class counts for less.

A further factor which needs to be considered in any discussion of intelligence is a phenomenon known as 'the Flynn effect'. It has been observed for several years now that, across the population, the average IQ has increased about three points every ten years. This is puzzling and it is unclear whether this offers support for inherited intelligence or not. Suggested causes include:

- improved nutrition;
- smaller families;
- better access to education and greater familiarity with testing procedures;
- earlier intervention;
- increasingly complex environment – increasing the flexibility and adaptability of the brain.

(based on Pound 2008: 38)

Are intelligence tests biased?

The difficulty of defining intelligence inevitably means that it is difficult to know what is or what should be tested. What is considered to be intelligence varies markedly from one culture to another (Deary 2001). For some such as American middle-class groups it may be abstract thinking and technical ability while for others such as Ugandan villagers it has been identified as 'knowing how to and acting in socially appropriate ways' (Pound 2008: 42, citing Deary).

In addition, it is clear that many, particularly of the early tests, were outrageously biased – asking about things that could only be known by people with particular life experiences. However the American Psychological Association identified one of the problems of intelligence testing as being that 'people who devise intelligence tests value most the things that they themselves are good at. Intelligence tests therefore tend to focus on things which enabled them to succeed at school' (Pound 2008: 42).

In the 1960s work by Bernstein (Nicholls and Wells 1985) and Labov (Singer 1992) claimed that the language use of working-class children was different but not inferior to that of middle-class children. Singer (1992: 113) continues:

> Tests for measuring the IQ became the subject of a scientific and political battle. In an historical study, Kamin (1977) showed how IQ tests had been entwined with racist, eugenic and social-political programmes since their development. The favouring of children from the middle class (cultural bias) by the use of IQ

tests was thus exposed. Black political groups advised parents and children not to cooperate with IQ and school achievement tests, because the results would be used against them.

Understanding human behaviour

Distinct types of scientific thinking have been used to explain our behaviour and thinking in biological terms. Genetics and evolution; models of the brain which liken it to a computer; and neuroscience are all used in a search to understand thinking, learning and development.

Evolutionary theories

Darwin was responsible for thinking in this area – his theory was developed in the mid-nineteenth century but since that time psychologists have attempted to make sense of our behaviour and cognition in evolutionary terms. Some early explanations of play, for example, owe much to evolutionary psychology. Herbert Spencer and Charles Darwin both offered the need to get rid of surplus energy as an explanation – an evolutionary explanation. In the 1890s, Groos (Millar 1968) put forward a different theory in which he regarded play in animals as well as humans as being about practising and perfecting skills that will be needed in adult life. Millar (1968) cites his description of play fighting, in particular, as being linked to human evolution.

Recapitulation theory – which proposes that processes of evolution are mirrored in the individual development of a child – was explored by Darwin, Preyer (said to have created child psychology) and Hall – all of whom kept detailed observations of their own children. Millar (1968: 18) writes:

> Unfortunately, the theory was based on the assumption that skills learned by one generation, and the cultural experience it has, can be inherited by the next. … Most western geneticists reject the notion that acquired characteristics can be inherited – at least in any form which could make Hall's recapitulation theory plausible. There is no tidy linear progress from 'primitive' to more complex civilisations.… But theory does not have to be correct to be of use. Hall's recapitulation theory had the excellent effect of stimulating interest in children's behaviour at various ages.

In the twenty-first century Steven Pinker is perhaps the best known of the evolutionary psychologists. He is variously described as an:

> evolutionary psychologist with a popular touch and a mission to explain how the brain works … (with) the looks of a rock star, a fondness for early Woody Allen movies, and a world-class reputation as a scientist and writer.
>
> (Pound, 2009: 43, citing Crace 2008)

His writings, questioning as he does 'the very nature of our thinking – the way we use words, how we learn, and how we relate to others' (Pound 2009: 43), have captured the popular imagination and this has raised the level of debate and thinking. However his explanations and conclusions are often heavily criticised by other scientists. Rose and Rose (2000: 2) argue that:

> To evolutionary psychologists, everything from children's alleged dislike of spinach to our supposed universal preferences for scenery featuring grasslands and water derives from this mythic human origin in the African savannah. And of course, there are more serious claims such as those legitimising men's 'philandering' and women's 'coyness', our capacity to detect cheaters, to favour our genetic kin, to be aggressive. Evolutionary psychologists claim to have identified and explained all these as biological adaptations – that is, behaviours that have been selected during human evolution to assist in survival and hence the propagation of our ancestors' genes.

Evolutionary psychologists such as Pinker and Dawkins counter such arguments by claiming that humans have free will and can resist genetic tyranny. Rose (2000: 262–3) rejects this resort to free will in their otherwise 'genetically and evolutionarily determined universe' and points out a fundamental flaw in this argument:

> The evolutionary path that leads to humans has produced organisms with profoundly plastic, adaptable brains/minds and ways of living. Humans have created societies, invented technologies and cultures. We, the inheritors of not merely the genes, but also the cultures and technologies of our forebears, are profoundly shaped by them in ways that make our future as individuals, societies and species, radically unpredictable. In short, the biological nature of being human enables us to create individual lives and collective societies whose futures lie at least in part in our own hands.

Stephen Jay Gould (see for example 2007), a highly respected evolutionary biologist, opposes Pinker's views. Gould argues that although our brains were shaped by evolution, individuals rather than their genetic make up are the driving force behind evolution. While we are the architects of our own brains – our contexts and behaviour constantly change which means that genetic shaping would be for too slow to respond – 'we cannot afford to be servants of our genes' (Pound 2009: 44). Steven Mithen, a professor of prehistory, has studied the evolution of the brain and, in relation to the role of music in developing language in the human race, comes up with a very different explanation (1996, 2005). While Pinker famously has declared music to have no evolutionary role – in fact to be of no more value that strawberry cheescake, Mithen argues that music is the origin of language and thought. Mithen's view is widely supported (see for example Malloch and Trevarthen 2008).

Three further criticisms of Pinker's analysis of our evolution should be aired. One suggests that we simply have too few genes for language to have dedicated genes. The second major criticism is that while some aspects of human behaviour clearly are rooted in the evolutionary process, much more of our behaviour cannot be attributed to evolution. Penn (2005: 71) summarises a third area of criticism. She writes 'what in other circumstances might be regarded as the most outrageous sexism has found an academic respectability in evolutionary psychology'.

Information processing models

Humans have long been interested in developing machines that behave like humans (Gardner et al. 1996). Gardner and his colleagues describe devices in Ancient Egypt which gave prophesies – speaking and gesturing. The seventeenth-century philosopher Descartes, seeing machines which moved like humans, queried whether machines would ever think. By the eighteenth century highly sophisticated machines – musicians playing instruments and a boy who could write – had been developed. Gardner et al. (1996) highlight the fact that such machines simply reproduced the movements that accompany thought – rather than thought itself.

In the nineteenth century calculation was still generally thought of as an intellectual, rather than a mechanical, skill. Steam-powered machines began to do tasks that had hitherto been thought of as entirely human and these in turn led to the calculators and highly sophisticated computers that we have today. Information processing theories were derived from the interest in what these increasingly powerful machines could do and their development was part of the cognitive revolution (see Part 4). Information processing theorists:

> do not literally believe that the mind is a computer. Rather they see the computer as a tool for testing models of cognitive development. In essence, the goal is to test whether a theory of intelligent behaviour can be accounted for by a computational system, whether the computations are run in a brain or on a computer.
>
> (Keenan 2002: 138)

Keenan (2002: based on 138) identifies those assumptions which underpin information processing theories:

1. *'the mind is a system which manipulates symbols according to a set of rules'.*
2. *'thinking is information processing* ... any thought processes such as remembering or perceiving involves the processing of information'
3. *'self-modification'* drives information processing systems; 'that is earlier knowledge and strategies can modify thinking and thus lead to higher levels of development.' In short the brain and machine are said to learn.

While there was great interest in these theories during the 1960s and 1970s, increased understanding of the role of emotions in learning (see for example Goleman 1996 and LeDoux 1998) and of complex neuroscientific processes have made these models often appear simplistic.

Neuroscientific research

Research into developmental psychology has been furthered by audio and video recording and by a range of devices such as electronic switches, timing devices, detailed databases and computerised preferential looking techniques (Karmiloff and Karmiloff-Smith 2001). Similarly, neuroscientific research has been furthered by the development of brain imaging techniques. What has been discovered about brain functions goes far beyond the scope of this book. However, this does not mean that neuroscience does not impact on early childhood care and education.

Neuroscience has been widely embraced in early childhood care and education as furthering the beliefs of practitioners that early childhood has its own imperatives and vulnerabilities – that it deserves a special place in society's values since the shaping of these young children determines the future of humanity. The respected neuroscientist Susan Greenfield (1996, 1997) has highlighted specific aspects of current research which do impinge on early childhood practice. Her assertion for example that if we didn't move we wouldn't need a brain (Greenfield 1997) has clear implications for the pressures to 'disembody' early childhood care and education (Tobin 2004). Similarly her statement that 'play is fun with serious consequences' (Greenfield 1996: 75) offers important food for thought for practitioners.

Caution in the face of neuroscientific findings

Bruer (1999) has long been critical of neuroscience, claiming that the first three years of life are not as critical as many believe – that, in short, the plasticity of the brain means that humans can overcome difficulties in early childhood. He believes that young children ought not to be privileged over older ones – that all have age-related needs. More recently, MacNaughton (2004) also challenges a reliance on the findings of neuroscience. Her criticism begins by questioning practitioners' acceptance of neuroscientific findings:

> Early childhood educators' and researchers' century-old desire to legitimise their pedagogies using hard scientific data continues. The certainties of new truth about the child, such as those generated in the neurosciences (often referred to as 'the brain research') ... are widely claimed to prove that the early years are significant to later development ... in areas such as our capacity to develop, control emotions and be disease free.... More specifically, neuroscience is seen as the source of hard, scientific data that supports the view that early experiences, including nutritional and emotional experiences, stimulate brain activity and influence how neural pathways develop. The ideas have considerable currency and authority, and are promulgated by key international institutions such as the World Bank ...
>
> (MacNaughton 2004: 92)

MacNaughton's argument continues by calling into question what she calls 'tree logic' – a linear, hierarchical view of development – which she suggests should be replaced by post-structuralist 'rhizomatic logic'. In this view change and development is lateral, dynamic and ever-changing, always 'becoming' rather than a finished product – heading off in sometimes unpredicted directions. She therefore (MacNaughton 2004) urges that neuroscientific research should be viewed with caution since:

- it does not fully reflect our changeability;
- it does not fully reflect our diversity;
- it does not fully reflect (or like) our complexity (or 'noisiness' – as she terms it. Human beings have too many variables to be sufficiently limited to mirror 'hard' scientific data.)

Reflective questions

It is hoped that the following questions (based on MacNaughton 2004: 97) will encourage you to weigh up evidence rather than taking it at face value:

- Where has this piece of research come from?
- What groups of people or animals was it done with?
- How generalisable is it to the groups of people I work with?
- Who is suggesting it can be generalised and with what degree of confidence?
- Is their confidence justified?
- Can I be confident about the methods and ethics employed in the research?

Further reading

Blakemore, S-J and Frith, U. (2005) *The Learning Brain: lessons for education*. Oxford: Blackwell. Publishing

Mukherji, P. and Albon, D. (2010) *Research Methods in Early Childhood*. London: Sage. (See Chapters 1–4.)

Wyse, D. (2006) *Rose Tinted Spectacles: synthetic phonics, research evidence and the teaching of reading*. www.tactyc.org.uk/pdfs/2006conf_wyse.pdf (accessed 19 May, 2010).

Final thoughts

The important thing is what those who live with, or work with and for young children in our present times and settings say and do. The important thing is that the new pioneers, those working in early childhood settings and elsewhere in the pursuit of the best provision for young children, take these ideas (from the past) into the future and make them their own. There is no better tribute to those who have gone than to remould, revisit and revise their ideas for a new today.

(Nutbrown et al. 2008: 181)

If you have simply used this book as a reference book – something to dip into – it is likely that you have found some immediate answers. However, if you have read this book in more depth – perhaps even from cover to cover – you have probably been left with many more questions than answers.

One set of questions relate to the relationship between formal and informal theories – a topic explored in the introduction to this book. Common to all the theories explored has been some aspect of reflective practice – listening, questioning, observing and analysing. This takes us back – again to the introduction to the book and Gardner's view that no one can consider themselves a professional unless they are prepared to engage in reflective practice. These seem to be not questions so much as imperatives – whether like Paley, or as in Reggio; whether in Dewey's or Darwin's mould. Without data there are no answers!

A second set of questions relate to the way in which theories overlap – influenced by historical and political events and by one another. Darwin's and Piaget's theories for example made possible the thinking of others that followed or challenged them. These questions prompt us to think about why theories, such as those of Vygotsky or even Piaget, lie apparently unnoticed and certainly not acted on for a period of time but then begin to be given a high profile. Sometimes the answers to these questions are little more than accidents – who happened to be selected to sit on a particular committee, who happened to be noticed or influenced by someone at a particular point in history. What will have been noticeable in these pages are some key or pivotal figures who have influenced many others – many of whom have gone on to greatness themselves. Binet is one such example; Pestalozzi another; and of course Piaget.

Egan (2002: 185) argues that developmental theories which attempt to link education to theories of learning are fruitless. Progressive educational theories, he continues, which attempt to harness practice to the nature of the child have also proved over many centuries to be futile. He argues that research will not give answers to the questions we ask – analysis is what is needed. For Egan the analysis he has in mind is of 'the cultural-cognitive tools that shape and mediate our learning, development and everything else to do with the conscious world of educational activity'. He claims that 'by climbing on the shoulders of giants and stealing their ideas' he has been able to identify 'a conception of education and derive from it a curriculum, an educationally relevant developmental scheme, and methods of teaching that encourage educational learning'. For the early years these are the somatic and the mythic – to do with the body and with stories.

Concern with the physical and with narrative (which of course includes dramatic play and language play, song, rhythm and rhyme) looks remarkably close to the concerns of many of the educators which have been discussed in this book. There are a number of themes which emerge time after time – active learning, dance, outdoor play perhaps form one cluster, but emotional well-being, respect, acknowledgement of the need for attachment and so on certainly form another.

Education takes many forms and has many motives but it has to be concerned both with the individual and with the cultural. Early education shares this complexity but has, I believe, another layer – the children with whom we work are our future as well as their own. We cannot know what will be needed in the future but, as practitioners engaged in work with children and their families from their earliest days, we can work to champion their rights and develop their sense of being a member of a culture. Early care and education must strive in its beliefs and practices to engage and support the development of young children in ways which ensure the flexibility, diversity and complexity needed for their future.

Bibliography

Adey, P. and Shayer, M. (2002) Cognitive acceleration comes of age. In M. Shayer and P. Adey (eds) *Learning Intelligence: cognitive acceleration across the curriculum from 5 to 15 years*. Buckingham: Open University Press.

Ainsworth, M., Blehar, M., Waters, E. and Wall, S. (1978) *Patterns of Attachment*. Hillsdale, NJ: Erlbaum.

Albon, D. (2011) Postmodern and post structuralist perspectives on early childhood education. In L. Miller and L. Pound (eds) *Theories and Approaches to Learning in the Early Years*. London: Sage.

Alderson, P. (2000) *Young Children's Rights*. London: Jessica Kingsley Publishers Ltd.

Alexander, R. (ed.) (2010) *Children, their World, their Education*. London; Routledge.

Alexander, R., Rose, J. and Woodhead, C. (1992) *Curriculum Organisation and Classroom Practice in Primary Schools: a discussion paper*. London: DES.

Alloway, N. (1997) Early childhood encounters the postmodern: What do we know? What can we count as 'true'? *Australian Journal of Early Childhood* 22(2): 1–5.

Anning, A. Cullen, J. and Fleer, M. (2004) (eds) *Early Childhood Education; society and culture*. London: Sage.

Apple, M. and Teitelbaum, K. (2001) John Dewey 1859–1952. In J. Palmer (ed.) *Fifty Major Thinkers: from Confucius to Dewey*. London: Routledge.

Apple, M., Gandin, L. and Hypoliti, A. (2001) Paulo Freire 1921–97. In J. Palmer (ed.) *Fifty Modern Thinkers on Education: from Piaget to the present*. London: Routledge.

Aries, P. (1962) *Centuries of Childhood: a social history of family life*. New York: Knopf.

Aspin, D. (1983) Friedrich Froebel: visionary, prophet and healer? *Early Childhood Development and Care* 12: 3/4.

Athey, C. (1990) *Extending Thought in Young Children*. London: Paul Chapman Publishing Ltd.

Athey, C. (2007) (2nd edn) *Extending Thought in Young Children*. London: Paul Chapman Publishing Ltd.

Ball, C. (1994) (ed.) *Start Right – the importance of early learning*. London: Royal Society of Arts.

Bartholomew, L. and Bruce, T. (1993) *Getting to Know You*. London: Hodder and Stoughton.

Bateman, A. and Holmes, J. (1995) *An Introduction to Psychoanalysis: contemporary theory and psractice*. London: Routledge.

Bathurst, K. (1905) The need for national nurseries, *Nineteenth Century* May.

Bauman, Z. (1995) *Life in Fragments*. Oxford: Blackwell.

Belsky, J. (2008) Quality, quantity and type of child care: effects on child development in the USA. In G. Bentley and R. Mace (eds) *Substitute Parenting; alloparenting in human societies*. Oxford: Berghahn Books.

Berk, L. and Spuhl, S. (1995) Maternal interaction, private speech, and task performance in pre-school children. *Early Childhood Research Quarterly* 10: 145–69.

Berube, M. (2004) *Radical Reformers: the influence of the left in American education*. Charlotte, NC: Information Age Publications Inc.

Bilton, H. (2010) (3rd edn) *Outdoor Learning in the Early Years*. London: Routledge.

Bishop, M. (ed.) (1986) *Portage: more than a teaching programme*. London: Routledge.

Blackstone, T. (1971) *A Fair Start: the provision of pre-school education*. London: Allen Lane/LSE.

Blackwell, S. and Pound, L. (2011) Forest Schools in the early years. In L. Miller and L. Pound (eds) *Theories and Approaches to Learning in the Early Years*. London: Sage.

Blakemore, S. J. and Frith, U. (2005) *The Learning Brain lessons for education*: Oxford-Blackwell Publishing.

Bleakley, A. (1999) From reflective practice to holistic reflexivity. *Studies in Higher Education* 24: 315–30.

Boaler, J. (2009) *The Elephant in the Classroom*. London: Souvenir Press Ltd.

Board of Education (1933) *Report of the Consultative Committee on Infant and Nursery Schools*. London: HMSO.

Board of Education (educational reconstruction/White Paper) (1943) *Report of the Women Inspectors on Children Under Five years of Age in Public Elementary Schools 1905*. London: HMSO.

Bogdan, R. and Biklen, S. (1998) *Qualitative Research Education: an introduction to theories and methods*. Boston MA: Allyn and Bacon.

Bolton, G. (2005) (2nd edn) *Reflective Practice*. London: Sage Publications Ltd.

Bostridge, M. (2008) *Florence Nightingale*. London: Penguin.

Bower, T. (1973) *The Perceptual World of the Child*. London: Fontana.

Bowlby, J. (1951) *Maternal Care and Mental Health*. World Health Organisation.

Bowlby, J. (1969) *Attachment and Loss Vol. 1 Attachment*. London: Hogarth Press.

Bowlby, J. (1973) *Attachment and Loss Vol. 2 Separation: anxiety and anger*. London: Hogarth Press.

Bowlby, J. (1992) *Charles Darwin: a new life*. London: WW Norton and Co. Ltd.

Bowlby, J. (nd) www.robertsonsfilms.info/ (accessed 1 July 2010).

Bradley, M., Isaacs, B., Livingston, L., Nasser, D., True, A-M. and Dillane, M. (2011) Maria Montessori in the United Kingdom. In L. Miller and L. Pound (eds) *Theories and Approaches to Learning in the Early Years*. London: Sage.

Bredekamp, S. (ed.) (1987) *Developmentally Appropriate Practice in Early Childhood Programs Serving Children from Birth Through Age 8*. Washington DC: NAEYC.

Bredekamp, S. and Copple, C. (eds) (1997) *Developmentally Appropriate Practice in Early Childhood Programs – Revised Edition*. Washington DC: NAEYC.

Brehony, K. (2000) English revisionist Froebelians and the schooling of the urban poor. In M. Hilton and P. Hirsch (eds) *Practical Visionaries: Women, Education and Social Progress*. Edinburgh: Pearson Education.

Bretherton, I. and Waters, E. (1985) Growing points of attachment theory and research. *Monographs of the Society for Research in Child Development* 50(209): 1–211.

Bromfield, R. (2003) Psychoanalytic play therapy. In C. Schaefer (ed.) *Foundations of Play Therapy*. Hoboken NJ: John Wiley and Sons Inc.

Bronfenbrenner, U. (1979) *The Ecology of Human Development*. London: Harvard University Press.

Bronfenbrenner, U. (ed.) (2005) *Making Human Beings Human: bioecological perspectives on human development*. London: Sage.

Brown, B. (1998) *Unlearning Discrimination in the Early Years*. Stoke on Trent: Trentham Books.

Brown, P. and Lauder, H. (1992) Education, Economy and Society: an introduction to a new agenda. In P. Brown and H. Lauder (eds) *Education for Economic Survival: From Fordism to Post-Fordism?* London: Routledge.

Browne, N. (2004) *Gender Equity in the Early Years*. Maidenhead: Open University Press.

Bruce, T. (2011) Froebel today. In L. Miller and L. Pound (eds) *Theories and Approaches to Learning in the Early Years*. London: Sage.

Bruce, T. (2005) (3rd edn) *Early Childhood Education*. London: Hodder Education.

Bruer, J. (1999) *The Myth of the First Three Years*. New York: The Free Press.

Bruner, J. (1960) *The Process of Education*. London: Harvard University Press.

Bruner, J. (1966) *Towards a Theory of Instruction*. Cambridge, MA: Harvard University Press.

Bruner, J. (1971) *The Relevance of Education*. New York: Norton.

Bruner, J. (1972) The nature and uses of immaturity. *American Psychologist* 27: 687–708.

Bruner, J. (1980) *Under Five in Britain*. London: Grant McIntyre Ltd.

Bruner, J. (1983) *Child's Talk; learning to use language*. Oxford: Oxford University Press.

Bruner, J. (1986) *Actual Minds, Possible Worlds*. London: Harvard University Press.

Bruner, J. (1990) *Acts of Meaning*. Cambridge, MA: Harvard University Press.

Bruner, J. (1996) *The Culture of Education*. London: Harvard University Press.

Bruner, J., Jolly, A. and Sylva, K. (eds) (1976) *Play: its role in development and evolution*. Harmondsworth: Penguin Books.

Burman, E. (1994) *Deconstructing Developmental Psychology*. London: Routledge.

CACE (Central Advisory Council for Education) (1959) *15 to 18, Vol. 1* (The Crowther Report). London: HMSO.

CACE (Central Advisory Council for Education) (1963) *Half our Future* (The Newsom Report). London: HMSO.

CACE (Central Advisory Council for Education) (1967) *Children and their Primary Schools Vol.1* (The Plowden Report). London: HMSO.

Caldwell Cook, H. (1917) *The Play Way*. London: William Heinemann.

Callaway, W. (2001) *Jean Piaget: a most outrageous deception*. New York: Nova Scientific Publications Inc.

Cannella, G. (1997) *Deconstructing Early Childhood Education: social justice and revolution*. New York: Peter Lange Publishing Inc.

Carr, M. (2001) *Assessment in Early Childhood Settings: learning stories*. London: Paul Chapman Publishing.

Case, R. (1995) *Intellectual Development: a systematic reinterpretation*. Orlando: Academic Press.

Case, R. and Yakamoto, Y. (1996) *The Role of Central Conceptual Structures in the Development of Knowledge and Thought*. Chicago: University of Chicago Press.

Casement, P. (1992) *Learning from the Patient*. New York: Guilford Press.

Chomsky, N. (1959) Review of 'Verbal Behaviour' by B.F. Skinner. *Language* 35.

Chonchaiya, W. and Pruksananonda, C. (2008) Television viewing associated with delayed language development. *Acta Paedictrica* 7: 977–82.

Christmas, S. (1998) 1968 and after. In J. Teichman and G. White (eds) *An Introduction to Modern European Philosophy*. London: Palgrave Macmillan.

Clark, A., Kjorholt, A. and Moss, P. (eds) (2005) *Beyond Listening: children's perspectives on early childhood services*. Bristol: Policy Press.

Claxton, G. (1997) *Hare Brain, Tortoise Mind*. London: Fourth Estate Ltd.

Claxton, G. (2000) The Anatomy of Intuition. In T. Atkinson and G. Claxton (eds) *The Intuitive Practitioner*. Buckingham: Open University Press.

Claxton, G. (2008) *What's the Point of Schooling?* Oxford: One World.

Claxton, G., Swann, W. and Salmon, P. (1985) *Psychology and Schooling: what's the matter?* London: Bedford Way Papers 25.

Clift, P., Cleave, S. and Griffin, M. (1980) *The Aims, Role and Development of Staff in the Nursery*. Slough: NFER.

Cohen, D. (2002) *How the Child's Mind Develops*. Hove, Sussex: Routledge.

Cole, M. (1998) Culture in development. In M. Woodhead, D. Faulkner and K. Littleton (eds) *Cultural Worlds of Early Childhood*. London: Routledge/The Open University.

Collins, J., Insley, K. and Soler, J. (eds) (2001) *Developing Pedagogy*. London: Paul Chapman Publishing.

Conroy, J., Hulme, M. and Menter, I. (2008) *Primary Curriculum Futures: The Primary Review Research Survey 3/3*. Cambridge: University of Cambridge.

Crace, J. (2008) Steven Pinker: the evolutionary man, *Guardian*, 17 June.

Crain, W. (1995) (3rd edn) *Theories of Development*. Englewood Cliffs, NJ: Prentice-Hall.

Curtis, P. (2009) Tories pledge return to rote learning and sets in school, *The Guardian*, 5 October.

Curtis, S. (1963) (5th edn) *History of Education in Great Britain*. London: University Tutorial Press.

Curzon, L. (2003) *Teaching in Further Education: an outline of principles and practice*. London: Continuum.

Dahlberg, G. Moss, P. and Pence, A. (2007) (2nd edn) *Beyond Quality in Early Childhood Care and Education*. London: Routledge.

Darder, A. (2002) (ed.) *Reinventing Paulo Freiere: a pedagogy of love*. Boulder, CO: Westview Press.

David, T. Gooch, K. Powell, S. and Abbott, L. (2003) *Birth to Three Matters: A Review of the Literature*. Nottingham DfES Publications.

Davies, P. (2004). 'Is evidence-based government possible?' The 2004 Jerry Lee Lecture, Campbell Collaboration Colloquium, Washington DC, 19 February.

DCSF (Department for Children, Schools and Families) (2008) *Every Child a Talker guidance for consultants*. Annesley, Notts: DCFS Publications.

Deary, I. (2001) *Intelligence: a very short introduction*. Oxford: Oxford University Press.

Derman-Sparks, L. (1989) *Anti-bias Curriculum: tools for empowering young children*. Washington, DC: NAEYC.

DES (Department for Education and Science) (1990) *Starting with Quality* (The Rumbold Report). London: HMSO.

Devlin, K. (2003) *Millennium Problems*. New York: Basic Books.

De Vries, R. and Kohlberg, L. (1987) *Constructivist Early Education: overview and comparison with other programs*. Washington DC: NAEYC.

Dewey, J. (1910) *How We Think*. Cincinnati, OH: LLC Publishers.

Donaldson, M. (1978) *Children's Minds*. London: Fontana.

Donaldson, M. (1992) *Human Minds*. London: The Penguin Press.

Donnachie, I. (2000) *Robert Owen: Owen of New Lanark and New Harmony*. E. Lothian: Tuckwell Press.

Drummond, M-J. (1999) Another way of seeing: perceptions of play in a Steiner kindergarten. In L. Abbott and H. Moylett (eds) *Early Education Transformed*. London: Falmer Press.

Drummond, M-J. (2010) Editorial. *Early Education* 61 Summer.

Drummond, M-J. and Jenkinson, S. (2009) *Meeting the Child: approaches to observation and assessment in Steiner Kindergartens*. Plymouth: University of Plymouth/Steiner Waldorf Early Years Research Group.

Drummond, M-J., Lally, M. and Pugh, G. (1989) *Working with Children: developing a curriculum for the early years*. London: NCB/NES.

du Sautoy, M. (2010) *The Number Mysteries*. London: Fourth Estate.

Edwards, C., Gandini, L. and Forman, G. (1995) *The Hundred Languages of Children*. Norwood, NJ: Ablex Publishing Corporation.

Egan, K. (1983) *Education and Psychology: Plato, Piaget and scientific psychology*. New York: Teachers' College Press.

Egan, K. (1984) *Education and psychology: Plato, Piaget and scientific psychology*. London: Methuen and Co. Ltd.

Egan, K. (1991) *Primary Understanding – education in early childhood*. London: Routledge.

Egan, K. (2002) *Getting it Wrong from the Beginning: our progressivist inheritance fro Herbert Spencer, John Dewy and Jean Piaget*. London: Yale University Press.

Elfer, P., Goldschmied, E. and Selleck, D. (2003) *Key Persons in the Nursery*. London: David Fulton Publishers.

Elias, C. and Berk, L. (2002) Self-regulation in young children: is there a role for sociodramatic play? *Early Childhood Research Quarterly* 17: 1–17.

Epstein, A., Johnson S. and Lafferty P. (2011) The HighScope approach. In L. Miller and L. Pound (eds) *Theories and Approaches to Learning in the Early Years*. London: Sage.

Ezell, M. (1983) *John Locke's Images of Childhood*. Liverpool: John Hopkins University Press.

Farenga, P. (nd) www.HoltGWS.com (accessed 24 July, 2010).

Feinberg, E. and Feinberg, W. (2001) Carl Rogers 1902–1987. In J. Palmer (ed.) *Fifty Modern Thinkers on Education: from Piaget to the present*. London: Routledge.

Flax, J. (1990) *Thinking Fragments: Psychoanalysis, Feminism and Postmodernism in the Contemporary West*. Oxford: University of California Press.

Foucault, M. (1980) *Power/Knowledge: selected interviews and other writings 1972–1977*. London: Harvester Wheatsheaf.

Fraser, S. and Robinson, C. (2004) *Paradigms and Philosophy*. In S. Fraser, V. Lewis, S. Ding, M. Kellett and C. Robinson (eds) *Doing Research with Children and Young People*. London: Sage.

Freire, P. (1972) *Pedagogy of the Oppressed*. Harmondsworth: Penguin Books.

Freud, S. (1955) The psychogenesis of a case of homosexuality in a woman. In E. Strachey (ed. and trans.) *The Standard Edition of the Complete Psychological Works of Sigmund Freud* (18: 145–172). London: Hogarth Press. (Original work published 1920.)

Froebel, F. ([1826] 2009) *The Education of Man*. New York: Dover Publications Inc.

Furedi, F. (2001) *Paranoid Parenting*. London: Penguin Press.

Gabbard, D. and Stuchal, D. (2001) Ivan Illich 1926–. In J. Palmer (ed.) *Fifty Modern Thinkers on Education: from Piaget to the present*. London: Routledge.

Gardner, H. (1983) *Frames of Mind*. London: Fontana Press.

Gardner, H. (1993) (2nd edn) *Frames of Mind*. London: Fontana Press.

Gardner, H. (1999) *Intelligence Reframed*. New York: Basic Books.

Gardner, H. (2001) Jerome S. Bruner 1915–. In J. Palmer (ed.) *Fifty Modern Thinkers on Education from Piaget to the present*. London: Routledge.

Gardner, H. (2006) *Five Minds for the Future*. Boston, MA: Harvard Business School Press.

Gardner, H., Kornhaber, M. and Wake, W. (1996) *Intelligence: multiple perspectives*. Fort Worth, TX: Harcourt Brace.

Gatto, J. (1996) The Public School Nightmare: why fix a system designed to destroy individual thought. In M. Hern (ed.) *Deschooling our Lives*. Gabriola Island, BC, Canada: New Society Publisher.

Gerhardt, S. (2004) *Why Love Matters*. Hove, E. Sussex: Brunner-Routledge.

Giroux, H. (1991) *Postmodernism, Feminism and Cultural Politics*. New York: State University of New York Press.

Giroux, H. (1992) *Border Crossings: cultural workers and the politics of education*. London: Routledge.

Goleman, D. (1996) *Emotional Intelligence*. London: Bloomsbury Publishing.

Gopnik, A., Meltzoff, A. and Kuhl, P. (1999) *How Babies Think*. London: Weidenfeld and Nicolson.

Gould, S. J. (2007) *The Richness of Life*. London: Vintage Press.

Graham, P. (2009) *Susan Isaacs: a life freeing the minds of children*. London: Karnac Books Ltd.

Graue, E. (2005) (De)centering the kindergarten prototype in the child-centred classroom. In S. Ryan and S. Grieshaber (eds) *Practical Transformations and Transformational Practices: globalization, postmodernism and early childhood education*. Kidlington, Oxford: Elsevier Ltd.

Green, J. and Collie, F. (1916) *Pestalozzi's Educational Writings*. London: Edward Arnold.

Greenfield, S. (1996) *The Human Mind Explained*. London: Cassell.

Greenfield, S. (1997) *The Human Brain – a guided tour*. London: Weidenfeld and Nicolson.

Greenfield, S. (2009) *The Quest For Meaning*. London: Hodder.

Grieshaber, S. and Ryan, S. (2005) Transforming ideas and practices. In S. Ryan and S. Grieshaber (eds) *Practical Transformations and Transformational Practices*. Kidlington, Oxford: Elsevier Ltd.

Gura, P. (ed.) (1992) *Exploring Learning*. London: Paul Chapman Publishing.

Habermas, J. (1986) Taking aim at the heart of the present. In D. Hoy (ed.) *Foucault: a critical reader*. Oxford: Blackwell.

Hailmann, W. ([1887] 2009) Introduction. In *The Education of Man*. New York: Dover Publications Inc. (Translation of Froebel's *The Education of Man*, first published in 1826.)

Halliday, M. (1975) *Learning How to Mean*. London: Hodder Arnold.

Healy, J. (1999) *Failure to Connect*. New York: Touchstone.

Heckman, H. (2008) *Childhood's Garden*. Spring Valley, NY: WECAN Books.

Hendrick, H. (1997) *Children, Childhood and English Society 1880–1990.* Cambridge: Cambridge University Press.

Hendrick, H. (1997) Constructions and reconstructions of British childhood: an interpretative survey, 1800 to the present. In A. James and A. Prout (eds) *Constructing and Reconstructing Childhood.* London: Falmer Press.

Hern, M. (1996) *Deschooling our Lives.* Gabriola Island, BC, Canada: New Society Publisher.

Hobson, P. (2002) *The Cradle of Thought.* London: MacMillan.

Holland, P. (2004) *Picturing Childhood: the myth of the child in popular imagery.* New York: Tauris and Co. Ltd.

Holmes, E. (1911) (2008) *What is and What Might Be.* Cincinnati, OH: LLC Publishing.

Holmes, J. (1993) *John Bowlby and Attachment Theory.* Hove, E. Sussex: Brunner-Routledge.

Holt, J. (1964) *How Children Fail.* Harmondsworth: Penguin Books.

Holt, J. (1967) *How Children Learn.* Harmondsworth: Penguin Books.

Holt, J. (1976) *Instead of Education.* Boston: Holt Associates.

Holt, J. (1981) *Teach your Own.* New York: Dell.

Holt, J. (1984) *Never Too Late.* New York: Delacourte.

Holt, J. (1996) Instead of education. In M. Hern (ed.) *Deschooling our Lives.* Gabriola Island, BC Canada: New Society Publishers.

Holzman, L. (2000) Performance, criticism and postmodern psychology. In L. Holzman and J. Morss (eds) *Postmodern Psychologies, Societal Practice and Political Life.* London: Routledge.

Hughes, P. (2001) Paradigms, methods and knowledge. In G. MacNaughton, S. Rolfe and I. Siraj-Blatchford (eds) *Doing Early Childhood Research: international perspectives on theory and practice.* Maidenhead: Open University Press.

Hunt, J. (1969) The Impact and Limitations of the Giant of Development. In D. Elkind, and J. Flavell, (eds) *Studies in Cognitive Development: essays in honor of Jean Piaget.* Oxford: Oxford University Press.

Hurst, V. and Joseph, J. (1998) *Supporting Early Learning: the way forward.* Buckingham: Open University Press.

Illich, I. (1970) *Deschooling Society.* Harmondsworth: Penguin Books.

Illich, I. (1977) *Disabling Professions.* London: Marion Boyers.

Isaacs, B., (2007) *Bringing the Montessori Approach to Your Early Years Practice.* London: David Fulton.

Isaacs, S. (1929) *The Nursery Years.* London: Routledge Kegan Paul.

Isaacs, S. (1930) *Intellectual Growth in Young Children.* London: Routledge.

Isaacs, S. (1932) *The Children We Teach.* London: University of London Press.

Isaacs, S. (1948) The nature and function of phantasy. *International Journal of Psycho-Analysis* 29: 73–98.

Isaacson, W. (2007) *Einstein: his life and universe.* London: Simon and Schuster UK Ltd.

James, A. and Prout, A. (eds) (1997) *Constructing and Reconstructing Childhood.* London: Falmer Press.

James, A., Jenks, C. and Prout, A. (1998) *Theorizing Childhood.* Cambridge: Polity Press.

Janzen, M. (2008) Where is the (postmodern) child in early childhood education research? *Early Years* 28(3): 287–8.

Jimack, P. (1762) (1974) Introduction. In J-J. Rousseau (ed.) *Emile.* London: Dent and Sons.

Johns, C. (2nd edn) (2004) *Becoming a Reflective Practitioner*. Oxford: Blackwell Publishing.

Johnson, S. P. (2010) (ed.) *Neoconstructivism: the new science of cognitive development*. New York: Oxford University Press.

Jones, C. and Pound, L. (2008) *Leadership and Management in the Early Years: from principles to practice*. Maidenhead: Open University Press.

Kagan, J. (1998) *Three Seductive Ideas*. Cambridge, Mass: Harvard University Press.

Kamin, L. (1977) *The Science and Politics of IQ*. Harmondsworth: Penguin.

Karmiloff, K. and Karmiloff-Smith, A. (2001) *Pathways to Language*. London: Harvard University Press.

Keenan, T. (2002) *An Introduction to Child Development*. London: Sage.

Keenan, T. and Evans, S. (2009) (2nd edn) *An Introduction to Child Development*. London: Sage.

Kincheloe, J. (1997) Introduction. In G. Cannella (ed.) *Deconstructing Early Childhood Education: social justice and revolution*. New York: Peter Lange Publishing Inc.

Klein, M. (1988) *Envy and Gratitude*. London: Virago Press.

Knight, S. (2009) *Forest Schools and Outdoor Learning in the Early Years*. London: Sage.

Kohn, A. (1993) *Punished by Rewards*. New York: Houghton Mifflin Co.

Kozol, J. and Coles, R. (1967) *Death at an Early Age*. Harmondsworth: Penguin.

Kramer, R. (1961) (1995) Preface. In C. Rogers (ed.) *On Becoming a Person*. New York: Houghton Mifflin Co.

Lawrence, D.H. (1923) *Psychoanalysis and the Unconscious*. London: William Heinemann.

LeDoux, J. (1998) *The Emotional Brain*. London: Weidenfeld and Nicolson.

Lewis, M. and Brooks, J. (1978) Self-knowledge and emotional development. In M. Lewis and L. Rosenblum (eds) *The Development of Affect*. New York: Plenum Press.

Lillard, A. and Else-Quest, N. (2006) Evaluating Montessori Education. *Science* 313: 1893–4.

Lindon, J (1999) *Too Safe for Their Own Good?* London: National EarlyYears Network.

Lobman, C. (2005) Improvisation: postmodern play for early childhood teachers. In S. Ryan and S. Grieshaber (eds) *Practical Transformations and Transformational Practices: globalization, postmodernism and early childhood education*. Kidlington, Oxford: Elsevier Ltd.

Lowndes, G. (1960) *Margaret McMillan: the children's champion*. London: Museum Press Ltd.

Lyotard, J-F. (1984) *The Postmodern Condition*. Minneapolis: University of Minnesota Press.

Mackenzie, N. and Knipe, S. (2006) Research dilemmas: paradigms, methods and methodology. *Issues in Educational Research* 16: 193–205.

MacNaughton, G. (2003) *Shaping Early Childhood*. Maidenhead: Open University Press.

MacNaughton, G. (2004) The politics of logic in early childhood research: a case of the brain, hard facts, trees and rhizomes. *The Australian Educational Researcher* 31, 3 December.

Main, M., Kaplan, N. and Cassidy, J. (1985) Security in infancy, childhood and adulthood: a move to the level of the representation. *Monographs of the Society for Research in Child Development* 50(1–2 Serial no. 209).

Malloch, S. and Trevarthen, C. (2008) (eds) *Communicative Musicality*. Oxford: Oxford University Press.

Manning-Morton, J. (2011) Psychoanalytic ideas and early years practice. In L. Miller and L. Pound (eds) *Theories and Approaches to Learning in the Early Years*. London: Sage.

Manning-Morton, J. and Thorp, M. (2003) *Key Times for Play*. Maidenhead: Open University Press.

Marmot, M. (2010) *Fair Society, Healthy Lives: strategic review of health inequalities in England post-2010*. London: University College London.

Mayes, L., Fonagy, P. and Target, M. (2007) *Developmental Science and Psychoanalysis: integration and innovation*. London: Karnac.

McArdle, F. (2005) Teaching Notes. In S. Ryan and S. Grieshaber (eds) *Practical Transformations and Transformational Practices: globalization, postmodernism and early childhood education*. Kidlington, Oxford: Elsevier Ltd.

McLaren, P. (1995) *Critical Pedagogy and Predatory Culture*. London: Routledge.

McMillan, M. (1919) *The Nursery School*. London: Dent.

McMillan, M. ([1904] 1923) *Education Through the Imagination*. London: Sonnenschein.

McMillan, M. (1927) *The Life of Rachel McMillan*. London: Dent.

McMillan, M. (1930) (revised edition) *The Nursery School*. London: Dent.

Meade, A. and Cubey, P. (2008) *Thinking Children: learning about schemas*. Maidenhead: Open University Press.

Mepham, T. (2009) Introduction. In M-J. Drummond and S. Jenkinson (eds) *Meeting the Child: approaches to observation and assessment in Steiner Kindergartens*. Plymouth: University of Plymouth/Steiner Waldorf Early Years Research Group.

Mercer, J. (2010) *Child Development: myths and misunderstandings*. London: Sage.

Millar, S. (1968) *The Psychology of Play*. Harmondsworth: Penguin Books.

Millar, F. (2010) Free schools will benefit some children at the expense of others, *Guardian*, 18 June.

Mithen, S. (1996) *The Prehistory of the Mind*. London: Thames and Hudson Ltd.

Mithen, S. (2005) *The Singing Neanderthals*. London: Weidenfeld and Nicolson.

Monahan, J. (2009) How to smile after a battering, *Guardian*, 21 July.

Montessori, M. (1912) (2nd edn) *The Montessori Method*. New York: Frederick A. Stokes Company. (Translator George, A.)

Montessori, M. (1919) *The Montessori Method*. New York: Schocken Books.

Montessori, M. (1948) *From Childhood to Adolescence*. New York: Schocken Books.

Montessori St Nicholas (2008) *Guide to the Early Years Foundation Stage in Montessori Settings*. London: Montessori St Nicholas.

Morrison, K. (2001) Henry Giroux 1943–. In J. Palmer (ed.) *Fifty Modern Thinkers on Education: from Piaget to the present*. London: Routledge.

Morss, J. (1990) *The Biologising of Childhood*. New Jersey: Erlbaum.

Morss, J. (1996) *Growing Critical*. London: Routledge

Moss, P. and Petrie, P. (2004) *From Children's Services to Children's Spaces Public Policy, Children and Childhood*. London: Routledge.

Mukherji, P. and Albon, D. (2010) *Research Methods in Early Childhood*. London: Sage.

Murray, E. R. and Brown Smith, H. (nd) *The Child Under Eight*. http: infomotions.com/etexts/Gutenberg/dirs/1/0/0/4/10042/10042.htm) (accessed 25 May, 2010.)

Murray, L. and Andrews, E. (2000) *The Social Baby*. Richmond, Surrey: CP Publishing.

Namy, L. (ed.) (2005) *Symbol Use and Symbolic Representation*. Mahwah, NJ: Lawrence Erlbaum Assoc. Inc.

Neisser, U. (1967) *Cognitive Psychology.* New York: Prentice Hall.

NESS (National Evaluation of Sure Start) (2005) *Changes in the Characteristics of Sure Start Local Programmes Areas in Round 1 to 4 Between 2000/2001 and 2002/2003.* London: NESS Birkbeck College.

NESS (National Evaluation of Sure Start) (2008) *The impact of Sure Start Local Programmes on Three Year Olds and Their Families.* London: NESS.

Nicholls, J. and Wells, G. (1985) Editors' introduction. In G. Wells and J. Nicholls (eds) *Language and Learning: an interactional perspective.* Lewes, E. Sussex: Falmer Press.

Nicol, J. (2007) *Bringing the Steiner Waldorf Approach to Your Early Years Practice.* London: David Fulton.

Nieto, S. (1999) *The Light in Their Eyes: creating multicultural learning communities.* Stoke on Trent: Trentham Books.

Nisbett, R. (2003) *The Geography of Thought.* London: Nicholas Brealey Publishing.

Nutbrown, C., Clough, P. and Selbie, P. (2008) *Early Childhood Education: history, philosophy and experience.* London: Sage Publications.

Oakley, A. (2005) *The Ann Oakley Reader: gender, women and social science.* Bristol: The Policy Press.

Oden, S., Schweinhart, L., Lawrence, J. and Weikart, D. (2000) *Into Adulthood: a study of the effect of Head Start.* Ypsilanti, MI: HighScope Press.

Opie, I. and Opie, P. (1977) *The Lore and Language of Schoolchildren.* Oxford: Oxford University Press.

Orr, D. (2010) Neglected children affect all our lives, *Guardian,* 8 July.

Owen, R. (1858) (1920) *The Life of Robert Owen by Himself.* London: Bell.

Pahl, K. (1999) *Transformations: meaning making in nursery education.* Stoke on Trent: Trentham Books.

Paige-Smith, A. and Craft, A. (2008) (eds) *Developing Reflective Practice in the Early Years.* Maidenhead: Open University Press.

Paley, V.G. (1979) *White Teacher.* London: Harvard University Press.

Paley, V.G. (1981) *Wally's Stories.* London: Harvard University Press.

Paley V.G. (2004) *A Child's Work: the importance of fantasy play.* London: The University of Chicago Press.

Paley, V.G. (2010) *The Boy on the Beach.* London: The University of Chicago Press.

Palmer, J. (ed.) (2001) *Fifty Modern Thinkers on Education.* London: Routledge.

Palmer, S. (2006) *Toxic Childhood: How Modern Life is Damaging our Children.* London: Orion Books.

Patzlaff, R., Sassmannshausen, W. et al. (2007) *Developmental Signatures: core values and practice in Waldorf education for children aged 3–9.* New York: AWSNA Publications .

Penn, H. (2005) *Understanding Early Childhood.* Maidenhead: Open University Press.

Percy, E. (1958) *Some Memories.* London: Eyre and Spottiswood.

Pestalozzi, J.H. (1746–1827) *The Approach and Method of Education,* Pestalozziworld, http://www.pestalozziworld.com/pestalozzi/methods.html (accessed 18 May, 2010).

Peters, M. (2001) Michel Foucault 1926–1984. In J. Palmer (ed.) *Fifty Modern Thinkers on Education: from Piaget to the present.* London: Routledge.

Petrie, P., Boddy, J., Cameron, C., Heptinstall, E., McQuail, S., Simon, A. and Wigfall, V. (2009) *Pedagogy – a holistic, personal approach to work with children and young people across services*. London: Thomas Coram Research Unit/Institute of Education.

Phillips, A. (2007*) Winnicott*. London: Penguin Books.

Piaget, J. ([1923] 2002) *The Language and Thought of the Child*. London: Routledge Classics.

Piaget, J. ([1932] 1999) *The Moral Judgement of the Child*. Abingdon: Routledge.

Piaget, J. (1962) *Play, Dreams and Imitation in Childhood*. New York: Norton.

Piaget, J. (1970) *Science of Education and the Psychology of the Child*. New York: Orion Press.

Piaget, J. (1976) *To Understand is to Invent: the future of education*. Harmondsworth: Penguin Books.

Piaget, J. and Inhelder, B. (1956) *The Child's Conception of Space*. London: Routledge and Kegan Paul.

Pinker, S. (1994) *The Language Instinct*. London: Penguin Books.

Pinker, S. (2002) *The Blank Slate*. London: Penguin Books.

Pollard, A. (2002) *Readings for Reflective Teaching*. London: Continuum.

Pollock, L. (1983) *Forgotten Children: parent-child relations from 1500–1900*. Cambridge: Cambridge University Press.

Postman, N. and Weingartner C. (1971) *Teaching as a Subversive Activity*. Harmondsworth: Penguin.

Pound, L. (1986) *Perceptions of Nursery Practice: an exploration of nursery teachers' views of the curriculum*. (Unpublished MA (ed studies) thesis) Roehampton Institute/Surrey University.

Pound, L. (2005) *How Children Learn*. Leamington Spa: Step Forward Publishing.

Pound, L. (2008) *How Children Learn Book 2*. London: Step Forward Publishing Ltd.

Pound, L. (2009a) *How Children Learn Book 3. Contemporary thinking and theorists*. London: Practical Pre-School Books.

Pound, L. (2009b) Postmodern thinking. *Early Years Educator* March: 16–18.

Prout, J. and James, A. (1997) A new paradigm for the sociology of childhood? Provenance, promise and problems. In A. James and A. Prout (eds) *Constructing and Reconstructing Childhood*. London: Falmer Press.

Pugh, G. (2002) *The Consequences of Inadequate Investment in the Early Years*. Buckingham: Open University Press.

QCA (2007) *Early Years Foundation Stage*. London: DfES.

Ramesh, R. (2010) *How to Bridge Britain's Divide Between Health and Wealth* 23/6/10 www.guardian.co.uk (accessed 23 July, 2010).

Raskin, J. (2002) Constructivism in psychology: personal construct psychology, radical constructivism and social constructionism. In J. Raskin and S. Bridges (eds) *Studies in Meaning: exploring constructivist psychology*. New York: Pace University Press.

Read, J. (1992) A short history of children's building blocks. In P. Gura (ed.) *Exploring Learning*. London: Paul Chapman Publishing.

Reggio Children (1995) *A Journey into the Rights of Children*. Reggio Emilia: Reggio Children.

Riley, D. (1983) *War in the Nursery*. London: Virago.

Rinaldi, C. (2007) Preface. In G. Dahlberg, P. Moss and A. Pence (eds) *Beyond Quality in Early Childhood Care and Education*. London: Routledge.

Ringen, S. (1997) Families and Social Services. In S. Kamerman and A. Kahn (eds) *Family Change and Family Policies in Great Britain, Canada, New Zealand and the United States*. Oxford: Clarendon Press.

Ritchie, J. (2005) Implementing Te Whariki as postmodernist practice: a perspective from Aotearoa/ New Zealand. In S. Ryan and S. Grieshaber (eds) *Practical Transformations and Transformational Practices: globalization, postmodernism and early childhood education*. Kidlington, Oxford: Elsevier Ltd.

Rizzolatti, G. and Craighero, L. (2004) The Mirror-Neuron System. *Annual Review of Neuro-science* 27: 169–92.

Robertson, A. (2002) Pupils' understanding of what helps them learn. In M. Shayer and P. Adey (eds) *Learning Intelligence: cognitive acceleration across the curriculum from 5 to 15 years*. Buckingham: Open University Press.

Robson, S. (2006) *Developing Thinking and Understanding in Young Children*. Abingdon, Oxon: Routledge.

Rogers, C. (1961) *On Becoming a Person*. New York: Houghton Mifflin Co.

Rogers, C. (1969) *Freedom to Learn*. Princeton: Merrill.

Rogers, C. (1980) *A Way of Being*. New York: Houghton Mifflin Co.

Rogers, C. (1983) *Freedom to Learn for the 80s*. New York: Merril.

Rogers, N. (nd) www.rogers.com/carlrogersbio/html (accessed 8 July, 2010).

Rogoff, B. (nd) http://people.ucsc.edu/~brogoff/ (accessed 23 July, 2010).

Rogoff, B. (1990) *Apprenticeship in Thinking: cognitive development in social context*. Oxford: Oxford University Press.

Rogoff, B. (2002) *Learning Together: children and adults in a school community*. Oxford: Oxford University Press.

Rogoff, B. (2003) *The Cultural Nature of Human Development*. Oxford: Oxford University Press.

Rose, H. and Rose, S. (2000) (eds) *Alas Poor Darwin*. London: Jonathan Cape.

Rose, S. (2000) Escaping evolutionary psychology. In H. Rose and S. Rose (eds) *Alas Poor Darwin*. London: Jonathan Cape.

Rose, J. (2005) Independent review of the teaching of early reading: Interim report. http://www.standards.dfes.gov.uk/new/#rose (accessed 27 June, 2010).

Rose, J. (2009) *Independent Review of the Primary Curriculum: final report*. London: DCSF.

Rutter, M. (1972) *Maternal Deprivation Reassessed*. Harmondsworth: Penguin.

Ryan, S. and Grieshaber, S. (eds) (2005) *Practical Transformations and Rransformational Prac-tices: globalization, postmodernism and early childhood education*. Kidlington, Oxford: Elsevier Ltd.

Scarr, S. and Dunn, J. (1987) *Mothercare Othercare*. Harmondsworth: Penguin Books.

School of Barbiana (1970) *Letter to a Teacher*. Harmondsworth: Penguin Books.

Schwartz, J. (1999) *Cassandra's Daughter: a history of psychoanalysis*. London: Viking/Allen Lane.

Schweinhart, L. J., Montie, J., Xiang, Z., Barnett, W.S., Belfield, C.R. and Nores, M. (2005) *Life-time effects: The HighScope Perry Preschool Study Through Age 40*. Ypsilanti, MI: HighScope Press.

Selleck, R. (1972) *English Primary Education and the Progressives 1914–1939*. London: Routledge and Kegan Paul.

Shaull, R. (1972) Foreword. In P. Freire (ed.) *Pedagogy of the Oppressed*. Harmondsworth: Penguin Books.

Shayer, M. (2002) Not just Piaget, not just Vygotsky, and certainly not Vygotsky as *alternative to Piaget*. In M. Shayer and P. Adey (eds) *Learning Intelligence: cognitive acceleration across the curriculum from 5 to 15 years*. Buckingham: Open University Press.

Shayer, M. and Adey, P. (eds) (2002) *Learning Intelligence: cognitive acceleration across the curriculum from 5 to 15 years*. Buckingham: Open University Press.

Shepherd, J. (2010) Khyra Ishaq tragedy: ministers urged to tighten law on home education, *Guardian*, 27 July.

Siegel, D. (1999) *The Developing Mind*. New York: The Guilford Press.

Siegler, R. (1996) *Emerging Minds*. New York: Oxford University Press.

Singer, E. (1992) *Child-care and the Psychology of Development*. London: Routledge.

Singer, D. and Singer, J. (1990) *The House of Make Believe: play and the developing imagination*. London: Harvard University Press.

Siraj-Blatchford, I. and Siraj-Blatchford, J. (1997) Reflexivity, Social Justice and Educational Research. *Cambridge Journal of Education* 27(2): 235–48.

Siraj-Blatchford, I., Sylva, K., Muttock, S., Gilden, R. and Bell, D. (2002) *Researching Effective Pedagogy in the Early Years*. London: Institute of Education/Dept. of Educational Studies, Oxford.

Skinner, B. (1948) Superstition in the Pigeon. *Journal of Experimental Psychology* 38: 168–72.

Skinner, B. (1976) Particulars of my life. *Verbal Behaviour* 75.

Slater, L. (2004) *Opening Skinner's Box: great psychological experiments of the twenteeth century*. London: Bloomsbury Publishing.

Slater, A. and Quinn, P. (2001) Face recognition in the newborn infant. *Infant and Child Development* 10: 21–4.

Slentz, K. and Krogh, S. (2001) *Teaching Young Children: contexts for learning*. New Jersey: Lawrence Erlbaum Associates.

Smith, A. (2011) Te Whariki. In L. Miller and L. Pound (eds) *Theories and Approaches to Learning in the Early Years*. London: Sage.

Smith, L. (1985) *To Understand and to Help: the life and work of Susan Isaacs (1885–1948)*. London: Associated University Presses.

Smith, L. (1996) The social construction of rational understanding. In A. Tryphon and J. Voneche (eds) *Piaget-Vygotsky: the social genesis of thought*. Hove, East Sussex: Psychology Press.

Smith, L. (2001) Jean Piaget 1896–1980. In J. Palmer (ed.) *Fifty Modern Thinkers on Education: from Piaget to the present*. London: Routledge.

Steiner, R. ([1904] 1923) Margaret MacMillan and her work. *Anthroposophy* II, 11: 141–3.

Steiner, R. (1907) (1996) *The Education of the Child*. Hudson, NY: Anthroposophic Press.

Steiner Waldorf Education (2009) *Guide to the Early Years Foundation Stage in Steiner Waldorf Early Childhood Settings*. Forest Row, East Sussex: The Association of Steiner Waldorf Schools.

Stern, D. (1985) *The Interpersonal World of the Infant*. New York: Basic Books.

Sternberg, R. (2009) Sketch of a componential subtheory of human intelligence. In J. Kaufman and E. Grigorenko (eds) *The Essential Sternberg*. New York: Springs Publishing Co.

Suggate, S. (2009a) School entry age and reading achievement in the 2006 programme for International Student Assessment (PISA): *International Journal of Education Research* 48: 151–61.

Suggate, S. (2009b) www.otago.ac.nz/news/news/otago006408.html (accessed 19 June, 2010).

Sumsion, J. (2005) Putting postmodern theories into practice in early childhood teacher education. In S. Ryan and S. Grieshaber (eds) *Practical Transformations and Transformational Practices: globalization, postmodernism and early childhood education.* Kidlington, Oxford: Elsevier Ltd.

Sylva, K., Melhuish, E., Sammons, P., Siraj-Blatchford, I. and Taggart, B. (2004) *The Effective Provision of Pre-school Education (EPPE) Project. Final report.* London: DfES/Institute of Education, University of London.

Talay-Ongan, A. (1998) *Typical and Atypical Development in Early Childhood.* Leicester: BPS Books.

Taplin, J. (2011) Steiner Waldorf Early Childhood Education – offering a curriculum for the twenteeth century. In L. Miller and L. Pound (eds) *Theories and Approaches to Learning in the Early Years.* London: Sage.

Tizard, B. (1974) *Early Childhood Education.* Windsor: NFER.

Tizard, B. and Hughes, M. (1984) *Young Children Learning.* London: Fontana.

Tobin, J. (2004) The disappearance of the body in early childhood education. In L. Bresler (ed.) *Knowing Bodies: moving minds.* Dordrecht, The Netherlands: Kluwer Academic Publishers.

Torgerson, C.J., Brooks, G. and Hall, J. (2005) *A Systematic Review of the Research Literature on the Use of Phonics in the Teaching of Reading and Spelling.* London: Department for Education and Science (DfES).

Tovey, H. (2007) *Playing Outdoors.* Maidenhead: Open University Press.

Tryphon, A. and Voneche, J. (eds) (1996) *Piaget-Vygotsky: the social genesis of thought.* Hove: Psychology Press.

van der Eyken, W. (1967) *The Pre-School Years.* Harmondsworth: Penguin Books.

van der Eyken, W. and Turner, B. (1969) *Adventures in Education.* Harmondsworth: Penguin Press Ltd.

Viruru, R. (2005) Postcolonial theory and the practice of teacher education. In S. Ryan and S. Grieshaber (eds) *Practical Transformations and Transformational Practices: globalization, postmodernism and early childhood education.* Kidlington, Oxford: Elsevier Ltd.

Vygotsky, L. (1978) *Mind in Society.* Mass: Massachusetts Institute of Technology.

Vygotsky, L. (1962) (1986) *Thought and Language.* Mass: Massachusetts Institute of Technology.

Vygotsky, L. (1981) The genesis of higher mental functions. In J. Wertsch (ed.) *The Concept of Activity in Soviet Psychology.* New York: M.E. Sharpe.

Vygotsky, L. (1988) The genesis of higher mental functions. In K. Richardson and S. Sheldon (eds) *Cognitive Development to Adolescence.* Hove, Sussex: Erlbaum.

Vygotsky, L. (1934) (1994) Academic concepts in school aged children. In R. van der Veer and V. Valsiner (eds) *The Vygotsky Reader.* Oxford: Blackwell.

Walkerdine, V. (1989) *Democracy in the Kitchen.* London: Virago.

Walsh, D. (2004) Frog Boy and the American Monkey: the body in Japanese early schooling. In L. Bresler Dordrecht (ed.) *Knowing Bodies, Moving Minds*. The Netherlands: Kluwer Academic Publishers.

Wardle, C.J. (1991) Twentieth-century influences on the development in Britain of services for child and adolescent psychiatry. *The British Journals of Psychiatry* 159: 53–68.

Watson, J. (1934) *Behaviorism*. New York: Norton.

Wells, G. (1985a) *The Meaning Makers: children learning language and using language to learn*. London: Heinemann.

Wells, G. (1985b) *Language Development in the Pre-school Years*. Cambridge: Cambridge University Press.

Weston, P. (1998) *Friedrich Froebel: His Life, Times and Significance*. London: Roehampton Institute.

Whalley, M. (2001) *Involving Parents in their Children's Learning*. London: Paul Chapman Publishing.

Whitbread, N. (1972) *The Evolution of the Nursery-infant School*. London: Routledge and Kegan Paul Ltd.

White, J. (2008) *Playing and Learning Outdoors*. London: Routledge/Nursery World.

Wills, D. (1978) Fifty years of child guidance: a psychologist's view. *Journal of Child Psychotherapy* 4(4) 97–102.

Winnicott, D. (1957) *Mother and Child – a primer of first relationships*. New York: Basic Books.

Winnicott, D. (1960) The theory of the parent-child relationship. *International Journal of Psychoanalysis* 41: 585–95.

Winnicott, D. (1965) *The Maturational Processes and Individual Development*. London: Hogarth Press.

Winnicott, D. (1967) The location of cultural experience. *International Journal of Psychoanalysis* 48: 368–72.

Winnicott, D. (1971) *Playing and Reality*. London: Tavistock.

Wokler, R. (2001) *Rousseau: a very short introduction*. Oxford: Oxford University Press.

Wood, D., Bruner, J. and Ross, G. (1976) The role of tutoring in problem-solving. *Journal of Child Psychology and Psychiatry* 17, 89–100.

Woodham-Smith, P. (1952) History of the Froebel movement in England. In E. Lawrence (ed.) *Friedrich Froebel and English Education*. London: Routledge and Kegan Paul.

Woodhead, M. (2003) The child in development. In M. Woodhead and H. Montgomery (eds) *Understanding Childhood: an interdisciplinary approach*. Chichester: John Wiley and Sons Ltd.

Woodhead, M. and Montgomery, H. (2003) *Understanding Childhood – an interdisciplinary approach*. Chichester: John Wiley and Sons Ltd.

Wright, K. (2001) The interface between mother and baby. In M. Bertolini, A. Giannakoulas, M. Hernandez and A. Molino (eds) *Squiggles and Spaces Vol. 2 – revisiting the work of D.W. Winnicott*. London: Whurr Publishers Ltd.

Wyse, D. (2006) *Rose Tinted Spectacles: synthetic phonics, research evidence and the teaching of reading*. www.tactyc.org.uk/pdfs/2006conf_wyse.pdf

Index

THE TROUBLE WITH PLAY

Susan Grieshaber and Felicity McArdle

978-0-335-23791-3 (Paperback)
2010

eBook also available

The Trouble with Play is a radical departure from some of the ideas about play that are held dear by many in early childhood education. For many, play is considered essential to children's development and learning, and is often promoted as a universal and almost magical 'fix'. Although play does have many proven benefits for children, the authors show that play in the early years is not always innocent, fun and natural. Play can also be political and involve morals, ethics, values and power.

So, what if . . .

- Play is not fair
- Play is not equitable
- Play is not innocent
- Play is not fun
- Play is not natural

Through vignettes, practical activities and reflection points the authors encourage discussion about new ways of seeing and thinking about play and argue for new approaches to pedagogy and the role of the teacher.

www.openup.co.uk

OPEN UNIVERSITY PRESS
McGraw · Hill Education

PARENTS AND PROFESSIONALS IN EARLY CHILDHOOD SETTINGS

Glenda Mac Naughton and Patrick Hughes

978-0-335-24373-0 (Paperback)
February 2011

eBook also available

The book addresses the real and often complex, difficult and even controversial issues that real staff and families face daily. Such issues may include bereavement; food and diet preferences; circumcision; challenging behaviour; discrimination; and bullying.

Key Features

- Covers a range of 'issue stories' which the reader can dip into as appropriate and which draw on research into relationships between staff and families
- Each chapter or story will feature the voices and perspectives of 'real staff' and families, illustrating the complex, difficult and/or controversial issue and high-lighting the questions of power and knowledge that emerge
- Fairness Alerts to help the reader see, understand and break unfair thinking habits

www.openup.co.uk

OPEN UNIVERSITY PRESS
McGraw - Hill Education

MAKING SENSE OF THEORY AND PRACTICE IN EARLY CHILDHOOD

Tim Waller, Judy Whitmarsh and Karen Clarke

978-0-335-24246-7 (Paperback)
March 2011

eBook also available

This accessible book demystifies the links between theory and practice for those studying in the field of early childhood. The book encourages those new to research to develop their investigations as straightforward narrative accounts of the phenomenon that they are investigating.

Throughout the book the authors demonstrate the influence of theoretical perspectives on their own practice and research. They articulate how this adds depth to their studies by linking into wider and more enduring themes.

Each chapter includes:

- Theoretical concepts, which are related to practice and/or research
- Case studies
- Examples from research practice enabling readers to explore the practical application of the 'big ideas'
- Further reading appropriate to the theoretical construct

www.openup.co.uk

OPEN UNIVERSITY PRESS
McGraw - Hill Education